Astrology on Your Personal Computer

Astrology on Your Personal Computer

Hank Friedman

SYBEX® Berkeley • Paris • Düsseldorf • London

Cover art: Peter Bartczak
Project Editor: Karl Ray

*This book is dedicated
to Bud Livingston.
Thank you Bud.*

Acknowledgements

I would like to thank all of the people who have made this book possible. Many people and companies have supplied me with documentation, hardware, and software to evaluate for the book: Michael Erlewine and Doug Pierce of Matrix Software; Rob Hand, Doug Kellogg, and Pat White of AGS Software; Nicki Michaels, representative for Digicomp Research, Mark Hayes of McT, Steve Hines of Microcycles, Andy Jong of Winners Circle, and the folks at M Systems, Inc.

I would particularly like to thank Pat White for all of the hours of assistance she gave me. She was patient, warm, and open and always willing to find the answers I needed. I also appreciate the time Robert Hand took to explain some of the more advanced techniques to me, and his willingness to let me evaluate all of his software.

I became interested in astro-computing when my friend Carolyn Brien bought her first computer system for astrology. At first I was envious, but before long I realized that I could get a system too. Michael Erlewine was the only person selling astrology programs for microcomputers at the time, and he helped me to get started. I appreciate all of Michael's efforts to advance astro-computing.

I also have received a great deal of support and guidance from Doug Pierce, and am very thankful for our friendship. He has given me a great deal over the years, and accepted my feedback readily.

Many people have supported the creation of this book from the very beginning. Karl Ray conceived of the book, found me, and stood by me at every step. Dr. Rudolph Langer accepted the project from the start, and helped it get under way. Joel Kreisman, computer genius, helped me get started on the IBM system, and solved all of the hardware problems I encountered. And my special thanks to Jonathan Kamin, who was the best editor I could have hoped for. I thank Jonathan for his excellent editing, his valuable suggestions on format, and his sympathetic ear and heart. I thank all of the people at SYBEX, for each of their parts in making this book possible.

Many of my friends have encouraged me, consoled me, and helped the book grow: George and Sue Norton, Steve Lett, Steve Pincus, Kimn Neilson, Steve Hines, Tom Lieber, Christine Blomquist, Harold and Lucerne Wahlfors, and Barbara LaRocca.

For much of the quality of this book, I am especially indebted to my wife Kathi, who shared her love, her ideas, and her presence, and helped me grow, renew, and shine.

I am grateful to my mother Sue, for helping me become who I am today, and for all of her care.

Finally, I thank God, for always being There.

Table of Contents

Chapter One

Computers and Astrology

I had just finished dinner when I suddenly remembered that a couple would be arriving in an hour for an astrological consultation. I needed to prepare two charts, a comparison between them, and a set of progressions for each person. In the old days, before I'd purchased my computer system and astrological software, my goose would have been cooked. It took me at least four hours to prepare all of that material using my reference books and a calculator. Instead of frantically rushing to get everything done, I calmed myself down, turned on my computer, and got to work.

First, I had to look up the longitude, latitude, and time zone information in the *American Atlas,* and jot it down. I then started the procedure that let the computer know I wanted it to calculate a new birth chart by pressing N for New Chart, when the computer displayed the *menu* illustrated in Figure 1.1.

Each time the program prompted me, for example by displaying on the screen FIRST NAME = , I entered the first name, last name, birth date, birth time, AM/PM, time zone information, longitude, latitude, and place of birth, and reviewed my entry to be sure it was correct. Next, I told the computer to record what I had entered, including the request to calculate the new chart, (this process is called posting the job), by hitting the Return key. The entry screen is shown in Figure 1.2.

```
+------------------------------------------+
! NAME: NO CHART POSTED YET                !
! DATE:                        ZONE        !
! TIME:                                    !
!PLACE:                                    !
+------------------------------------------+
+------------------------------------------+
!*********** COMMAND MENU ************!
!                                          !
!                                          !
!                                          !
!                                          !
!                                          !
!                                          !
!                                          !
!                                          !
!  SAME CHART OUTPUT NEW FILE GET FILE!
+------------------------------------------+
+------------------------------------------+
! EXIT & PROCESS   DELETE FILES            !
!                                          !
! 00 JOBS POSTED 40 JOBS OPEN LIST OFF!
+------------------------------------------+
```

Figure 1.1: *The first screen display of an astrology program.*

```
+------------------------------------------+
! NAME: ECLIPSE,SOLAR                      !
! DATE: JUN 10, 1983        ZONE+ 8:00!
! TIME:   9:38:00 AM PDT    122W16'00"!
!PLACE: BERKELEY CA         37N52'00"!
+------------------------------------------+
+------------------------------------------+
!****** JOB PROCESSING MENU ********!
!                                          !
! 1 TROPICAL* 2 PROGRESS   3 RELOCATE !
!                                          !
! 4 SIDEREAL  5 SOLUNARS   6 HOUSES   !
!                                          !
! 7 COMMENT   8 LOCAL SPC  9 PSSRS    !
!                                          !
! : OPTIONS   ; SYNASTRY   < RE-ENTER !
!PRESS <SPACE*BAR> TO POST ENTERED JOB!
+------------------------------------------+
+------------------------------------------+
!  OUTPUT                  ?=SCREEN DUMP!
!                                          !
! 00 JOBS POSTED 40 JOBS OPEN LIST OFF!
+------------------------------------------+
```

Figure 1.2: *Display of data entered before posting the chart.*

Since I also wanted a printout of the chart, I had to let the computer know that, so I pressed O for output, 2 to print a wheel, and 1 for the standard wheel printout (which included an aspect page). The menu from which I made those choices appears in Figure 1.3.

Finally, when the menu shown in Figure 1.4 appeared, I pressed 3 to tell the computer I wanted to do more with the same chart, followed by 2 for progressions, 1 for secondary progressions, after which the computer asked me to enter the progressed date, which I typed in.

Again I had to post the job by hitting return. To get the program to print out the progressed chart I again entered O, 2, and then 1 as before.

I repeated this series of steps for the second person, and then had the program print the interaspects, for my chart comparison, by pressing S to work with the same chart again, O to output the printout, and 3 to select the biwheel module. The program then listed a directory of the names on my file disk (alphabetically listed by last names, and starting at the beginning or at whatever letter I chose), and I selected the other person. Since I wanted both a printout of both people's planets positioned on one chart wheel and a page of interaspects, I pressed the 1 key, when

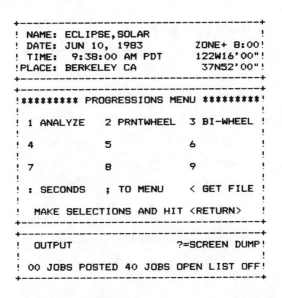

```
+-------------------------------------------+
! NAME:  ECLIPSE,SOLAR                      !
! DATE:  JUN 10, 1983          ZONE+ 8:00!
! TIME:    9:38:00 AM PDT      122W16'00"!
!PLACE:  BERKELEY CA             37N52'00"!
+-------------------------------------------+
+-------------------------------------------+
!******** PROGRESSIONS MENU ********!
!                                           !
! 1 ANALYZE    2 PRNTWHEEL   3 BI-WHEEL !
!                                           !
! 4            5             6               !
!                                           !
! 7            8             9               !
!                                           !
! : SECONDS    ; TO MENU     < GET FILE !
!                                           !
!  MAKE SELECTIONS AND HIT <RETURN>   !
+-------------------------------------------+
+-------------------------------------------+
!  OUTPUT                   ?=SCREEN DUMP!
!                                           !
! 00 JOBS POSTED 40 JOBS OPEN LIST OFF!
+-------------------------------------------+
```

Figure 1.3: Display of screen for choosing printout selection.

the computer asked which type of printout I wanted (as I had preset the computer to give me both pages of printout if I chose option 1).

Finally, I entered X to exit, and responded to the computer's query, ARE YOU SURE? with Y for yes, and sat back and let the computer do the rest of the work. It took me about ten minutes to complete all of these steps, and the computer about 15 minutes to calculate and print out a complete set of wheels and aspects for both people, both of their progressed charts including timed progressed hits, and a combined bi-wheel with interaspects. I even had enough time left over to review the charts before they arrived.

The Advantages of a Computer

One primary reason to use a computer, of course, is speed. A computer can do many kinds of work much faster than a human being. For example, it typically takes a person at least half an hour to calculate an astrological chart, but, given all the data, a personal computer can do so

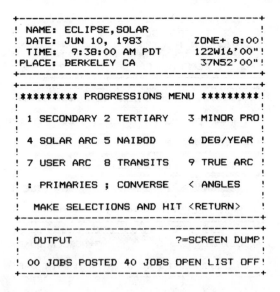

Figure 1.4: *Display of progressions menu.*

in under half a minute. And after calculating the chart, the computer can print out a complete chart wheel in another couple of minutes— much more quickly and more legibly than most astrologers can.

The computer's speed not only reduces work time; it also permits the machine to perform highly complex tasks simply as a matter of routine. Consider the computer's ability to search through hundreds of chart files in seconds for the specific files that have say, the Moon in Aries. Computers can process multiple requests easily. For example, you can get your computer to calculate and print out five natal charts, three progressions, four comparison charts, and three bi-wheels in one run, simply by spending a few minutes entering raw data and then instructing the computer to process the whole batch. To call a computer a labor-saving device is quite an understatement. For astrologers, computers and the appropriate software can save hours of tedious calculations. I have yet to meet an astrologer who loves doing the necessary calculations by hand, or who would turn away this kind of assistance.

Perhaps the computer's greatest value is its accuracy. Anyone who has miscalculated a chart knows how serious even a single mistake can be, and at the same time how easy it is both to make mistakes and to fail to notice that you have done so. I have seen charts done by well-respected astrologers that contained serious errors (such as the wrong rising sign) caused by simple arithmetic mistakes. With a computer, though, all you have to do is enter the correct birth information and time-zone data, and you can rest assured as to the accuracy of your chart. The reason is that once a computer program is loaded, the computer undeviatingly follows the program's rules. The only possible errors are those that result from bad instructions (programs that are defective or poorly written) or from mechanical failures (which are quite rare in most systems). For people who prepare charts on a regular basis and for whom accuracy is a significant concern, investing in a computer might be considered a necessity rather than a luxury.

Both the speed and accuracy of computers, then, allow the astrologer to make on-the-spot analyses of events, relationships, and individuals. Thus, a computer will enable you to gain immediate insights into events and interactions and will encourage you to look at many more charts than you would have otherwise. The overall result is that you will learn a great deal about astrology, yourself, and your relationships, and enjoy yourself more in the process.

The power of a good computer-astrology system can go much further than that. One benefit stems from the computer's storage power: you can save all you do—on disk or tape, depending on the type of system— so you never have to enter a person's birth data again, even though you may later prepare, for example, solar returns, progressions, or comparison charts, or other jobs for that person. Clearly this capacity will save you time and ensure your accuracy, since repeatedly entering data increases the chance for errors to occur.

Using astrological programs on your personal computer gives you access to areas you probably would never explore were you limited to manual calculations: advanced progressed or sidereal work, for example, or local-space charts, harmonic charts, ancient and future horoscopes, or relocation charts. The most advanced programs even allow you to ask simple and complex questions about the charts you have on file—who has Mercury in Scorpio? for example, or who has the ruler of the Tenth House in the Second House and in a fire sign? Such programs gather names of the people on file who meet your criteria and then display them and, if you wish, print them out. What better way to test your theories than to look at a group of familiar charts all exhibiting the same factors? Futher, many programs can be modified or customized to do exactly what you want. For example, a few programs now on the market can be preset to choose the zodiac, house system, and types of printouts you want automatically, so you do not have to select them each time.

Moreover, some programs not only calculate charts but interpret them as well. Thus, computers can be wise investments for those new to astrology—and for those looking for a second opinion in interpreting charts—as well as for more advanced astrologers seeking to extend their expertise. With interpretive programs, you merely enter the necessary data and the program will display or print out interpretations of birth charts, transits, relationships, or even your sex life.

An Overview of the Options

Those of you who are new to computers may wish at this point to read Appendix A, An Introduction to Computers in Astrology. This appendix also includes tips on how to optimize your system for astrology—for example, how to shorten processing and printing time. Appendix B, on the other hand, will introduce you to the areas of astrology that a computer can assist you in investigating, with references to the programs that are capable of each type of calculation.

Chapter Two, Basic Chart Software, reviews the smallest astrological packages, for those whose needs are simple.

Chapter Three, Multifunction Astrological Software, examines multifunction programs for those who want more powerful programs.

Chapter Four looks at transit programs, for those who wish to automate their transit calculations.

Chapter Five covers programs that interpret charts, including the smallest packages, which are suitable for students and beginners.

If you are interested in the most powerful astrological software available, complete with research capabilities and file generation, see Chapter Six, State-of-the-Art Software.

Chapter Seven reviews little-known astrological programs, used for special applications.

Chapter Eight looks at the latest developments in the field, and at the future of computer astrology.

You should know that, when you start off using a computer system, whether for astrology or other purposes, all is not a bed of roses (unless you count the thorns). First, many of the basic manuals that are supplied with computer systems are poorly written and inadequate for the needs of a beginner. You may be able to get some help from your dealer, but local users' groups (like the Apple Core for Apple users) are much more likely to have both the time and the patience to answer many of your questions. It is often a very worthwhile investment to buy additional books, written by companies other than your computer's manufacturer, that introduce you to using your computer, or specific software packages that teach you about your computer as you use them (e.g., Know Your Apple, by Muse Software). Corresponding with the companies that write the programs can be a frustrating experience. Neither of the firms that publish the astrological programs mentioned in this book respond to letters, and telephone communication is costly and cannot always be depended on for quick answers.

It is also important to realize that not all computers are completely reliable. The majority of dealers selling Commodore 64 computers have reported quality control problems. Many of the units fail shortly after purchase. Once you start using programs, it is essential that you keep copies of all of the programs stored safely, as anything from coffee spills to line surges can destroy the data on the disk in your drive.

Astrological Software

It is very common in the software industry to advertise products before they are available. An unfortunate consequence of this practice is that many people become impatient waiting for the programs to be finished, and software publishers may compromise themselves by sending out versions that are not completely debugged. The two astrological software firms, Astro-Graphics Services, Inc. (referred to from now on as AGS), and Matrix Software, are both culpable of these practices, with users waiting many months for software to be finished, or ending up with a product that has serious flaws.

One case in point is the AGS Transit Package. This program was released and sold for years with a bug that caused the program to mislabel all of the retrograde transits (as entering when they were leaving, and vice versa). When I discovered this bug while testing programs for this book, I was told by AGS that they were aware of the problem and would fix it when they had time (they were busy working on new programs). Three months later, after my impressing on them the seriousness of this bug, the problem was fixed and I was sent a new copy. Matrix frustrated even more people with both the long delay in readying and releasing their master program, M-65, and then with the dozens of bugs contained in the released version, a few of which remained to be fixed three years later.

Clearly, both companies do their best to market reliable products, and the cases I've cited are the exception, as opposed to the rule; but you can still expect many programs to have a bug here or there. That is why you should be cautious when considering buying new astrological software, and test any software you purchase at least once for accuracy. You will also have to read the instructions that come with the programs very carefully, because neither company's instructions for using their programs are well-written.

Matrix has a network of local representatives to help you with your questions both before and after you purchase Matrix software, as well as people on hand at Matrix to assist you. For questions about AGS products, you can call AGS directly.

Both companies have been writing software for astrology for many years, have improved their programs considerably over time, and have continued to refine their products. They offer programs of various types, and the products reflect each company's distinctive style.

Computer hardware is covered in detail in the following section. It's important to state here, though, that not all programs run on all computers. In shopping for software, a crucial first step is determining whether the package you are considering will actually run on your machine. At the time of this writing, if you have a Commodore system, you will need to purchase from Matrix exclusively. Both AGS and Matrix make software for the Apple II series, the IBM/MS-DOS series, and the TRS-80 models I and III. AGS publishes many programs for CP/M-based computers, and Matrix has also begun offering CP/M programs, beginning with chart-interpretation programs.

A wide range of astrological software is available from Matrix and AGS. The range starts with simple programs that can perform only basic tasks and ends with highly complex (and therefore more expensive) programs that perform complicated and sophisticated jobs. To choose software that meets your needs and matches your particular level of expertise, you'll need to know what to look for and what questions to ask of the people at AGS or Matrix. The following checklist of characteristics lays the groundwork for judging a program's suitability for your astrological work.

1. *Power.* Programs vary widely in the specific jobs they can do. It is imperative that you choose astrological software that can actually do the work you require. Can the program you are considering prepare returns, progressions, comparison charts, midpoint analyses? Does it offer advanced features like harmonic charts, parallax correction, local-space charts, or heliocentric charts?

2. *Adaptability.* If your needs are simple—say you only do a few charts a week—most programs will work well for you. If you increase your output to many jobs per week, however, details that were once little annoyances (such as the need to swap disks constantly or to wait through slow routines) become tiresome and inefficient. Make sure you buy a package that will serve you as learn and do more.

3. *Batch processing.* You'll need to know whether the program does batch processing. This is the feature that allows you, at one sitting, to instruct the computer to perform a number of jobs—for example, to create several chart printouts—and then to leave the computer while it does its work.

4. *File storage.* File storage is simply the saving of information. Computers store data in electronic "files" on disks, that are analogous to file folders in a paper-based file system. Programs may or may not store files. Those that do enable you to use them in various ways.

    a. *Simple files.* Programs with simple files permit you to call up files and reuse them in the same program.

    b. *Modular files.* Modular files can be used for different types of jobs. For example, with modular files you can use a person's natal-chart file to create his or her solar-return charts, either with the same or a different program.

C. *Research files.* This is the most advanced type of file system. With research files, besides being able to use these files for a variety of jobs, you can ask your program specific questions and it will find all the files in your directory that meet your specified criteria. For example, you could ask your program to find everyone in your files who had any planet conjunct your Moon.

5. *Printouts.* The ability of different programs to produce "hard copy"—that is, to print charts, interpretations, and so on, onto paper—varies considerably. Some programs make no printouts; with these you are restricted to screen displays of data. Some simple programs have usable but crude printouts; others produce high-quality chart wheels and other kinds of output.

6. *Glyphs and graphics.* The simplest programs print out letter symbols for the sun, signs, and so on (e.g., SU for the sun, AR for Aries), but the more powerful software gives you the ability to print out charts and tables using astrological symbols. With these symbols, you can interpret a chart straight from the printout, since glyphs are much easier to use intuitively. However, if you are planning to buy a program that prints glyphs, *make sure* your printer can generate graphics, and that the program you intend to purchase will work with your computer/printer/printer-interface combination. Also note that even some the more powerful programs produce printouts that offend some people's sensibilities. If you are planning to spend several hundred dollars on software, be sure you can live with the type of printout it will produce.

7. *Time Periods.* Some software is accurate only for the twentieth century, while other software may accurately cover the years from 1800 to 2000 or even 1700 to 2300. If your needs go beyond (or before) the twentieth century, make sure the program you are buying will be accurate for the time period you wish to study.

8. *Modifiability:* Unless you plan to learn computer programming, whether the program is modifiable is not an important issue. If you do want to customize calculation routines, however, this feature is important. Matrix will send you modifiable versions of its programs on request (otherwise they send protected versions). Most AGS programs are modifiable.

9. ***Upgrades.*** If you purchase one of the largest software systems (M-65, Nova, Astro Star), you will become part of a software family. Where that is the case, the company will make available to you file-swapping options, additional modules, and regular improvements to the program. Unless you have purchased these large programs, do not count on as much support—that is, updated information and software.

Hardware

If you have not purchased a computer system yet, a few points bear consideration. As noted earlier, compatibility between software and hardware is a chief concern. In other words, you have to be sure that the program you want to purchase is available for the computer you own.

Because the astrological-software market is small, it is impractical for Matrix and AGS, the two firms writing programs for it, to create software for all types of computers. Therefore, if you plan to use your system for astrology and you want the latest and most powerful software, you should limit your choice of computer to four major groups: Commodore 64, IBM and its MS-DOS work-alikes, the Apple II series, and CP/M computers. Each of these computer families has certain advantages and disadvantages, considered below. Note that astrology software for the TRS (Radio Shack) line of computers is falling off, and it is unlikely that anything but the most basic astrological programs for Atari or other computers with their own dialects and operating systems will be created in the near future. (The one exception to this is the Macintosh, for which a lot of new software is likely to appear, including some in the astrology field.)

Many personal-computer companies have run into financial difficulties, among them Osborne, Victor, Texas Instruments, and Zorba. To ensure that reliable service and support (advice and help) will continue to be available for the computer you choose, it's a good idea to stick to a major company with a reputation for supporting its customers. Apple and IBM are excellent examples.

Finally, consider a machine's versatility. You will want to be able to use your computer for a variety of applications—not simply making astrological charts, doing word processing, or organizing data. Why choose a machine that is limited in its functions when you can buy a system that can perform a wide range of tasks? Again, most software is written for the popular computers, and hardware add-ons are also made mostly for the best-selling computers. IBM (and its true compatibles),

Apple II series computers, and popular CP/M computers such as Kaypro have the most versatility and the greatest long term value.

Recommended Hardware Systems

The Commodore 64 has been the computer most recommended by Matrix Software. There are two major reasons: ease of programming (for the Matrix programmers, that is; not necessarily for home users) and very low cost. Indeed, you can get more computing power for your money with the C-64 than with any other machine.

However, the Commodore 64 has some notable disadvantages. Less software of other types is written for the C-64, fewer hardware add-ons are available, and it has poor record for quality control. Also, the C-64 comes with only the most primitive of BASIC dialects (making programming more difficult for the novice), and its disk operating system (DOS) is both very slow and unreliable. When I worked on a Commodore system myself, I was very frustrated with the poor quality of the disk operations (e.g., file saving and loading) and the frequency of crashes (total system failures). If, despite these problems, you choose a C-64 system, you are better off buying one from a large chain rather than a small computer store, since the chains will usually replace your machine quickly from stock if you have received a lemon. I've been told that once you have a C-64 that works well it will continue to serve reliably, but I have also talked to people who had serious overheating problems with their C-64s and had to exchange them several times. Obviously, I cannot recommend Commodore 64 systems given their present unreliability.

The CP/M computers have long been the favored system of AGS. The term CP/M refers to the computer's operating system—the computer's built-in system for organizing the instructions it receives from programs and the means at its disposal for carrying them out. When you choose a CP/M-based system, you will be making two additional choices at the same time: you will be limiting yourself mostly to business software (as opposed to games, educational programs, and so on) and you will be electing to purchase your astrological software largely from AGS (since currently Matrix offers only a few programs for CP/M computers). Like the C-64, the CP/M systems offers a lot of power for your money. They are usually equipped with double-density disk drives (doubling the usual storage capacity) and plenty of memory, include a large bundle of free software with the purchase, and, in some cases, are transportable. My biggest complaint about the transportable CP/M computers is that most utilize small display screens. After writing this book on a Kaypro II, I hope to never have to use a 9-inch screen again.

Nonetheless, AGS will continue to provide their most sophisticated software (e.g., Nova and Astro Star II) for CP/M systems, and as a result, the Kaypro II and other CP/M computers are an excellent choice for astrologers who want to use their systems for only astrology and/or business.

As for the IBM personal computer, quite simply, it is a more expensive computer than many astrologers will buy. The machine is reasonably powerful, reliable, and fast, but the price is high. IBM computers will continue to sell well and new software for them will continue to appear, but the rise of the IBM work-alikes—similar machines compatible with the software designed for the IBM—is in part due to the fact that other companies can offer more for the money with relative ease. Note that not all of the "IBM/MS-DOS compatible computers" are truly compatible—that is, not all can run most IBM software and use IBM hardware add-ons. If you purchase one of these "clones," therefore, make sure that the software you want—both general and astrological—will run on your machine. The Compaq, for instance, has the reputation of being almost completely compatible, while the Sanyo is rumored to run only about two-thirds of the IBM software available. If you are considering a work-alike, check with AGS or Matrix directly before buying to see which machines can run their programs. Both companies are making an effort to create programs that are compatible with the majority of MS-DOS (i.e., IBM-compatible) machines. For those who can afford an MS-DOS computer (and the price of these computers keeps dropping) they are the best choice for astrology. Not only are they faster than comparable computers, but both Matrix and AGS have started writing all of their latest astrological software on and for these machines before writing them for any other computers. Many new programs will never be released for the Commodore or Apple computers, because they lack the capacity to run more complex programs. IBM deliberately crippled their PC*jr* by preventing it from using two disc drives. As a result, while there will be programs written for the machine, much less sophisticated software will be written for it. At present, there are no astrology programs for the PC*jr*, but by the time you read this, both AGS and Matrix will have written some, and AGS plans to offer a scaled-down version of Astro Star II for the PC*jr*. Call AGS for more details. (See Appendix E for addresses and telephone numbers of suppliers of astrological software.)

The Apple II is neither a bargain nor overpriced. It offers the largest library of software in most fields, the most hardware add-ons, and some of the best customer support. Unfortunately, Apple has yet to supply its computers with double-density disk drives. As a result, while Apple drives are very reliable, they store only about half the amount of data that CP/M-based and IBM computers do. You can get disk drives for the Apple that do have a larger capacity (from other companies, like Rana Systems), but since most Apple users don't have such drives, few programs can take advantage of the additional disk space. Nevertheless, at this time, Apple II computers provide the most reliable low-cost computer system for astrologers besides the CP/M systems. You can purchase the powerful Matrix M-65 series for the Apple, as well as many other astrological programs. Matrix has published more astrological programs for the Commodore 64 than for the Apple, but the Apple is faster, offers a much wider range of other software, and is much more reliable.

I do not recommend the new Apple IIc, for astrological or other uses. First, the IIc's keyboard is not as good as those on other Apples. Also, the IIc is a little too large for the lap, and a bit small for the desk. More important reasons however, are that the IIc cannot run an appreciable amount of Apple software, and has no slots for hardware add-ons. The latter is important in light of the new fast 6502 cards—e.g., the SpeeDemon card from McT—available for the Apple IIs. These new cards increase the Apple's speed by $3^1/2$ times, making it about as fast as the IBM for much less money.

In summing up, it is well to admit that, objective comparisons aside, the 16-bit brains of the IBM-type computers (compared with the 8-bit brains of the C-64, CP/M, and Apple II computers) are conducive to the creation of more powerful and sophisticated software, both for astrological and other purposes, and that these systems are the wave of the future. You may be able to do quite well in astrology with an Apple II or CP/M computer system, but if you want the latest and most powerful programs as they come out, you would be wise to purchase an MS-DOS (IBM-compatible) computer, or the much more powerful Macintosh/ Lisa systems (for which astrogical software is just now being released).

Chapter Two

Basic Chart Software

Basic chart software consists of small astrological programs suitable for the curious, beginners, students, and professional astrologers. These programs do chart calculations and perform other tasks for a relatively low price ($30–50), and they are generally easy to use.

Hardware Considerations

If you are using a computer other than an Apple, Commodore, TRS-80, CP/M-compatible, or IBM/MS-DOS-compatible computer, there is very little astrological software for your machine. You will probably be able to use only the M-0 program from Matrix. This program calculates planetary positions, house cusps and aspects, and is priced at $30–50. For some computers, M-0 has additional features. Call Matrix for details.

M-0 Natal Starter Package

Matrix Software, $30-$50

Principal Functions Calculates natal positions for a variety of small computer systems

Types of Calculations *Aspects included:* Some versions include major aspects

Custom aspects: None

Number of house systems: 1 (usually Koch)

Heliocentric charts: In some versions

Methods of progression: None

Solar and lunar returns: No

Midpoint analysis: No

Chart comparisons: No

Harmonics: No

Defaults *Preset calculation defaults:* No

Preset printout defaults: No

File Management *Batch processing:* No

Saves files: No

Printouts *Glyphs:* No

Type of printouts: Prints or displays lists of positions

Computers *Computer required:* VIC-20, PET, TRS-80 Color Computer, TRS-80 Pocket Computer I and II, TI-99/4A, Timex/Sinclair ZX-80, Atari 400 and 800

Other hardware required: None

If you own a CP/M-compatible computer, your only choices in the low price range are Astrotalk by Matrix and Astroscope by AGS (both small packages that interpret charts). The rest of the programs by AGS for CP/M machines start at $130. And although IBM and MS-DOS-compatible machines are well-supported by both companies at the high end of the price scale, Astrotalk and Astroscope are the only software packages available for these machines in the low price range.

If you have or plan to purchase a computer in the Apple II series, a TRS-80 (Model I or III), or a Commodore computer system, a number of programs are available for $50 or less.

Simple Versus Complex Programs

The advantage of using these basic chart programs is that for a small outlay, you can do quite a bit of astrology. However, as you will learn as you become familiar with the available software, there is also a serious disadvantage in starting with a simple, inexpensive program: you will need to buy a new program for every additional astrological function you want to perform.

For example, as a new user I might buy a program that compares charts and calculates progressions (Matrix's M-31), and then want to analyze midpoints. I then buy a small program with this feature (M-30), and become fascinated with solar returns. I then have to buy a new program (M-32), and so on. Not only would I have to keep buying new programs (in the example so far I've spent $150), but, since my programs cannot share data, every time I want to examine a chart in the three ways mentioned I have to run three different programs, entering the raw data for each one every time. Not only is this time-consuming and irritating, it also invites errors.

Therefore, if you anticipate wanting to do different types of astrological work, even if you don't do so now, you will be much better off buying a bigger package containing all the functions you might need. Moreover, if you buy a larger program package, you can often count on its being made more powerful, and you can generally purchase the upgrade for much less than the price of the program. The smaller packages, on the other hand, are seldom upgraded, and even if they are, owners are not notified.

Nevertheless, if you are new to computer astrology, if your needs are simple at present, and particularly if your resources are limited, a small package might be just what you want. You have two choices in this category: small interpretive programs and chart-calculation packages. Both types of programs will calculate birth data, but the interpretive packages will also display (and print) interpretations of astrological factors. Interpretive programs are ideal for users who want to begin learning astrology casually, or who want to show off their computer at social gatherings.

Three small interpretive packages are currently available: Astroscope and Sexoscope by AGS and Astrotalk by Matrix. These programs are discussed in detail in Chapter 5. AGS publishes no other astrological software in this price range. Matrix, on the other hand, offers a whole series of programs.

Obviously, the strength of interpretive programs lies in the quality of their interpretations. These programs do perform natal calculations, with an accuracy of one-tenth of one degree, and they also indicate aspects, but they do not construct charts or perform any other functions. Therefore, for most astrological purposes, they are of limited use.

The chart-calculation packages, on the other hand, do more accurate and thorough astrological analyses. Although they do no interpreting, they contain features more useful both to the astrology student and the practicing astrologer.

Small Chart-Calculation Programs

As noted, Matrix publishes a range of small chart-calculation packages for the astrologer. Only one of these programs (called M-30) creates files of chart data that can be saved on a disk, and the files can only be used by M-30. The others offer more options, however, and are certainly worth considering.

M-1 Natal Horoscopes

Matrix Software, $30

Principal Functions	Displays and prints planets in houses, aspects and midpoints
Types of Calculations	*Aspects included:* Major aspects plus semisquare, sesquiquadrate, quintile, and inconjunct
	Custom aspects: No
	Number of house systems: 1 (choice from 4 major systems)
	Heliocentric charts: Yes
	Methods of progression: None
	Solar and lunar returns: No
	Midpoint analysis: No
	Chart comparisons: No
	Harmonics: No
Defaults	*Preset calculation defaults:* No
	Preset printout defaults: No
File Management	*Batch processing:* No
	Saves files: No
Printouts	*Glyphs:* No
	Types of wheels: Square wheels
	Quality of printouts: Fair
Computers	*Computer required:* Commodore 64, PET, VIC-20, Atari 400 and 800
	Other hardware required: None

M-4 Local Space (Locality Charts)

Matrix Software, $30

Principal Functions

Displays and in some versions prints charts for five coordinate systems: heliocentric, geocentric, right ascension, azimuth & altitude, prime vertical

Types of Calculations

Aspects included: None

Custom aspects: No

Number of house systems: None

Heliocentric charts: Yes

Methods of progression: None

Solar and lunar returns: No

Midpoint analysis: No

Chart comparisons: No

Harmonics: No

Defaults

Preset calculation defaults: No

Preset printout defaults: No

File Management

Batch processing: No

Saves files: No

Printouts

Glyphs: No

Types of wheels: None

Quality of printouts: Fair

Computers

Computer required: Commodore 64, PET, VIC-20, TRS-80 Models I, III, and 4

Other hardware required: None

M-5: Transit & Secondary Progressions

Matrix Software, $30

Principal Functions	Displays and prints interaspects between two charts, and progressed positions with timed hits
Types of Calculations	*Aspects included:* Major aspects plus semisquare, sesquiquadrate, quintile, inconjunct
	Custom aspects: No
	Number of house systems: None
	Heliocentric charts: Yes
	Methods of progression: Secondary progressions
	Timed progressed hits: Yes
	Solar and lunar returns: No
	Midpoint analysis: No
	Chart comparisons: List of interaspects (between planets)
	Harmonics: No
Defaults	*Preset calculation defaults:* No
	Preset printout defaults: No
File Management	*Batch processing:* No
	Saves files: No
Printouts	*Glyphs:* No
	Types of wheels: None
	Quality of printouts: Fair
Computers	*Computer required:* Commodore 64, PET, VIC-20, Atari 400 and 800
	Other hardware required: None

M-7 Solar Returns

Matrix Software, $30

Principal Functions	Displays and in some versions prints listing of solar return positions of planets and house cusps

Types of Calculations

Aspects included: None

Custom aspects: No

Number of house systems: 1 (choice from 4 major systems)

Heliocentric charts: No

Methods of progression: None

Solar and lunar returns: Prints list of solar return positions

Midpoint analysis: No

Chart comparisons: No

Harmonics: No

Defaults

Preset calculation defaults: No

Preset printout defaults: No

File Management

Batch processing: No

Saves files: No

Printouts

Glyphs: No

Types of wheels: None

Quality of printouts: Fair

Computers

Computer required: Commodore 64, PET, VIC-20

Other hardware required: None

M-8 Lunar Returns

Matrix Software, $30

Principal Functions	Displays and in some versions prints listing of lunar return positions of planets and house cusps

Types of Calculations

Aspects included: None

Custom aspects: No

Number of house systems: 1 (choice from 4 major systems)

Heliocentric charts: No

Methods of progression: None

Solar and lunar returns: Prints list of lunar return positions

Midpoint analysis: No

Chart comparisons: No

Harmonics: No

Defaults

Preset calculation defaults: No

Preset printout defaults: No

File Management

Batch processing: No

Saves files: No

Printouts

Glyphs: No

Types of wheels: None

Quality of printouts: Fair

Computers

Computer required: Commodore 64, PET, VIC-20

Other hardware required: None

M-10: Solar Arc Directions

Matrix Software, $30

Principal Functions   Displays and in some versions prints listings of solar arc positions and timed aspect hits

Types of Calculations   *Aspects included:* Majors plus semisquare, sesquiquadrate, semisextile, inconjuct; quintile, septile, novile series

Custom aspects: No

Number of house systems: None

Heliocentric charts: No

Methods of progression: Solar arc directions

Timed hits: Yes

Solar and lunar returns: No

Midpoint analysis: No

Chart comparisons: No

Harmonics: No

Defaults   *Preset calculation defaults:* No

Preset printout defaults: No

File Management   *Batch processing:* No

Saves files: No

Printouts   *Glyphs:* No

Types of wheels: None

Quality of printouts: Fair

Computers   *Computer required:* Commodore 64, PET, VIC-20

Other hardware required: None

M-17: Composite & Relationship Charts

Matrix Software, $30

Principal Functions	Displays and in some versions prints composite and relationship chart positions and aspects in the charts
Types of Calculations	**Aspects included:** Major aspects plus semisquare, sesquiquadrate, quintile, inconjunct
	Custom aspects: No
	Number of house systems: 1 (choice of 4 major systems)
	Heliocentric charts: Yes
	Methods of progression: None
	Solar and lunar returns: No
	Midpoint analysis: No
	Chart comparisons: Displays/prints composite and relationship chart positions and aspects
	Harmonics: No
Defaults	**Preset calculation defaults:** No
	Preset printout defaults: No
File Management	**Batch processing:** No
	Saves files: No
Printouts	**Glyphs:** No
	Types of wheels: None
	Quality of printouts: Fair
Computers	**Computer required:** Commodore 64, PET, VIC-20
	Other hardware required: None

The smallest programs from Matrix are M-1, M-4, M-5, M-7, M-8, M-10, and M-17. Most of these programs are available only for the Commodore (VIC, PET, and C-64) computers, and will create printed output only on the latter two machines. M-1 and M-5 are now being sold in printing versions for the Atari 400 and 800 computers. All of these programs are priced at $30, but they are less accurate than the other low-priced packages (up to five minutes of arc off for the outer planets, and less accurate in labeling planets retrograde and direct; making them unacceptable for the professional astrologer).

These programs do have such features as major aspect tables, midpoint listings, one house system, square-wheel screen display, and the basic planetary positions. One of the better buys is the M-5 program; it computes progressions and compares two dates (as does M-31, reviewed below). M-7 calculates accurate solar returns. M-8 calculates lunar returns. M-10 computes solar-arc directions. M-17 prepares composite and relationship charts. M-4 creates local-space charts. M-1 performs basic chart calculations.

The Matrix M-30 Series

The Matrix programs in the $50 price range—M-30, M-31, M-32, M-34, and M-35—have many features similar to those of the less expensive programs, plus some additional ones. All are extremely accurate for the period 1900–2000, most let you choose any of the nine most popular house systems, and all perform *screen dumps*—they can print whatever is on the screen. Their screen dumps are not elegant, but they are certainly functional enough for the average astrologer. Most of these programs produce square chart wheels on the screen with an aspect grid in the center, complete with midpoints and angular separations (see Figure 2.1). They list heliocentric positions, Vertex, latitudes, declinations, and sidereal positions if needed.

These programs are available for the Apple II series, TRS-80 models I and III, and the Commodore 64 and PET (on disk and in some cases cassette versions).

```
UR 05CN122VE 00GE082          2NO 02AR42
SU 05CN195ME 20GE015          5
        G         T           A
        E         A           R
        3         3           3
*25CN35**5***SUN***5***MIDPT*5**25PI35*
PL 16LE33*1MON   :149:19VI37*JUR07PI26
        *2MER    : 15:27GE41*
        *3VEN    : 35:17GE44*
        *4MAR*SQR: 91:20LE53*
        *5JUP*TRI:118:06TA23*
*25LE35***6SAT   : 69:09LE44***25AQ35*
SA 14VI07*7URA*CJN:  0:05CN16*
        *8NEP    : 99:24LE57*
        *9PLU    : 41:25CN56*
        *:NOD*SQR: 93:19TA01*
        * ASPECTS RUN MORE  *
*25VI35**2**EQUA***2*HOUSES**2**25CP35*
MA 06LI265          5MO 03SA545
NE 14LI34L          S          S
        I           C          A
        3           3          3
        5           5          5
```

Figure 2.1: *Matrix square wheel.*

M-30: Advanced Natal Package

Matrix Software, $50

Principal Functions	Displays and prints planets in houses, aspects and midpoints, harmonics, sorted midpoints
Types of Calculations	**Aspects included:** Major aspects plus semisquare, sesquiquadrate, inconjunct, quintile
	Custom aspects: No
	Number of house systems: 9 major house systems
	Heliocentric charts: Yes
	Methods of progression: None
	Solar and lunar returns: No
	Midpoint analysis: Displays and prints sorted list of midpoints (selectable dial)
	Chart comparisons: No
	Harmonics: Displays and prints harmonic planetary positions
Defaults	**Preset calculation defaults:** No
	Preset printout defaults: No
File Management	**Batch processing:** No
	Saves files: Yes (if disk drive present)
	File access: Excellent (includes file utilities)
Printouts	**Glyphs:** No
	Types of wheels: Square wheels
	Quality of printouts: Fair
Computers	**Computer required:** Commodore 64, PET, Apple II, TRS-80 Models I, III, and 4
	Other hardware required: Apple version requires one disk drive

M-30 is an excellent small program to start with, to create and examine natal charts. It is available on either cassette or disk, and is limited to jobs involving only one chart—that is, you cannot use it to compare charts. This program offers batch processing (if you have a disk drive), allowing you to process up to a hundred chart jobs at one sitting. The files created by M-30 can be stored (again, if you have a disk drive) for later use. M-30's strong point is calculating quite accurate charts and then examining them. You can sort midpoints for whatever dial you select (see Figure 2.2), with planets inserted in the sort, and you can calculate any harmonic you wish (see Figure 2.3). Unfortunately, the Ascendant and M. C. are not included in the harmonic routine, but the routine does allow you to change orbs, and the conjunctions in each harmonic are starred for emphasis.

M-30 handles well. The program doesn't crash or respond disconcertingly if you hit the wrong key. Saving and calling up files is simple, and entering data is easy. Screens display data sorted by latitude, declination, and longitude. The documentation—computer jargon for written

```
!    5  12!05AR12 ****URA!
!    5  16!05AR16=SUN/URA!
!    5  20!05AR20 ****SUN!
!    5  49!05AR49=MAR/URA!
!    5  53!05AR53=SUN/MAR!
!    6  04!06AR04=PLU/ASC!
!    6  27!06AR27 ****MAR!
!    7  12!07AR12=MC /ASC!
!    8  21!08AR21=VEN/PLU!
!    8  39!08AR39=NEP/NOD!
!    9  29!09AR29=VEN/MC !
!    9  32!09AR32=NOD/VTX!
!    9  53!09AR53=URA/NEP!
!    9  57!09AR57=SUN/NEP!
!   10  14!10AR14=MON/PLU!
!   10  31!10AR31=MAR/NEP!
!   10  35!10AR35 ****ASC!
!   10  47!10AR47=URA/VTX!
!   10  50!10AR50=SUN/VTX!
!   11  22!11AR22=MON/MC !
!   11  24!11AR24=MAR/VTX!
!   12  00!12AR00=JUP/PLU!
!   12  52!12AR52=VEN/ASC!
***PRESS=FORWARD* (R) EVERSE* (M) ORE*
```

Figure 2.2: M-30 midpoint sort.

instructions—is skimpy, and it's slightly outdated in some technical aspects, but it's sufficient nonetheless.

Overall, the program is worth the price—but, remember: only if you'll be looking at charts one at a time and don't need fancy printouts. Most beginners will be willing to sacrifice M-30's batch-processing capability, midpoint sorts, and harmonic routines for M-31's ability to compare charts and its many other features.

```
*001=HAR***  *002=HAR***  *003=HAR***
  60 09=VE    12 54=MA     11 45=MO
  80 02=ME    29 09=NE     49 40=PL
  95 12=UR*   120 17=VE    132 24=SA
  95 20=SU*   127 50=MO    180 26=VE
  136 33=PL   160 04=ME    199 20=MA
  164 08=SA   190 24=UR*   223 44=NE
  186 27=MA   190 39=SU*   240 06=ME
  194 35=NE   273 07=PL    285 36=UR*
  243 55=MO   314 54=JU    285 59=SU*
  337 27=JU   328 16=SA    292 20=JU
*004=HAR***  *005=HAR***  *006=HAR***
  20 48=UR*   40 09=ME      52=VE
  21 18=SU*   100 40=SA    23 30=MO
  25 47=MA*   116 00=UR*   38 41=MA
  58 18=NE    116 38=SU*   87 28=NE
  186 13=PL   139 35=MO    99 20=PL
  240 35=VE   212 14=MA    120 11=ME
  255 40=MO   247 14=JU    211 12=UR*
  269 47=JU   252 53=NE    211 58=SU*
  296 32=SA   300 43=VE    224 41=JU
  320 07=ME   322 46=PL    264 48=SA
1=CONT*2=HAR?*3=NEW*ORB?*4=MENU***
```

Figure 2.3: M-30 harmonic display.

M-31: Transits & Progressions

Matrix Software, $50

Principal Functions
Displays and prints interaspects between two charts, progressed chart positions with timed hits

Types of Calculations
Aspects included: Major aspects plus semisquare, sesquiquadrate, inconjunct, quintile

Custom aspects: No

Number of house systems: 9 major house systems

Heliocentric charts: Yes

Methods of progression: Secondary progressions

Timed progressed hits: Yes

Solar and lunar returns: No

Midpoint analysis: No

Chart comparisons: Displays and prints interaspects between planets

Harmonics: No

Defaults
Preset calculation defaults: No

Preset printout defaults: No

File Management
Batch processing: No

Saves files: No

Printouts
Glyphs: No

Types of wheels: None

Quality of printouts: Fair

Computers
Computer required: Commodore 64, PET, Apple II, TRS-80 Models I, III, and 4

Other hardware required: Apple version requires one disk drive

M-31 has most of the features of M-30 and can also compute second-ary progressions and "transits." I put the word *transits* in quotation marks here because M-31 can only compare one date to another, rather than look at a several-month period of aspects between the sky and a birth chart, which is the standard definition of the term. Therefore, the transit routine is only useful for comparing one date at a time to the natal chart, and does not give timed hits, only angular separations and the aspects formed. Still, the single-date approach is useful for chart comparisions—for example, comparing your chart with your wife's, your boss's, and so on. The interaspects (aspects between the two charts) can be printed out, but doing so is laborious. You must print a separate screen for each transiting planet. Also, the Ascendants of both charts are not included in the inter-aspecting, an unfortunate deficiency if you plan to use the program for chart comparisons.

The secondary progression routine is quite useful: timed hits are printed on the screen and easily sent to the printer, and secondary positions are listed. You can look at secondary-to-secondary aspects, as well as secondary-to-natal aspects with this routine (see Figure 2.4).

RADIX	YEAR'S ASPECTS		PROGRESSED
06.271950	SUN		06.271984
---------	MON		----------
3H5M27S	SQR*MER	6-03-85	5H21M57S
MC 18TA49	OPP*SAT	12-18-84	MC 21GE16
AS 25LE35	SXT*MC	4-30-85	AS 22VI27
VT 16CP21	MER		VT 09PI34
---------	VEN		----------
	MAR		
SUN 05CA20	JUP		SUN 07LE46
MON 03SA56	SAT		MON 07PI58
MER 20GE02	URA		MER 27LE30
VEN 00GE09	NEP		VEN 10CA36
MAR 06LI27	PLU		MAR 24LI03
JUPRO7PI27	NOD		JUPRO5PI36
SAT 14VI08	ASC		SAT 17VI10
URA 05CA12	MC		URA 07CA10
NEP 14LI35			NEP 14LI55
PLU 16LE33			PLU 17LE30
NOD 02AR51			NOD 29PI25

NEW CONT MENU

Figure 2.4: M-31 progression display.

M-31 is a good program to start with, if you can live without fancy printouts, batch processing, file storage, and charts for periods other than the twentieth century. The program is easy to handle, and you can examine progressions to a birth chart, then a transit, followed by another transit or a second progression, all without re-entering the original chart data.

M-32: Solar & Lunar Returns

Matrix Software, $50

Principal Functions
Displays and prints solar and lunar returns, wheels with aspects and midpoints

Types of Calculations
Aspects included: Major aspects plus semisquare, sesquiquadrate, inconjunct, quintile

Custom aspects: No

Number of house systems: 9 major house systems

Heliocentric charts: Yes

Methods of progression: None

Solar and lunar returns: Displays and prints solar and lunar return positions around square wheel with aspects, demi-returns and lunar returns to a specific zodiac point

Midpoint analysis: No

Chart comparisons: No

Harmonics: No

Defaults
Preset calculation defaults: No

Preset printout defaults: No

File Management
Batch processing: No

Saves files: No

Printouts
Glyphs: No

Types of wheels: Square wheels

Quality of printouts: Fair

Computers
Computer required: Commodore 64, PET, Apple II, TRS-80 Models I, III, and 4

Other hardware required: Apple version requires one disk drive

M-32 is specifically designed to generate solar- and lunar-return charts. You can specify sidereal or tropical zodiacs and can include precession correction. The program is quite accurate, and calculates demi-returns as well as lunar returns to specified points.

M-33: Advanced Local Space

Matrix Software, $50

Principal Functions

Displays and prints charts for five coordinate systems: heliocentric, geocentric, right ascension, azimuth & altitude, prime vertical

Types of Calculations

Aspects included: None

Custom aspects: No

Number of house systems: None

Heliocentric charts: Yes

Methods of progression: None

Solar and lunar returns: No

Midpoint analysis: No

Chart comparisons: No

Harmonics: No

Defaults

Preset calculation defaults: No

Preset printout defaults: No

File Management

Batch processing: No

Saves files: No

Printouts

Glyphs: No

Types of wheels: None

Quality of printouts: Fair

Computers

Computer required: Commodore 64, PET, Apple II

Other hardware required: Apple version requires one disk drive

M-33 enables you to examine charts from other coordinate systems: heliocentric, right ascension/declination, azimuth/altitude, and prime vertical perspectives. The program is useful in relocation work, as you can use it to calculate relocated chart angles, and is sold with several articles from Michael Erlewine, who has pioneered research in this field.

M-34: Composite & Relationship Charts

Matrix Software, $50

Principal Functions	Displays and prints composite and relationship chart positions and aspects in the charts
Types of Calculations	**Aspects included:** Major aspects plus semisquare, sesquiquadrate, quintile, inconjunct
	Custom aspects: No
	Number of house systems: 9 major house systems
	Heliocentric charts: Yes
	Methods of progression: None
	Solar and lunar returns: No
	Midpoint analysis: No
	Chart comparisons: Displays and prints composite and relationship chart positions and aspects
	Harmonics: No
Defaults	**Preset calculation defaults:** No
	Preset printout defaults: No
File Management	**Batch processing:** No
	Saves files: No
Printouts	**Glyphs:** No
	Types of wheels: None
	Quality of printouts: Fair
Computers	**Computer required:** Commodore 64, PET, Apple II, TRS-80 Models I, III, and 4
	Other hardware required: Apple version requires one disk drive

M-34 prepares charts based on the theories of Rob Hand, who invented composite charts, and those of Ronald Davidson, who pioneered the use of relationship charts. The most important method of comparing charts is looking at the interconnections—interaspects—between two people's charts, but these new types of charts afford astrologers valuable insights. M-34 will display house cusps, as well as aspects, for the charts generated.

M-35: Solar Arc Directions

Matrix Software, $30

Principal Functions   Displays and prints listings of solar arc positions and timed aspect hits

Types of Calculations   *Aspects included:* Majors plus semisquare, sesquiquadrate, semisextile, inconjuct; quintile, septile, novile series

Custom aspects: No

Number of house systems: None

Heliocentric charts: No

Methods of progression: Solar arc directions

Timed hits: Yes

Solar and lunar returns: No

Midpoint analysis: No

Chart comparisons: No

Harmonics: No

Defaults   *Preset calculation defaults:* No

Preset printout defaults: No

File Management   *Batch processing:* No

Saves files: No

Printouts   *Glyphs:* No

Types of wheels: None

Quality of printouts: Fair

Computers   *Computer required:* Commodore 64, PET, TRS-80 Models I, III, and 4

Other hardware required: None

Solar arcs are a popular method of prediction, and with M-35 you can choose the mean arc, true arc, or degree-for-a-year method of arcing. The program displays dates of exact aspect (i.e., timed hits) for a year period, as well as the planetary positions by solar arc.

M-77: The Time Traveler

Matrix Software, $30

Principal Functions   Displays and in some versions prints square chart wheels for planetary positions from 4713 B. C.

Types of Calculations

Aspects included: Major aspects plus semisquare, sesquiquadrate, quintile, inconjunct

Custom aspects: no

Number of house systems: One

Heliocentric charts: No

Methods of progression: None

Solar and lunar returns: No

Midpoint analysis: No

Chart comparisons: No

Harmonics: No

Defaults

Preset calculation defaults: No

Preset printout defaults: No

File Management

Batch processing: No

Saves files: No

Printouts

Glyphs: No

Types of wheels: Square wheels

Quality of printouts: fair

Computers

Computer required: Commodore 64, PET, VIC-20, Apple II, TRS-80 Models I, III, and 4

Other hardware required: Apple version requires one disk drive

If you have a TRS-80 or a computer in the Apple II or Commodore series, this $30 package will permit you to calculate charts with reasonable accuracy for the period from 4713 B. C. to the present. The program is designed to prepare charts for dates before 1900, but some planetary positions are up to a degree off. Like the other Matrix programs, M-77 displays a square chart wheel with aspect grid in the center, but it cannot produce printouts with TRS, Apple, or VIC systems. This program is not intended to replace other programs for the twentieth century, as its calculation of the outer planet positions for this century can be off by a few minutes of arc.

Chapter Three

Multifunction
Astrological
Software

This chapter is devoted to programs specifically designed to interest and serve those seriously interested in astrology who want programs that perform a multiplicity of functions, including fast calculation and printing. The *most* advanced software is covered not in this chapter but in Chapter 6, where state-of-the-art software for the professional astrologer is reviewed. If you want to acquaint yourself fully with the range of software currently available, consult that chapter as well as this one.

The multifunction packages reviewed here will all create and print natal charts and their accompanying tables. Most of the programs in this category will do all of the following:

1. Calculate planetary positions, Ascendant, M. C., Vertex, Part of Fortune, and true node quickly and accurately;

2. Calculate charts for tropical and sidereal zodiacs and heliocentric positions;

3. Work with at least the four most popular house systems: Equal, Placidian, Campanus, and Koch;

4. Print chart wheels with glyphs and aspect tables;

5. Prepare progressed charts, solar arcs, and returns;

6. Make comparisons via interaspects and composite charts;

7. Print sorted midpoints and harmonics;

8. Batch process several jobs.

A limited number of the chart-program packages will also:

9. Create and store files for later use;

10. Calculate and print timed progressed hits;

11. Print two sets of data on one chart—that is, print bi-wheels;

12. Allow the user to customize the program so that the zodiac, house system, aspects, and so on can be selected once, rather than each time the program is run.

Two types of software are reviewed in this chapter:

1. *Natal-chart programs.* These programs—M-64; M-71; Blue Star 1, 2, and 3; Natal Horoscope 110, and Natal Package 410— deal exclusively with single birth charts. They will not compare charts, prepare progressed charts, or perform any functions involving charts other than natal charts.

2. *Secondary-chart programs.* These more powerful programs—Apple Star Track, Astro Star I and II, Blue Star 7, Blue Star 10, and CCRS—will create progressed, composite, and other types of charts and compare them with the natal chart.

Matrix and AGS Packages Compared

Matrix has paid a great deal of attention to its chart-wheel printouts. Its software can create wheels with planets spaced proportionately around the circle, open wheels, and in some cases bi-wheels. AGS's programs do not space planets proportionately around the houses, but instead list planets one above the next in each house (see Figures 3.2 and 3.10 for examples). Therefore, to insert aspect lines you must redraw the charts. Except for the CCRS program, which prints bi-wheel charts, AGS programs do not print open wheels or bi-wheels.

Most of the Matrix programs reviewed in this section can be customized: you can select the house system, zodiac, aspects, and other features you want. Only two AGS programs are fully customizable, Transit

Package 113 and the new Astro Star II. The rest require you to specify all your choices every time you use the program. (Astro Star I, however, allows the user to define and save a set of aspects.)

Matrix programs also handle files much more efficiently than AGS programs. Matrix programs that work with files display a directory of all of the files on disk, so you can select the file you want with a single keystroke. With AGS's programs, on the other hand, you must either remember (or keep written records of) all of the file names on a disk or leave the program to look at the disk directory of the file disk. And to call up a file, you then have to type in the entire file name rather than a single letter, which makes AGS programs tedious to use. (AGS has made improvements in Astro Star II—for example, the program can keep 24 chart files in memory—but you still cannot select disk files with a single keystroke.)

In any case, each publisher has its own format for storing files on disk. Files created by Matrix programs cannot be read by AGS programs, and vice versa. This is an important consideration if you hope to use the same files for different purposes in different programs.

On the other hand, most AGS programs have an important advantage over Matrix programs: you can edit any piece of birth information you enter, such as birth date, longitude, time zone. With Matrix programs, you have to start over from the beginning if you make a mistake. But some AGS programs require that you specify N or S latitude and E or W longitude for every birth entered. When you are entering lots of charts, it breaks the flow to have to specify N, S, E, or W every time. The method used in Matrix programs, on the other hand, is that you enter, say, 41.52 for 41N52. Thus, especially if you do charts for the U.S., and have a numeric keypad, the Matrix method is faster and easier.

Some of the AGS programs reviewed here also require that you enter the delta-T time correction yourself, while all of the Matrix programs enter it for you.

In general, the written instructions accompanying astrology programs by both firms are brief, and users must study them carefully to learn how to use the programs most effectively. However, both Matrix and AGS will answer questions on the phone, so don't hesitate to call them if you don't understand how to use the software.

Natal-Chart Programs

These programs work only with natal charts, and cannot compare charts or progress them.

Blue Star 1

Matrix Software, $150

Principal Functions Prints birth charts, harmonic charts, midpoint page with aspects noted

Types of Calculations *Aspects included:* Majors plus semisquare, sesquiquadrate, inconjunct

Custom aspects: 15 total

Number of house systems: 6 plus user-defined Ascendant

Heliocentric charts: Yes

Methods of progression: None

Solar and lunar returns: No

Midpoint analysis: Prints sorted midpoint list, selectable dial

Chart comparisons: No

Harmonics: Prints harmonic charts

Defaults *Preset calculation defaults:* House system, zodiac, coordinate system, dial, harmonic, type of sort

Preset printout defaults: Type of wheel, second page on/off

File Management *Batch processing:* No

Saves files: No

Printouts *Glyphs:* Yes

Types of wheels: Closed, open, spoke; all with proportionally spaced planets

Quality of printouts: Very good

Computers *Computer required:* Commodore PET/CBM 32K, Commodore 64

Other hardware required: One disk drive, compatible printer

Blue Star 2

Matrix Software, $150

Principal Functions	Prints birth charts, harmonic charts, aspect/midpoint page
Types of Calculations	***Aspects included:*** Majors plus semisquare, sesquiquadrate, inconjunct
	Custom aspects: 15 total
	Number of house systems: 6 plus user-defined Ascendant
	Heliocentric charts: Yes
	Methods of progression: None
	Solar and lunar returns: No
	Midpoint analysis: No
	Chart comparisons: No
	Harmonics: Prints harmonic charts
Defaults	***Preset calculation defaults:*** House system, zodiac, coordinate system, dial, harmonic
	Preset printout defaults: Type of wheel, second page on/off
File Management	***Batch processing:*** No
	Saves files: No
Printouts	***Glyphs:*** Yes
	Types of wheels: Closed, open, spoke; all with proportionally spaced planets
	Quality of printouts: Very good
Computers	***Computer required:*** Commodore PET/CBM 32K, Commodore 64
	Other hardware required: One disk drive, compatible printer

Blue Star 3

Matrix Software, $150

Principal Functions	Prints one page birth charts with aspect and midpoint table, harmonic charts page
Types of Calculations	*Aspects included:* Majors plus semisquare, sesquiquadrate, inconjunct
	Custom aspects: 15 total
	Number of house systems: 6 plus user-defined Ascendant
	Heliocentric charts: Yes
	Methods of progression: None
	Solar and lunar returns: No
	Midpoint analysis: Sorted midpoint table, selectable dial
	Chart comparisons: No
	Harmonics: Prints harmonic charts
Defaults	*Preset calculation defaults:* House system, zodiac, coordinate system, dial, harmonic
File Management	*Batch processing:* No
	Saves files: No
Printouts	*Glyphs:* Yes
	Types of wheels: Closed, open, spoke; all with proportionally spaced planets
	Quality of printouts: Very good, but a little crowded
Computers	*Computer required:* Commodore PET/CBM 32K, Commodore 64
	Other hardware required: One disk drive, compatible printer

Blue Star 1, 2, and 3 are very fast chart-printing programs available only for the Commodore CBM/PET and C-64 computers. Blue Star 7, reviewed in the second part of this chapter, is a much more powerful program at the same price. Blue Star 3 differs from the other Blue Star programs in that it produces a one-page chart printout complete with aspects, sorted midpoints, and chart wheel (see Figure 3.1), instead of a two-page printout. The only difference between Blue Star 2 and Blue Star 1 is in their second page of printout. Blue Star 1 creates a second page that is more suited to those who work primarily with midpoints, although it does include aspect and orb labeling. The second page of Blue Star 2's printouts is more easy to read and could be useful for beginners (with planet names and zodiac signs spelled out, as shown in Figures 3.5 and 3.6). Blue Star 1 will print charts for any harmonic you select, and it can print out a second-page table that may be sorted in a variety of ways, listing midpoints, angular separations, aspects, orbs, applying/separating, and waxing/waning labels.

These programs operate easily and quickly, and you can order them in cassette format if you don't have a disk drive. They can also be customized to your specific needs—name and address label, a specified set of aspects and orbs, house system, midpoint dial, and zodiac—so that every time you run the program, your choices are already selected.

The two programs from AGS in this category are stripped-down versions of their larger programs (Natal Horoscope 110 is a module of Apple Star Track, and Natal Package 410 is a module of Astro Star I). AGS has an upgrade policy, though, so you can first purchase these smaller programs and later add the other modules.

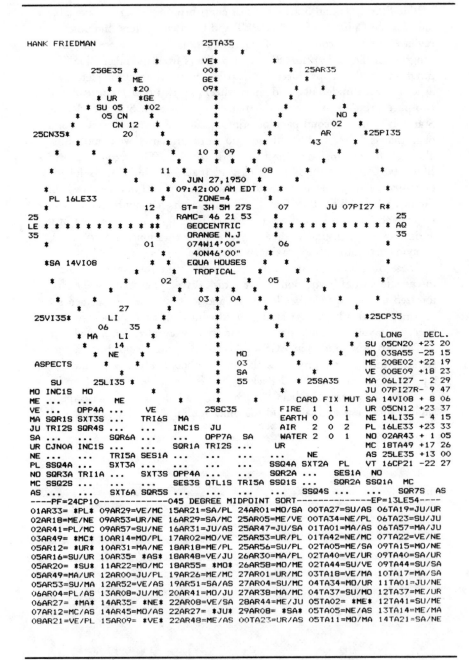

Figure 3.1: *A one-page chart wheel with aspects and midpoints from Blue Star 3 and M-64.*

Natal Horoscope 110

AGS Software, $125

Principal Functions	Prints birth charts and aspect/midpoint page
Types of Calculations	***Aspects included:*** Major plus semisquare, sesquiquadrate, semisextile, inconjunct, and quintile, septile, novile, and sixteenth aspect series
	Custom aspects: No
	Number of house systems: 7
	Heliocentric charts: No
	Methods of progression: None
	Timed progressed hits: No
	Solar and lunar returns: No
	Midpoint analysis: No
	Chart comparisons: No
	Harmonics: No
Defaults	***Preset calculation defaults:*** No
	Preset printout defaults: No
File Management	***Batch processing:*** No
	Saves files: Yes
	File access: None (files can be used by other modules)
Printouts	***Glyphs:*** Yes
	Types of wheels: Closed wheel
	Quality of printouts: Good
Computers	***Computer required:*** Apple II 48K
	Other hardware required: One disk drive, printer

Natal Horoscope 110 is a small and simple package for the Apple II computers. This program prints out a chart wheel with planet listings, complete with daily motion, latitude and declination, right ascension, heliocentric longitudes and latitudes, and planetary nodes. One thing I really like about the chart wheels in this program is that (unlike those of any other program that I've seen except Nova), on Equal House charts, it places the M. C. in the correct house as a point, instead of omitting it. The program also places the East Point, Part of Fortune, and Vertex in the wheel accurately by house (I wish these points were optional). See Figure 3.2 for an example of the wheel. Natal Horoscope doesn't use glyphs for the aspects in the second page of its printout, which Apple Star Track does, but that is actually not the disadvantage it might seem to be, since using them would slow down the printing process noticeably.

A second page of printout (Figure 3.3) displays planets in elements and modalities, planetary dignities, and includes an excellent aspect/midpoint table. This table can contain either the aspects and the midpoints or the aspects alone (making it very readable), and it uses the major aspects, the semisquare and sesquiquadrate, the quintile series, the novile series, the septile series, and the sixteenth series of aspects.

Users with even modest programming skills can rework a few lines of code and make the program list an even larger range of harmonic aspects. AGS uses a weighting system alongside its listing of planets in modalities and elements, to permit the user to better evaluate the strength of each of the modes and elements in the chart. While this weighting system might have some merit, it ignores focal-planet influence. A planet on the Descendant, for example, would highly color the actual weighting of elements. The weighting system is therefore of reduced value.

When I loaded the copy of Natal Horoscope I received, it gave me only a blinking cursor; I had to type in RUN AGSNATAL to get the program running. I strongly suspect, though, that by the time you read this, the program will run automatically once it's booted.

Neither Natal Horoscope 110 nor Apple Star Track offer heliocentric charts, and both give only the mean node, not the true node, position. You cannot customize the Natal Horoscope program, but you can store files with it, and the stored files can later be used by Apple Star Track if you upgrade.

Although Natal Horoscope 110 stores files, it cannot read the files and print out additional charts. Moreover, unless you buy the Multi-Loader #111 for an additional $65, you cannot batch process with Natal Horoscope, while you can do so with other programs in this price range. The

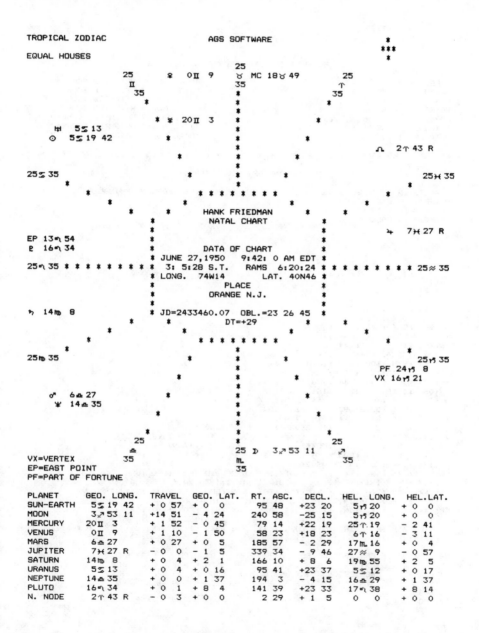

Figure 3.2: A Natal Horoscope 110 chart wheel.

PLANET	GEO. LONG.	TRAVEL	GEO. LAT.	RT. ASC.	DECL.	HEL. LONG.	HEL.LAT.
SUN-EARTH	5♋19 42	+ 0 57	+ 0 0	95 48	+23 20	5♑20	+ 0 0
MOON	3♐53 11	+14 51	− 4 24	240 58	−25 15	5♑20	+ 0 0
MERCURY	20♊ 3	+ 1 52	− 0 45	79 14	+22 19	25♈19	− 2 41
VENUS	0♊ 9	+ 1 10	− 1 50	58 23	+18 23	6♈16	− 3 11
MARS	6♎27	+ 0 27	+ 0 5	185 57	− 2 29	17♏16	+ 0 4
JUPITER	7♓27 R	− 0 0	− 1 5	339 34	− 9 46	27♒ 9	− 0 57
SATURN	14♍ 8	+ 0 4	+ 2 1	166 10	+ 8 6	19♍55	+ 2 5
URANUS	5♋13	+ 0 4	+ 0 16	95 41	+23 37	5♋12	+ 0 17
NEPTUNE	14♎35	+ 0 0	+ 1 37	194 3	− 4 15	16♎29	+ 1 37
PLUTO	16♌34	+ 0 1	+ 8 4	141 39	+23 33	17♌38	+ 8 14
N. NODE	2♈43 R	− 0 3	+ 0 0	2 29	+ 1 5	0 0	+ 0 0

```
        HANK FRIEDMAN


                         PLANETS IN ELEMENTS AND MODALITIES

FIRE      ☽  ♇  ☊  AS EP                          TOTAL NO.=5 WEIGHTED SCORE=8
EARTH     ♄  MC VX PF                             TOTAL NO.=4 WEIGHTED SCORE=4
AIR       ☿  ♀  ♂  ♆                              TOTAL NO.=4 WEIGHTED SCORE=7
WATER     ☉  ♃  ♅                                 TOTAL NO.=3 WEIGHTED SCORE=5
CARDINAL  ☉  ♂  ♅  ♆  ☊  VX PF                    TOTAL NO.=7 WEIGHTED SCORE=8
FIXED     ♇  AS MC EP                             TOTAL NO.=4 WEIGHTED SCORE=7
MUTABLE   ☽  ☿  ♀  ♃  ♄                           TOTAL NO.=5 WEIGHTED SCORE=9

WEIGHTS USED ABOVE: ☉ , ☽ ,AS,MC=3; ☿ , ♀ , ♂ =2; ♃ , ♄ , ♅ , ♆ , ♇ , ☊ =1; VX,EP,PF=0

                              PLANETARY DIGNITIES

PLANETS IN RULERSHIPS  ☿  ♃                       THERE ARE NO MUTUAL RECEPTIONS.
PLANETS IN EXALTATIONS ♇
PLANETS IN DETRIMENTS  ♂
PLANETS IN FALL


                              GEOCENTRIC ASPECTS
  :☉
☽ :QNX :☽
  :1A27:
☿ : ** : ** :☿
  :    :    :
♀ : ** :OPP : ** :♀
  :    :3S44:    :
♂ :SQU :SXT : ** :TRI :♂
  :1A 7:2A34:    :6A18:
♃ :TRI :SQU :7TH : ** :QNX :♃
  :2A 8:3A34:0A16:    :1A 0:
♄ : ** :9TH :SQU :7TH :16TH:OPP :♄
  :    :0S15:5S55:1A 8:0A11:6S41:
♅ :CON :QNX : ** : ** :SQU :TRI : ** :♅
  :0S 7:1A19:    :    :1S15:2A15:    :
♆ : ** : ** :TRI :SQQ : ** :BIQ :SSX : ** :♆
  :    :    :5S28:0S35:    :1S 7:0A26:    :
♇ : ** : ** :SXT : ** :7TH :9TH : ** : ** :SXT :♇
  :    :    :3S29:    :1A32:0A54:    :    :1S59:
☊ :SQU :TRI : ** :SXT :OPP : ** : ** :SQU : ** :SQQ :☊
  :2S37:1S11:    :2A33:3S45:    :    :2S30:    :1A 9:
AS:7TH : ** : ** :SQU :9TH : ** : ** :7TH : ** : ** :BIQ :AS
  :1S11:    :    :4S34:0S52:    :    :1S 4:    :    :1A 8:
MC:SSQ : ** :SSX : ** : ** :QNT :TRI :SSQ :BIQ :SQU :SSQ :SQU :MC
  :1S30:    :1S13:    :    :0A38:4A41:1S23:1S45:2A16:1S 7:6A45:
VX: ** : ** :7TH :SQQ : ** :7TH :TRI : ** :SQU :QNX : ** : ** :TRI :VX
  :    :    :0A36:1A12:    :0S20:2A13:    :1A47:0S12:    :    :2A28:
EP: ** : ** : ** :QNT :7TH : ** :SSX : ** :SXT :CON : ** : ** :SQU : ** :EP
  :    :    :    :1A45:1S 8:    :0S14:    :0S41:2S40:    :    :4A56:    :
PF:9TH :7TH :BIQ :TRI : ** :SSQ : ** :9TH : ** :16TH: ** :QNX :TRI : ** :9TH :PF
  :1S11:1S11:1S54:6S 1:    :1S41:    :1S 4:    :0A 5:    :1A27:5A19:    :0A14:

MAXIMUM ORBS--CON,OPP,TRI,SQU          --PLUS OR MINUS 7 DEGREES
              SXT                      --PLUS OR MINUS 5 DEGREES
              SSQ,SQQ,SSX,QNX,QNT,BIQ--PLUS OR MINUS 2 DEGREES
              MINOR HARMONICS          --PLUS OR MINUS 3% OF WAVE

AGS SOFTWARE
```

Figure 3.3: Natal Horoscope 110, page 2, displaying aspects without midpoints.

documentation is good, and contains a delta-T table, examples, and a time-zone table.

In summary, Natal Horoscope 110 is fine for the beginner who wants to stay in the AGS family and plans to upgrade later to the Apple Star Track program. The aspect/midpoint table is easy to read and the program is fast enough, but the quality of the chart wheel (without proportionately spaced planets) leaves something to be desired (see Figures 3.2 and 3.3). I recommend that you consider M-71 Natal Chart Service and M-64 from Matrix before making a choice.

M-71 Natal Chart Service

Matrix Software, $150

Principal Functions	Prints natal charts, aspect/midpoint page
Types of Calculations	*Aspects included:* Major plus semisquare, sesquiquadrate, inconjunct, quintile
	Custom aspects: No
	Number of house systems: 6 plus user-defined Ascendant
	Heliocentric charts: Yes
	Methods of progression: None
	Solar and lunar returns: No
	Midpoint analysis: No
	Chart comparisons: No
	Harmonics: No
Defaults	*Preset calculation defaults:* No
	Preset printout defaults: No
File Management	*Batch processing:* 10 jobs
	Saves files: No
Printouts	*Glyphs:* Yes
	Types of wheels: Closed, open; both with proportionally spaced planets
	Quality of printouts: Very good
Computers	*Computer required:* Apple II 48K, TRS-80 models I & III 48K, Commodore CBM/PET 32K, Commodore 64
	Other hardware required: printer

M-71 Natal Chart Service is also a fast and simple chart-generation program. It does not save files, and therefore cannot be used with other programs, but it makes up for this lack in its speed and power. There is no screen output, so this program is suited only to printing out charts; but it does offer batch processing—you can enter up to ten charts at one time. Its chart wheels are of superior quality, with a choice of open or closed wheels, and include such features as proportionately spaced planets and glyphs, a quadrant count, phase and speed of travel of the Moon, a mode/element grid, the Sun/Moon angle, the positions of the Part of Fortune, and East Point. The wheel page also includes a table complete with declinations, dignities, house positions, elements, and triplicities for each planet.

Although I prefer a chart wheel in which the planets are placed proportionately around the circle, as in this program, there are drawbacks to this approach. Some people can't get used to Matrix's convention of placing the degrees and minutes of the planet's position backwards for Sixth- and Seventh-House planets and upside down for Third- and Fourth-House positions (see Figures 3.4 and 3.5 for examples of open and closed wheels from M-71). Therefore, if you are considering buying this program, you should inspect the examples in Figures 3.2, 3.4, and 3.5 to see which type of output you prefer, AGS's or Matrix's.

M-71 can create a second page of printout, with a table of midpoints and aspects (major aspects plus the semisquare, sesquiquadrate, inconjunct, and quintile). It uses fewer aspects than the Natal Horoscope program (and there are no aspects to the Vertex, East Point, or Part of Fortune), and the M-71 aspect page is a little harder to read. Still, M-71 also supplies tables showing daily motion, tallies (number of planets per house, aspects per planet, type of each aspect in the chart), and a house-cusps listing (see Figure 3.6). The program calculates and uses the true node, and can create solar charts, Aries charts, user-specified house cusps, and heliocentric charts as well as the most popular house systems.

In summary, M-71 produces excellent charts and tables, operates easily and quickly, and could be used quite effectively as a chart-service program (Matrix will send a version that will print your own name and address at the top right-hand corner of each chart upon request). M-71 does nothing but prepare birth charts, but it does birth charts very well.

If M-71 saved files for use in other programs (it does not) or could be upgraded to a more powerful program (it cannot be) I would have recommended it over the AGS Natal Horoscope program, because I feel the quality of its chart wheels is higher. Since the Natal Horoscope package can be upgraded to Apple Star Track (with batch processing), for $170 it has the potential to be more powerful. However, if you plan to

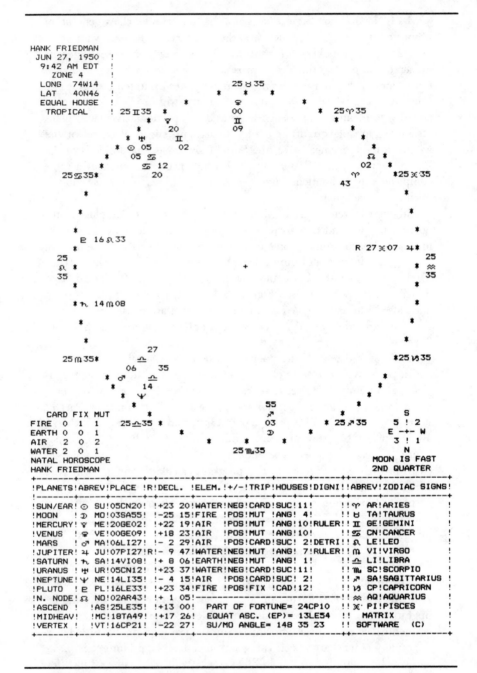

Figure 3.4: An open wheel produced by M-71.

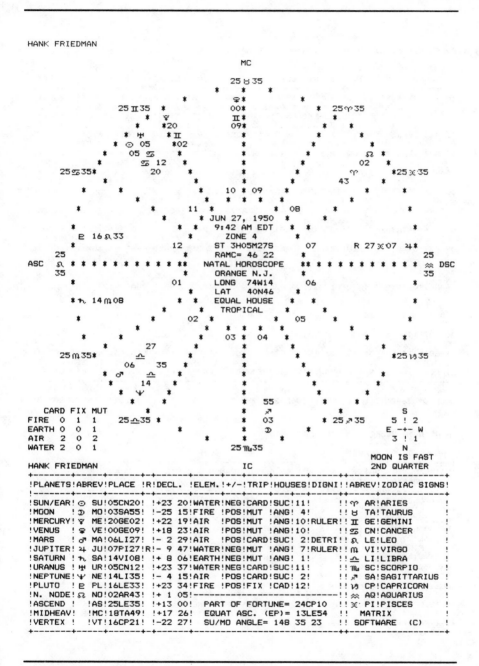

Figure 3.5: A standard wheel produced by M-71.

ASPECTS & 45 MIDPOINTS FOR HANK FRIEDMAN

```
  SU  !  MO  !  ME  !  VE  !  MA  !  JU  !  SA  !  UR  !  NE  !  PL  !  NO  !
05CN20!03SA55!20GE02!00GE09!06LI27!07PI27!14VIO8!05CN12!14LI35!16LE33!02AR43!
------+------+------+------+------+------+------+------+------+------+------+
--SU--! *INC*! 15 18! 35 11! *SQR*! *TRI*! 68 48! *CNJ*! 99 15! *SSQ*! *SQR*!
      ! 1 25A!      !      ! 1 07A! 2 07A!      !  08S!      ! 3 46S! 2 37S!
04TA37!--MO--!163 53! *OPP*! *SXT*! *SQR*! 79 47! *INC*! 49 20!107 22! *TRI*!
      !      !      ! 3 46S! 2 32A! 3 32A!      ! 1 17A!      !      ! 1 12S!
12TA41!26AR58!--ME--! 19 53!106 25!102 35! *SQR*! 15 10! *TRI*! *SXT*! 77 19!
      !      !      !      !      !      ! 5 54S!      ! 5 27S! 3 29S!      !
02TA44!17AR02!25AR05!--VE--! *TRI*! 82 42!103 59! 35 03! *SES*! 76 25! *SXT*!
      !      !      !      ! 6 18A!      !      !      !  34S!      ! 2 34A!
05AR53!05TA11!13TA14!03TA18!--MA--! *INC*! 22 19! *SQR*!  8 08! 49 54! *OPP*!
      !      !      !      !      ! 1 00A!      ! 1 15S!      !      ! 3 44S!
06TA23!20AR41!28AR44!18AR48!06TA57!--JU--! *OPP*! *TRI*!142 52!159 07! 25 16!
      !      !      !      !      !      ! 6 41S! 2 15A!      !      !      !
09TA44!24AR01!02TA05!22AR08!10TA17!25AR47!--SA--! 68 56! 30 27! 27 35!161 25!
      !      !      !      !      !      !      !      !      !      !      !
05AR16!04TA34!12TA37!02TA40!05AR49!06TA19!09TA40!--UR--! 99 23! *SSQ*! *SQR*!
      !      !      !      !      !      !      !      !      ! 3 39S! 2 29S!
09AR57!09TA15!02AR18!07TA22!10AR31!11TA01!14TA21!09AR53!--NE--! *SXT*!168 08!
      !      !      !      !      !      !      !      !      !      ! 1 59S!
25AR56!10AR14!18AR18!08AR21!26AR30!12AR00!15AR21!25AR53!00TA34!--PL--! *SES*!
      !      !      !      !      !      !      !      !      !      ! 1 09S!
04AR01!03TA19!11TA22!01TA26!04AR35!05TA05!08TA25!03AR57!08AR39!24AR38!--NO--!
      !      !      !      !      !      !      !      !      !      !      !
AS
 50 15! 98 20! *SXT*! *SQR*! 40 52!168 08! 18 33! 50 23! *SSQ*!  9 01!142 52!
      !      ! 5 33A! 4 34S!      !      !      !      ! 4 00S!      !      !
00TA27!14AR45!22AR48!12AR52!01TA01!16AR31!19AR51!00TA23!05TA05!06AR04!29AR09!
MC
 *SSQ*!164 54! 31 13! 11 19! *SES*! *QTL*! *TRI*! *SSQ*!145 45! *SQR*! *SSQ*!
 1 30S!      !      !      ! 2 38S!  37A! 4 41S! 1 23A!      ! 2 16S! 1 07S!
27AR04!11AR22!19AR26!09AR29!27AR38!13AR08!16AR29!27AR01!01TA42!02AR41!25AR46!
------+------+------+------+------+------+------+------+------+------+------+
  SU  !  MO  !  ME  !  VE  !  MA  !  JU  !  SA  !  UR  !  NE  !  PL  !  NO  !
05CN20!03SA55!20GE02!00GE09!06LI27!07PI27!14VIO8!05CN12!14LI35!16LE33!02AR43!
```

CHART DATA-SCOPE FOR HANK FRIEDMAN

```
+---------------------------+   +---------------------------+   +--------------+
! ASPECTS PER PLANET    !   !      ASPECT ANALYSIS      !   !   HOUSES     !
!--+------+-+---------+--!   !--+----------------+---+--!   +--------------+
!CO!PLANET! ! DAILY   ! !   ! ! ! ASPECT NAMES !DEG!O !   ! PLANETS      !
!DE! NAME!R! MOTION  !# !   ! #!                !ASP!RB!   !  PER HOUSE   !
+--+------+-+---------+--+   +--+----+-----------+---+--+   +---------+--+--+
!SU!05CN20! !   57 13! 7!   ! 1!CJN!CONJUNCTION!000! 7!   !01=25LE35! 1!
!MO!03SA55! ! 14 53 50! 6!   ! 3!OPP!OPPOSITION !180! 7!   !02=25VI35! 2!
!ME!20GE02! !  1 52 10! 4!   ! 6!TRI!TRINE      !120! 7!   !03=25LI35! 0!
!VE!00GE09! !  1 10 28! 5!   ! 8!SQR!SQUARE     ! 90! 7!   !04=25SC35! 1!
!MA!06LI27! !    27 04! 7!   ! 5!SXT!SEXTILE    ! 60! 6!   !05=25SA35! 0!
!JU!07PI27!R!    00 07! 6!   ! 6!SSQ!SEMI-SQUARE! 45! 3!   !06=25CP35! 0!
!SA!14VI08! !    04 09! 3!   ! 1!QTL!QUINTILE   ! 72! 3!   !07=25AQ35! 1!
!UR!05CN12! !    03 36! 7!   ! 3!SES!SESQUIQUAD.!135! 3!   !08=25PI35! 1!
!NE!14LI35! !    00 02! 4!   ! 3!INC!INCONJUNCT !150! 3!   !09=25AR35! 0!
!PL!16LE33! !    01 27! 6!   ! !-------------------------!   !10=25TA35! 2!
!NO!02AR43! !    03 00! 7!   ! ! COPYRIGHT (C) 1980      !   !11=25GE35! 2!
!AS!25LE35! !    00 00! 3!   ! ! MATRIX SOFTWARE         !   !12=25CN35! 1!
!MC!18TA49! !    00 00! 7!   ! ! BIG RAPIDS, MI          !   !         !
+--+------+-+---------+--+   +--+-------------------------+   +---------+--+--+
```

Figure 3.6: M-71 aspects and midpoints page.

spend that much altogether, you might consider either buying the more powerful M-65 from Matrix (at $300) or purchasing their M-64 module, which prints a one-page chart complete with midpoint sort and aspect table, maintains chart files, and will do batch processing, as well as analyzing charts many ways.

M-64 Natal Disk Package

Matrix Software, $125

Principal Functions
Prints one-page chart wheels with aspect and midpoint tables, analyzes charts on screen

Types of Calculations

Aspects included: Majors plus semisquare, sesquiquadrate, quintile, inconjunct

Custom aspects: No

Number of house systems: 9

Heliocentric charts: Yes

Methods of progression: None

Solar and lunar returns: No

Midpoint analysis: On-screen sorting, selectable dial, screen dumps to printer

Chart comparisons: No

Harmonics: No

Defaults

Preset calculation defaults: No

Preset printout defaults: No

File Management

Batch processing: Batch size limited only by disk space

Saves files: Yes

File access: Excellent, with directory and file utilities

Printouts

Glyphs: Only in Commodore version

Types of wheels: Open, closed; both with proportionately spaced planets

Quality of printouts: Very good, but a little crowded

M-64 Natal Disk Package *(continued)*

Computers

Computer required: Apple II 48K, TRS-80 Model I & III 48K, Commodore CBM/PET 32K, Commodore 64

Other hardware required: Two disk drives (one-drive versions available for Apple II and TRS-80), printer

M-64 is a modular program that generates chart files, prints out charts, and performs analyses on individual charts. It has no comparison or interchart functions, however, nor does it have predictive options (returns, progressions, directions), nor any degree of customizing.

M-64 was Matrix's first attempt at a multimodule program—that is, a program with a variety of functions in separate modules. As a result, M-64 is somewhat slower and more cumbersome to operate than the other natal-chart programs (remember, though, that the program does more than the others, too). For instance, this program has three interlocking menus for different kinds of functions. Moving between the menus can be confusing when you first start using the program. The analysis module takes about two minutes to prepare charts for analysis (although once the charts are prepared, the subsequent routines work quickly) and it takes almost four minutes to create and print a chart—without glyphs—(at least twice as long as other "glyph-less" programs). Nor does M-64 get any faster with multiple jobs. Glyphs are available only in the Commodore version, and only for certain combinations of printer and interface. Because you can't customize the program, you have to specify the house system, type of midpoint dial, tropical or sidereal zodiac, and standard or Uranian planets each time you process a chart.

M-64 supplies you with a great many options, nonetheless, including midpoint analysis, nine house systems, one-page chart wheels complete with aspects and sorted midpoints (selectable midpoint dial; see Figure 3.1), and aspect sorts of several types (such as by planet, aspect, and orb, as in Figures 3.7 and 3.8). It can save files, its file directories are easy to use, and it has utilities for such file-handling tasks as deleting files. It will also do batch processing.

```
!00AR15!SA/VT!122 13!TRI!+ 2 13!S!
!01AR33!PL***!******!***!******!*!
!02AR18!ME/NE!114 33!TRI!+ 5 27!S!
!02AR41!PL/MC! 87 44!SQR!+ 2 16!S!
!02AR43!NO***!******!***!******!*!
!03AR12!ME/VT!153 41!   !      ! !
!03AR49!MC***!******!***!******!*!
!03AR57!UR/NO! 92 30!SQR!+ 2 30!S!
!04AR01!SU/NO! 92 37!SQR!- 2 37!A!
!04AR35!MA/NO!176 16!OPP!+ 3 44!S!
!05AR12!UR***!******!***!******!*!
!05AR16!SU/UR!    08!CNJ!-   08!A!
!05AR20!SU***!******!***!******!*!
!05AR49!MA/UR! 91 15!SQR!+ 1 15!S!
!05AR53!SU/MA! 91 07!SQR!+ 1 07!S!
!06AR04!PL/AS!  9 01!   !      ! !
!06AR27!MA***!******!***!******!*!
!07AR12!MC/AS! 96 45!SQR!- 6 45!A!
!08AR21!VE/PL! 76 25!   !      ! !
!08AR39!NE/NO!168 08!   !      ! !
!09AR29!VE/MC! 11 19!   !      ! !
!09AR32!NO/VT! 76 21!   !      ! !
***PRESS=FORWARD*(R)EVERSE*(M)ORE*
```

Figure 3.7: An M-64 screen dump of a midpoint sort.

```
!11TA22!ME/NO! 77 19!   !      ! !
!05AR16!SU/UR!    08!CNJ!-   08!A!
!01TA27!PL/VT!149 48!INC!-   12!A!
!07TA22!VE/NE!134 26!SES!+   34!S!
!13AR08!JU/MC! 71 23!QTL!-   37!A!
!06TA57!MA/JU!151 00!INC!- 1 00!A!
!05AR53!SU/MA! 91 07!SQR!+ 1 07!S!
!25AR46!NO/MC! 46 07!SSQ!+ 1 07!S!
!24AR38!PL/NO!133 51!SES!+ 1 09!S!
!03TA19!MO/NO!118 48!TRI!+ 1 12!S!
!08TA15!VE/VT!133 47!SES!+ 1 13!S!
!05AR49!MA/UR! 91 15!SQR!+ 1 15!S!
!04TA34!MO/UR!148 43!INC!- 1 17!A!
!27AR01!UR/MC! 46 23!SSQ!- 1 23!A!
!04TA37!SU/MO!148 35!INC!- 1 25!A!
!27AR04!SU/MC! 46 30!SSQ!+ 1 30!S!
!15AR28!NE/VT! 91 47!SQR!+ 1 47!S!
!00TA34!NE/PL! 58 01!SXT!+ 1 59!S!
!06TA23!SU/JU!117 53!TRI!+ 2 07!S!
!00AR15!SA/VT!122 13!TRI!+ 2 13!S!
!06TA19!JU/UR!117 45!TRI!- 2 15!A!
!02AR41!PL/MC! 87 44!SQR!+ 2 16!S!
***PRESS=FORWARD*(R)EVERSE*(M)ORE*
```

Figure 3.8: An M-64 screen dump of an aspect sort by orb.

Once you get used to the way M-64 works, the program is not difficult to use, and it functions well both as a chart-service program and a tool for analyzing the charts on file. Because the program modules are so large, files load slowly. Loading could be speeded up considerably with a faster DOS, such as PRONTO-DOS on the Apple. Still, M-64 won't let you change the aspects and orbs used (major aspects plus the semisquare, sesquiquadrate, inconjunct, and quintile), and printing takes longer than in comparable programs. If you don't mind these limitations, then M-64 might be the program to buy. For $125, you do get more functions than in most programs sold for the same machines in this price range.

Natal Package 410

AGS Software, $130

Principal Functions	Fast computation and screen displays of aspect, midpoint, harmonic analysis, plus printouts
Types of Calculations	**Aspects included:** Majors plus semisextile, semisquare, sesquiquadrate, inconjunct
	Custom aspects: 25 total
	Number of house systems: 10 plus equal houses from planets, points
	Heliocentric charts: Yes
	Methods of progression: None
	Solar and lunar returns: No
	Midpoint analysis: Displays and prints sorted midpoint list, midpoint structures, aspects to midpoints
	Chart comparisons: No
	Harmonics: Displays and prints sorted harmonic positions
Defaults	**Preset calculation defaults:** No
	Preset printout defaults: No
File Management	**Batch processing:** No
	Saves files: Yes
	File access: Fair
Printouts	**Glyphs:** Yes
	Types of wheels: Spoke
	Quality of printouts: Fair
Computers	**Computer required:** TRS-80 I, III, 4 48K, CP/M Apple 48K, CP/M 48K
	Other hardware required: One disk drive

Natal Package 410 is a subset of Astro Star I; it is most suitable for those who plan to upgrade eventually to Astro Star. This program, like its parent, Astro Star, performs calculations with exceptional speed and is designed primarily as an interactive, screen-oriented program. In other words, the program responds so quickly to your input that you can sit at your computer screen and keep selecting tasks for it to perform, with practically no waiting between tasks. It does produce printouts, but it shines in its speed and versatility on the screen, and not in its printouts. You can analyze midpoints, examine several harmonics, and study the chart using a variety of aspect methods, switching between modules with ease and reliability.

Unfortunately, the screen displays and printouts of planets in houses of the Natal Package and Astro Star I are hard to read, because the programs do not place the positions in a wheel format or put spaces between houses (see Figure 3.9). The aspect displays are crowded and poorly spaced (see Figure 3.10), as are the midpoint displays, which fail to show the placing of planets (see Figure 3.11). The chart wheels are quite readable, but among the most primitive of those presently in use, with planets in each house printed in a column and house boundaries poorly constructed (see Figure 3.12). Its one visual quirk is the use of SO as the abbreviation for the Sun, instead of the usual SU. In all these cases, the displays and printouts are usable but simply not what they should be.

```
AS 25LE35  MC 18TA49  VX 16CP21   EP 13LE54

1    25LE35      4    25SC35      7    25AQ35     10    25TA35
     SA 14VI08        MO  3SG53        JU  7PI27        VE  0GE09
2    25VI35      5    25SG35      8    25PI35           ME 20GE03
     MA  6LI27   6    25CP35           NO  2AR43   11   25GE35
     NE 14LI35                    9    25AR35           UR  5CN12
3    25LI35                                             SO  5CN20
                                                   12   25CN35
                                                        PL 16LE31


1    25LE35      4    25SC35      7    25AQ35     10    25TA35
     SA 14VI08        MO  3SG53        JU  7PI27        VE  0GE09
2    25VI35      5    25SG35      8    25PI35           ME 20GE03
     MA  6LI27   6    25CP35           NO  2AR43   11   25GE35
     NE 14LI35                    9    25AR35           UR  5CN12
3    25LI35                                             SO  5CN20
                                                   12   25CN35
                                                        PL 16LE31
```

Figure 3.9: A house listing by Astro Star I.

Both programs lack batch processing, and are therefore unsuitable for a chart service. Their file-handling routines are as poor as those in most AGS software. When I first tried to create a chart file and save charts with Natal Package, I had a great deal of difficulty because I followed the example in the documentation too closely.

```
ASPECTS FROM POINTS OF kathi TO POINTS OF hank
SO :TRI SO   3 43 :CON JU   1 36 :OPP SA   5 05 :TRI UR   3 51
MO :CON ME   9 37 :CON VE  10 17 :TRI MA   3 59 :SQR JU   2 59
ME :CON NO   9 37
VE :QCX AS   0 58 :TRI MC   0 58
MA :CON JU  10 45 :OPP AS   1 07 :SQR MC   1 07
JU :CON MO   6 37 :OPP VE   2 53 :SQR AS   1 41 :OPP MC   1 41
SA :TRI MO   0 54 :TRI NO   0 16
UR :CON ME   2 18 :TRI NE   3 10 :SXT PL   1 14
NE :CON MA   3 47 :CON NE   4 21 :SSQ AS   0 21 :SQQ MC   0 21
PL :CON PL   4 55
NO :OPP MO   3 10 :CON VE   6 54 :TRI MA   0 36 :SQR JU   0 24 :CON MC  11 28
AS :OPP SO   2 31 :OPP UR   2 23 :SQQ PL   1 18 :SQR NO   0 06
MC :SQR SO   2 31 :SXT MO   1 04 :TRI VE   2 40 :CON MA   3 38 :SQR UR   2 23
      :CON NE  11 46 :SSQ PL   1 18 :OPP NO   0 06
ASPECTS FROM POINTS OF hank TO POINTS OF kathi
SO :TRI SO   3 43 :OPP AS   2 31 :SQR MC   2 31
MO :CON JU   6 37 :TRI SA   0 54 :OPP NO   3 10 :SXT MC   1 04
ME :CON MO   9 37 :CON UR   2 18
VE :CON MO  10 17 :OPP JU   2 53 :CON NO   6 54 :TRI MC   2 40
MA :TRI MO   3 59 :CON NE   3 47 :TRI NO   0 36 :CON MC   3 38
JU :CON SO   1 36 :SQR MO   2 59 :CON MA  10 45 :SQR NO   0 24
SA :OPP SO   5 05
UR :TRI SO   3 51 :OPP AS   2 23 :SQR MC   2 23
NE :TRI UR   3 10 :CON NE   4 21 :CON MC  11 46
PL :SXT UR   1 14 :CON PL   4 55 :SSQ AS   1 18 :SSQ MC   1 18
NO :CON ME   9 37 :TRI SA   0 16 :SQR AS   0 06 :OPP MC   0 06
AS :QCX VE   0 58 :OPP MA   1 07 :SQR JU   1 41 :SSQ NE   0 21
MC :TRI VE   0 58 :SQR MA   1 07 :OPP JU   1 41 :SQQ NE   0 21 :CON NO  11 28
```

```
POINTS OF kathi IN HOUSES OF hank
1   25LE35        4   25SC35        7   25AQ35        10   25TA35
2   25VI35            JU 27SC16         MA 26AQ42          NO  7GE03
    NE 10LI14     5   25SG35            SO  9PI03          MO 10GE26
3   25LI35            VE 24CP37         ME 23PI06          UR 17GE45
              6   25CP35        8   25PI35        11   25GE35
                                 9   25AR35        12   25CN35
                                                        SA  2LE59
                                                        PL 11LE36

POINTS OF hank IN HOUSES OF kathi
1   2CP49         4   2AR49         7   2CN49         10   2LI49
2   2AQ49         5   2TA49             UR  5CN12          MA  6LI27
3   2PI49             VE  0GE09         SO  5CN20          NE 14LI35
    JU  7PI27     6   2GE49             2LE49         11   2SC49
    NO  2AR43         ME 20GE03     8   PL 16LE31     12   2SG49
                                 9   2VI49              MO  3SG53
                                     SA 14VI08
```

Figure 3.10: A synastry output by Astro Star I.

In spite of these deficiencies, the Natal Package calculates natal charts very quickly (seven seconds), and includes heliocentric and local-space charts, plus powerful aspect analysis that finds aspects to a specified point, aspects to midpoints and aspect sorts. You can also define your own aspects and orbs (although doing so is pretty complex). In addition, the package contains a variety of harmonic routines and midpoint sorts and techniques (including midpoint trees), all of which compute at lightning-fast speeds (faster than any other program I tested) and work very well.

Many of the weaknesses of Natal Package and Astro Star I are being corrected in the new updated version of Astro Star (Astro Star II) and its subset, which will probably still be called Natal Package 410. See the review of Astro Star II in this chapter for further details. By the time you read this book, at least the first release of the new programs should be available.

```
SG/MO  19VI37     MO/SA  24LI01     ME/MC   7GE49     MA/AS  16VI01     UR/PL  25CN52
SO/ME  27GE42     MO/UR  19VI33     VE/MA   3LE18     MA/MC   1LE01     UR/NO  18TA58
SO/VE  17GE45     MO/NE   9SC14     VE/JU  18LI48     JU/SA  10SG48     UR/AS   OLE24
SO/MA  20LE54     MO/PL  10LI12     VE/SA  22CN09     JU/UR   6SC20     UR/MC  15GE24
SO/JU   6SC24     MO/NO   3LE18     VE/UR  17GE41     JU/NE  26SG01     NE/PL  15VI33
SO/SA   9LE44     MO/AS  14LI44     VE/NE   7LE22     JU/PL  26SC59     NE/NO   8CN39
SO/UR   5CN16     MO/MC  29LE44     VE/PL   8CN20     JU/NO  20VI05     NE/AS  20VI05
SO/NE  24LE58     ME/VE  10GE06     VE/NO   1TA26     JU/AS   1SG31     NE/MC   5LE05
SO/PL  25CN56     ME/MA  13LE15     VE/AS  12CN52     JU/MC  16LI31     PL/NO   9GE37
SO/NO  19TA02     ME/JU  28LI45     VE/MC  27TA52     SA/UR   9LE40     PL/AS  21LE03
SO/AS   OLE28     ME/SA   2LE06     MA/JU  21SG57     SA/NE  29VI22     PL/MC   6CN03
SO/MC  15GE28     ME/UR  27GE38     MA/SA  25VI18     SA/PL   0VI20     NO/AS  14GE09
MO/ME  11VI58     ME/NE  17LE19     MA/UR  20LE50     SA/NO  23GE26     NO/MC  29AR09
MO/VE   2VI01     ME/PL  18CN17     MA/PL  11VI29     SA/AS   4VI52     AS/MC  10CN33
MO/MA   5SC10     ME/NO  11TA23     MA/NO   4CN35     SA/MC  19CN52
MO/JU  20CP40     ME/AS  22CN49                       UR/NE  24LE54

HARMONIC     8 ORB    1 00
PL=ME/NE 0 48=MO/SA 0 01
NO=UR/PL 0 39=SO/PL 0 43=ME/NE 0 24=ME/VE 0 07=JU/SA 0 35
UR=MA/NO 0 37=PL/AS 0 51=PL/MC 0 51=MO/ME 0 44
SO=MA/UR 0 30=MA/NO 0 45=PL/AS 0 43=PL/MC 0 43=MO/ME 0 52=ME/JU 0 55
MA=NO/AS 0 12=PL/AS 0 24=NO/MC 0 12=PL/MC 0 24=ME/JU 0 12
AS=MA/NE 0 04=SO/NE 0 38=UR/NE 0 42=VE/MA 0 13=SO/VE 0 21=VE/UR 0 25=MO/NO 0 13
   =MO/PL 0 23=ME/SA 0 60
MC=MA/NE 0 04=SO/NE 0 38=UR/NE 0 42=VE/MA 0 13=SO/VE 0 21=VE/UR 0 25=MO/NO 0 13
   =MO/PL 0 23=ME/SA 0 60
NE=MO/MC 0 09=MO/AS 0 09=MA/JU 0 08=SO/JU 0 42=JU/UR 0 46=SA/PL 0 45
VE=MO/MC 0 25=MO/AS 0 25=MA/JU 0 42=SA/NO 0 47=SA/PL 0 11
MO=VE/JU 0 05=JU/NE 0 22=SA/MC 0 59=SA/AS 0 59=ME/NO 0 00=ME/PL 0 36
JU=VE/SA 0 19=SA/NE 0 36=ME/MC 0 22=ME/AS 0 22
SA=ME/JU 0 23=PL/MC 0 35=PL/AS 0 35=NO/MC 0 01=NO/AS 0 01
ME=JU/PL 0 34=JU/NO 0 02=MO/UR 0 31=SO/MO 0 27=MO/MA 0 07=VE/AS 0 19=NE/AS 0 02
   =VE/MC 0 19=NE/MC 0 02
```

Figure 3.11: Midpoints and midpoint structures printouts by Astro Star I.

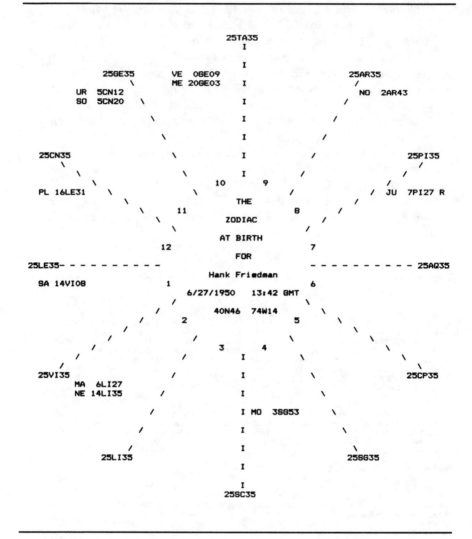

Figure 3.12: An Astro Star I chart wheel.

Astro Star I

AGS Software, $295

Principal Functions	Fast computation and screen displays of aspect, midpoint, harmonic analysis, predictive, chart comparison modules, plus printouts
Types of Calculations	***Aspects included:*** Majors plus semisextile, semisquare, sesquiquadrate, inconjunct
	Custom aspects: 25 total
	Number of house systems: 10 plus equal houses from planets, points
	Heliocentric charts: Yes
	Methods of progression: Secondary, minor, tertiary, with a variety of methods to progress the angles: solar arc, quotidian, degree/year, duodenary, vertical, user-specified arcs
	Solar and lunar returns: Full, half, quarter returns
	Midpoint analysis: Displays and prints sorted midpoint list, midpoint structures, aspects to midpoints
	Chart comparisons: Interaspects, inter-midpoints, composite charts, relationship charts, inter-house placements
	Harmonics: Displays and prints sorted harmonic positions
Defaults	***Preset calculation defaults:*** No
	Preset printout defaults: No
File Management	***Batch processing:*** No
	Saves files: Yes
	File access: Fair

Astro Star I (*continued*)

Printouts	*Glyphs:* Yes
	Types of wheels: Spoke
	Quality of printouts: Fair
Computers	*Computer required:* TRS-80 I, III, 4 48K, CP/M Apple 48K, CP/M 48K
	Other hardware required: One disk drive

AGS's Astro Star I is the pioneer program for CP/M and TRS-80 computers. When it was first released, nothing could match it for speed or power. Of course, even then better printouts were available in other programs, but no product offered Astro Star's range of options. Even today, there are no Matrix chart-service programs for the CP/M format, although Matrix is currently creating a version of M-65 for CP/M users.

In evaluating Astro Star I, you should first read the description of Natal Package 410, since the two function identically. The difference is that Astro Star I has two additional modules: a predictive module (412) and a chart-comparison module (413). Also, pay careful attention to the preliminary evaluation of Astro Star II below (I received a prerelease copy from AGS), which covers the new program's many improvements and enhancements.

Astro Star I will print astrological glyphs on certain printers, and one version includes Uranian planets (#405). Since I have already described the essential features of this program in my review of Natal Package 410, I will discuss only Astro Star's two additional modules.

The chart-comparison module will work with two charts at once, compare aspects between charts, create composite and relationship charts, find midpoints, and place one person's planets in the other's houses. While the screen displays and printouts are quite crowded to the eye, they are serviceable (see Figure 3.13).

The predictive module, which can calculate a variety of solar and lunar returns, makes it simple for you to examine a series of returns (year by year or month by month) and to compute demi-returns.

This part of the program will also prepare progressed charts, such as day-for-a-year (secondary progressed) charts, and several kinds of solar-arc charts. But while it does create progressed charts, it cannot calculate timed progressed hits, which should have been built in.

The documentation for Astro Star is good, and includes such nice touches as a list of additional possible aspects to use. The entry routine is also good, although fractional time zones cannot be entered, and you must convert the birth time to compensate.

Despite the poor quality of the screen displays and printouts I still think CP/M users are lucky to be able to purchase a program of this quality. Astro Star I involves no long waits compared with other programs, it's accurate, and it contains many features.

Astro Star II

AGS Software, $295

Principal Functions	Fast computation and screen displays of aspect, midpoint; harmonic analysis; prediction; chart comparison

Types of Calculations

Aspects included: Majors plus semisextile, semisquare, sesquiquadrate, inconjunct

Custom aspects: 25 total per set, unlimited number of sets

Number of house systems: 11 plus equal houses from planets, points

Heliocentric charts: Yes

Methods of progression: Secondary, minor, tertiary, with a variety of methods to progress the angles: solar arc, quotidian, degree for a year, duodenary, vertical, user-specified arcs

Solar and lunar returns: Full, half, quarter returns

Midpoint analysis: Displays and prints sorted midpoint list, midpoint structures, aspects to midpoints

Chart comparisons: Interaspects, inter-midpoints, composite charts, relationship charts, inter-house placements

Harmonics: Displays and prints sorted harmonic positions

Defaults

Preset calculation defaults: Extensive list including house system, method of progression, type of harmonics, coordinate system, type of return, type of aspect analysis, comparison method

Preset printout defaults: Extensive capacity including type of printer, glyph option, number of lines/page, print all jobs, expand/compress printouts; plus macro capacity to design templates for large calculation/printing jobs

Astro Star II *(continued)*

File Management	**Batch processing:** 24 charts in buffer, batch size limited only by disk space
	Saves files: Yes
	File access: Very good (includes file utilities)
Printouts	**Glyphs:** Yes
	Types of wheels: Spoke
	Quality of printouts: Good
Computers	**Computer required:** IBM PC and PC*jr*, CP/M computers
	Other hardware required: One disk drive

I received a preliminary version of Astro Star II from AGS to evaluate for this book. As soon as I ran the program for the first time, I noticed that some of the problems I encountered in Astro Star I had been fixed. Specifically: the new version has batch processing; it uses SU for the Sun (with the option to use SO if you prefer it); the spacing in some of its displays and printouts is less crowded; and it handles files more easily.

The entry routines for Astro Star II are good, and the program will now accept fractional time zones (e.g., 10.5), so you no longer have to correct the birth time.

With the new file-handling routines, you can now store up to twenty-four charts in memory, providing greater speed and versatility. Astro Star II also lets you list the contents of a file more easily than does Astro Star I, lets you create and delete files from within the program (without having to *reboot*, or reactivate, the program from the beginning), and lets you switch easily between groups of chart files.

Astro Star II will also include two of the most sophisticated customizing routines ever available in an astrological program. The preliminary version of Astro Star II did not contain these functions, but AGS assured me that they were close to completion.

The first of these customizing modules is called an *installation* routine; it allows you to control the flow of the options at almost every step of the program. In most such customizing routines, you have to specify which house system, which form of progressions, which comparison routine, and so on, you want to preset. With this installation module, you have an additional choice in each case: You can preset a specific house system, for example, or have the program present you with all the choices available whenever you come to this part of the program. In other words, the installation module lets you either choose a specific method for each step or review all the alternatives when you get to that step. If you always use one house system, and always want solar arcs, but still want to choose an aspect option when you calculate aspects, this program is a great boon.

As if that weren't enough customizing power, you can also generate a number of different installation files in case several different people will be using your computer, or if you yourself have different customizing needs at different times (for example, for research work and for client work).

The second customizing method involves the generation of *macros,* which are sets of instructions on the kinds of overall jobs you want to design. In using macros, which requires careful entry of information at each step, you essentially instruct the program to follow your agenda on a larger scale.

An example of a macro will illustrate what I mean. You could create a template (macro) to do the following jobs in order: ask for two sets of birth data; compute both charts; print the aspects for each chart; print the interaspects between the two charts; print a composite chart; print wheels with the first person's planets in the second person's houses and vice versa; and then determine midpoints between the charts.

After creating such a set of instructions, you would save the macro file. Whenever you wanted all this work done, you would simply call up the macro file, enter the two sets of birth data, and let the program do the rest. Macro files can work in the batch-processing mode, too. All versions of Astro Star II will use macros, but the 64K CP/M version will not permit you to create your own macros; on these machines you will have to use the templates that are provided with the program.

The aspect-dictionary module has been vastly improved in Astro Star II. Not only can you call up the aspect dictionary easily from within the program, but you can also easily change aspects and orbs in the dictionary, and even create several of your own aspect dictionaries with no difficulty. The dictionary allows you to define three sets of orbs: a set for synastry (interaspects between charts), a set indicating strong aspects, and a set indicating weaker aspects. Since you can switch dictionaries whenever you want, you have almost all the power you need. The only constraint is that each dictionary can only hold twenty-five aspects. Therefore, if you want to investigate a larger number of aspects you must use the harmonic routines or create several dictionaries.

My only disappointment with Astro Star II was that the chart wheels were no better than those in Astro Star I. But most people will be happy with the speed and power of this upgraded version. It offers all the options of Astro Star I plus many more.

AGS intends to include an enhanced version of Transit Star with Astro Star II, and eventually will also include Nova's dynamic transit and progression module as part of Astro Star II.

CCRS

AGS Software, $100

Principal Functions Prints charts and a wide variety of astrological tables

Types of Calculations *Aspects included:* Major plus quintile, septile, octile, novile series, semisextile, inconjunct, decile

Custom aspects: No, but custom orbs

Number of house systems: 4 (no Equal House System except for wheel routines)

Heliocentric charts: Yes

Methods of progression: Secondary, tertiary, minor

Solar and lunar returns: Yes, plus kinetic returns

Timed progressed hits: No

Midpoint analysis: Prints sorted midpoint list, selectable dial

Chart comparisons: Prints interaspect table (no orbs), composite charts

Harmonics: Prints list of 30 harmonics, list of harmonic conjunctions

Defaults *Preset calculation defaults:* Three ranges of aspect orbs (synastry, close, and wide), number of factors to include in aspecting

Preset printout defaults: Type of printer

File Management *Batch processing:* Yes

Saves files: Yes

File access: Good (includes file utilities)

CCRS *(continued)*

Printouts   *Glyphs:* Yes

Types of wheels: Bi-wheel

Quality of printouts: Good

Computers   *Computer required:* IBM PC, CP/M, Apple CP/M

Other hardware required: Two disk drives, 80 column printer CCRS may not be used for profit (e.g., chart casting service). Only program that includes asteroids, Chiron, and fixed stars.

Mark Pottenger, the creator of CCRS, has given the public one of the most powerful astrological programs ever written, at one of the lowest prices. This program is only available for CP/M- and IBM-format computers, its documentation is on disk only (you have to print it out yourself), and it's sold in an *uncompiled* form. (Briefly, a program that has been compiled runs faster than one that has not, but an uncompiled program is easier to modify, and can be compiled at any time to give you greater speed.) Also, it lacks sophisticated file access via directories. Nonetheless, CCRS is incredibly versatile. Because AGS is merely the distributor, not the publisher, of CCRS, AGS does not provide customer support for the program, so you have to get in touch with Mark if you have questions or difficulties. Fortunately, the program is not hard to work with, and Mark's address and telephone number are included in the documentation.

It is hard to believe that a $100 program could include so many powerful features. CCRS permits the full use of the four most popular asteroids and Chiron (which no other program I've examined does) complete with glyphs for them. Via a set of ephemeris disks, it can also to prepare accurate charts for ancient time periods. CCRS can make bi-wheels (that is, place two separate sets of chart data around one wheel) for six types of house systems. The chart files are stored, however, with only four house systems, not including the Equal House System. The program calculates the true node, and comes with chart-file utilities that allow you to copy, delete, and inspect files.

The chart-preparation module lets you customize the system for the zodiac and house system you use, lets you include asteroids or not, select your method of progressing the M. C., correct for precession or not, and choose aspect orbs in both synastry and single-chart work. The aspect-customizing routine is easy to use and powerful; the program uses the major aspects plus semisquares and sesquiquadrates; the quintile; septile and novile series aspects; and the semisextile, quincunx, and decile (see Figure 3.13).

Entering birth data in this program is a breeze. The documentation gets you started well, and the entry routines are the easiest and most flexible I've seen. You can create collections of charts with understandable file names such as Family Charts and, if you wish, store them on a separate disk. Even after you have entered all the data and made your choices, the program lets you change anything you want (if only most programs were this agreeable).

Since it is uncompiled, CCRS is a bit slow, but it can be speeded up considerably both by compiling and by using a printer buffer (see Appendix A for an explanation). The program is designed primarily for producing printouts, and offers a wide range of them. You can have the program calculate and print out natal charts, relationship charts, progressed charts (with secondary, tertiary, and minor progressions), and returns (solar and lunar returns, with the option to produce a series of returns, as well as demireturns and kinetic returns to the position of a secondary progressed Sun or Moon position). These charts are printed in the form of bi-wheels, but the outer ring can be empty if you choose. See Figure 3.13 for an example.

As if the program didn't already give you your money's worth, Mark has included many extras:

Composite charts;

Midpoint sorts;

Parans;

Harmonic positions and sorts (see Figure 3.14);

Arabian parts (a *large* list);

Gauquelin sector work;

Angular separations;

Detailed aspect tables (see Figure 3.15).

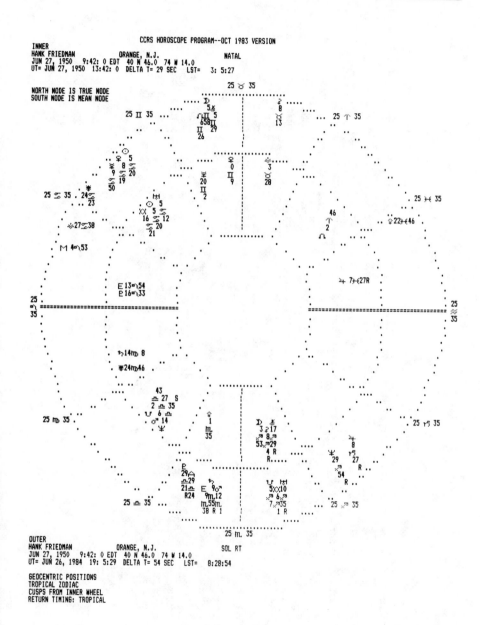

Figure 3.13: *A CCRS bi-wheel printout.*

```
HANK FRIEDMAN          JUN 27, 1950    9:42: 0  ZONE   5.00 D T
ORANGE, N.J.                         40 N 46.0  74 W 14.0
TROPICAL NATAL
```

HARMONIC POSITIONS

H #	5	6	7	8	9	10	11	12	13	14
☉	26 ♋39	1 ♏58	7 ♒18	12 ♉38	17 ♌58	23 ♏17	28 ♒37	3 ♊57	9 ♍16	14 ♐36
☽	19 ♌26	23 ♈19	27 ♐12	1 ♍ 6	4 ♉59	8 ♑52	12 ♍45	16 ♉38	20 ♑32	24 ♍25
☿	10 ♉10	0 ♌12	20 ♎14	10 ♑16	0 ♈18	20 ♊20	10 ♍22	0 ♐24	20 ♒26	10 ♉28
♀	0 ♒44	0 ♈52	1 ♊ 1	1 ♌10	1 ♎19	1 ♐27	1 ♒36	1 ♈45	1 ♊54	2 ♌ 2
♂	2 ♏14	8 ♉41	15 ♏ 8	21 ♉34	28 ♏ 1	4 ♊28	10 ♐55	17 ♊22	23 ♐49	0 ♋15
⚳	10 ♍18	18 ♉22	26 ♑25	4 ♎29	12 ♊33	20 ♒36	28 ♎40	6 ♋44	14 ♓47	22 ♏51
⚴	7 ♓54	9 ♎28	11 ♉ 3	12 ♐38	14 ♋12	15 ♒47	17 ♍22	18 ♈56	20 ♏31	22 ♊ 6
⚵	3 ♍50	28 ♒36	23 ♌22	18 ♒ 8	12 ♌54	7 ♒40	2 ♌26	27 ♑12	21 ♋58	16 ♑44
⚶	17 ♍19	20 ♎47	24 ♏15	27 ♐43	1 ♒11	4 ♓38	8 ♈ 6	11 ♉34	15 ♊ 2	18 ♋30
♃	7 ♐16	14 ♏43	22 ♎10	29 ♍37	7 ♍ 4	14 ♌31	21 ♋58	29 ♊25	6 ♊52	14 ♉19
♄	10 ♋40	24 ♐48	8 ♊56	23 ♏ 5	7 ♉13	21 ♎21	5 ♈29	19 ♍37	3 ♓45	17 ♌53
⚷	27 ♎24	14 ♋53	2 ♈22	19 ♐51	7 ♍20	24 ♉49	12 ♒17	29 ♎46	17 ♋15	4 ♈44
♅	26 ♋ 0	1 ♏12	6 ♒24	11 ♉36	16 ♌49	22 ♏ 1	27 ♒13	2 ♊25	7 ♍37	12 ♐49
♆	12 ♐53	27 ♊28	12 ♑ 2	26 ♋37	11 ♒11	25 ♌46	10 ♓21	24 ♍55	9 ♈30	24 ♎ 4
♇	22 ♒46	9 ♋20	25 ♏53	12 ♈26	28 ♌59	15 ♑33	2 ♊ 6	18 ♎39	5 ♓13	21 ♋46
☊	13 ♈48	16 ♈33	19 ♈19	22 ♈ 4	24 ♈50	27 ♈35	0 ♉21	3 ♉ 6	5 ♉52	8 ♉37
☋	13 ♎33	16 ♈15	18 ♎58	21 ♈41	24 ♎23	27 ♈ 6	29 ♎48	2 ♉31	5 ♏14	7 ♉56
XX	21 ♍46	8 ♑ 7	24 ♈29	10 ♌50	27 ♏11	13 ♓32	29 ♊54	16 ♎15	2 ♒36	18 ♉57
E	9 ♒29	23 ♊23	7 ♏17	21 ♓10	5 ♌ 4	18 ♐58	2 ♉52	16 ♍46	0 ♒39	14 ♊33
A	7 ♈54	3 ♍28	29 ♑ 3	24 ♊38	20 ♏13	15 ♈47	11 ♍22	6 ♒57	2 ♋32	28 ♏ 6
M	4 ♐ 7	22 ♑56	11 ♓45	0 ♉35	19 ♊24	8 ♌13	27 ♍ 3	15 ♏52	4 ♑41	23 ♒31

H #	15	16	17	18	19	20	21	22	23	24
☉	19 ♓56	25 ♊16	0 ♎35	5 ♑55	11 ♈15	16 ♋35	21 ♎54	27 ♑14	2 ♉34	7 ♌54
☽	28 ♉18	2 ♒11	6 ♎ 4	9 ♊58	13 ♒51	17 ♎44	21 ♊37	25 ♒30	29 ♎24	3 ♋17
☿	0 ♌30	20 ♎32	10 ♑34	0 ♈36	20 ♊38	10 ♍40	0 ♐42	20 ♒44	10 ♉46	0 ♌48
♀	2 ♎11	2 ♐20	2 ♒29	2 ♈37	2 ♊46	2 ♌55	3 ♎ 4	3 ♐12	3 ♒21	3 ♈30
♂	6 ♑42	13 ♋ 9	19 ♑36	26 ♋ 3	2 ♒29	8 ♌56	15 ♒23	21 ♌50	28 ♒17	4 ♍43
⚳	0 ♌55	8 ♈58	17 ♐ 2	25 ♌ 5	3 ♉ 9	11 ♑13	19 ♍16	27 ♉20	5 ♒24	13 ♎27
⚴	23 ♑41	25 ♌15	26 ♓50	28 ♎25	29 ♉59	1 ♑34	3 ♌ 9	4 ♓43	6 ♎18	7 ♉53
⚵	11 ♋30	6 ♑16	1 ♋ 2	25 ♐48	20 ♊34	15 ♐20	10 ♊ 6	4 ♐52	29 ♉38	24 ♏24
⚶	21 ♌58	25 ♍26	28 ♎53	2 ♐21	5 ♑49	9 ♒17	12 ♓45	16 ♈13	19 ♉40	23 ♊ 8
♃	21 ♈47	29 ♓14	6 ♓41	14 ♒ 8	21 ♑35	29 ♐ 2	6 ♐29	13 ♏56	21 ♎23	28 ♍50
♄	2 ♒ 1	16 ♋ 9	0 ♑17	14 ♊25	28 ♏33	12 ♉41	26 ♎49	10 ♈57	25 ♍ 6	9 ♓14
⚷	22 ♐13	9 ♍42	27 ♉11	14 ♒39	2 ♏ 8	19 ♋37	7 ♈ 6	24 ♐35	12 ♍ 4	29 ♉33
♅	18 ♓ 1	23 ♊13	28 ♍25	3 ♑37	8 ♈49	14 ♋ 1	19 ♎13	24 ♑25	29 ♈37	4 ♌49
♆	8 ♉39	23 ♏14	7 ♊48	22 ♐23	6 ♋57	21 ♑32	6 ♌ 6	20 ♒41	5 ♍16	19 ♓50
♇	8 ♐19	24 ♈52	11 ♍26	27 ♑59	14 ♊32	1 ♏ 6	17 ♓39	4 ♌12	20 ♐45	7 ♉19
☊	11 ♉23	14 ♉ 8	16 ♉54	19 ♉40	22 ♉25	25 ♉11	27 ♉56	0 ♊42	3 ♊27	6 ♊13
☋	10 ♏39	13 ♉21	16 ♏ 4	18 ♉46	21 ♏29	24 ♉12	26 ♏54	29 ♉37	2 ♐19	5 ♊ 2
XX	5 ♍19	21 ♐40	8 ♈ 1	24 ♋22	10 ♏44	27 ♒ 5	13 ♊26	29 ♍47	16 ♑ 9	2 ♉30
E	28 ♎27	12 ♓21	26 ♋15	10 ♐ 8	24 ♈ 2	7 ♍56	21 ♑50	5 ♊44	19 ♎37	3 ♓31
A	23 ♈41	19 ♍16	14 ♒51	10 ♋25	6 ♐ 0	1 ♉35	27 ♍10	22 ♒44	18 ♋19	13 ♐54
M	12 ♈20	1 ♊ 9	19 ♋59	8 ♍48	27 ♎37	16 ♐27	5 ♒16	24 ♓ 5	12 ♉55	1 ♋44

H #	25	26	27	28	29	30	31	32	33	34
☉	13 ♏13	18 ♒33	23 ♉53	29 ♌12	4 ♐32	9 ♓52	15 ♊12	20 ♍31	25 ♐51	1 ♈11
☽	7 ♓10	11 ♏ 3	14 ♋56	18 ♓50	22 ♏43	26 ♋36	0 ♈29	4 ♐22	8 ♌16	12 ♈ 9
☿	20 ♎50	10 ♑52	0 ♈54	20 ♊56	10 ♍58	1 ♐ 0	21 ♒ 2	11 ♉ 4	1 ♌ 6	21 ♎ 8
♀	3 ♊39	3 ♌47	3 ♎56	4 ♐ 5	4 ♒14	4 ♈22	4 ♊31	4 ♌40	4 ♎49	4 ♐57
♂	11 ♓10	17 ♍37	24 ♓ 4	0 ♎31	6 ♈57	13 ♎24	19 ♈51	26 ♎18	2 ♉45	9 ♏11
⚳	21 ♊31	29 ♒35	7 ♏38	15 ♋42	23 ♓46	1 ♐49	9 ♌53	17 ♈56	26 ♐ 0	4 ♍ 4
⚴	9 ♐28	11 ♋ 2	12 ♒37	14 ♍12	15 ♈46	17 ♏21	18 ♊56	20 ♑30	22 ♌ 5	23 ♓40
⚵	19 ♉10	13 ♏56	8 ♉42	3 ♏28	28 ♈14	23 ♎ 0	17 ♈46	12 ♎32	7 ♈18	2 ♎ 3
⚶	26 ♋36	0 ♍ 4	3 ♎32	7 ♏ 0	10 ♐28	13 ♑55	17 ♒23	20 ♓51	24 ♈19	27 ♉47
♃	6 ♍18	13 ♌45	21 ♋12	28 ♊39	6 ♊ 6	13 ♉33	21 ♈ 0	28 ♓27	5 ♓54	13 ♒21
♄	23 ♌22	7 ♒30	21 ♋38	5 ♑46	19 ♊54	4 ♐ 2	18 ♉10	2 ♏18	16 ♈26	0 ♎34
⚷	17 ♒ 1	4 ♏30	21 ♋59	9 ♈28	26 ♐57	14 ♍26	1 ♊55	19 ♒24	6 ♏52	24 ♋21
♅	10 ♏ 1	15 ♒14	20 ♉26	25 ♌38	0 ♐50	6 ♓ 2	11 ♊14	16 ♍26	21 ♐38	26 ♓50
♆	4 ♎25	18 ♈59	3 ♏34	18 ♉ 9	2 ♐43	17 ♊18	1 ♑52	16 ♋27	1 ♒ 2	15 ♌36
♇	23 ♍52	10 ♒25	26 ♊58	13 ♏32	0 ♈ 5	16 ♌38	3 ♑12	19 ♉45	6 ♎18	22 ♒51
☊	8 ♊58	11 ♊44	14 ♊29	17 ♊15	20 ♊ 0	22 ♊46	25 ♊31	28 ♊17	1 ♋ 3	3 ♋48
☋	7 ♐45	10 ♊27	13 ♐10	15 ♊52	18 ♐35	21 ♊17	24 ♐ 0	26 ♊43	29 ♐25	2 ♋ 8
XX	18 ♌51	5 ♐12	21 ♓34	7 ♋55	24 ♎16	10 ♒37	26 ♉59	13 ♍20	29 ♐41	16 ♈ 2
E	17 ♋25	1 ♐19	15 ♈13	29 ♌ 6	13 ♑ 0	26 ♉54	10 ♎48	24 ♒42	8 ♋35	22 ♏29
A	9 ♉28	5 ♎ 3	0 ♓38	26 ♋13	21 ♐47	17 ♉22	12 ♎57	8 ♓32	4 ♌ 6	29 ♐41
M	20 ♌33	9 ♎23	28 ♏12	17 ♑ 1	5 ♓51	24 ♈40	13 ♊29	2 ♌19	21 ♍ 8	9 ♏57

Figure 3.14: *CCRS harmonics.*

```
HANK FRIEDMAN          JUN 27, 1950    9:42: 0  ZONE   5.00 D T
ORANGE, N.J.                     40 N 46.0  74 W 14.0
TROPICAL NATAL

ASPECTS

CONJUN  5  8  SEMISX  1  2  decile  0  1  novile  0  1  OCTILE  1  2  septil  0  1
SEXTIL  2  4  qintil  0  2  binovl  0  1  SQUARE  3  7  bisept  0  1  TRINE   3  7
TRIOCT  1  2  biqntl  0  2  QINCNX  1  2  trispt  0  1  4novil  0  1  OPPOSI  4  8

DECIMAL COLUMN IS ORB AS PERCENT OF MAXIMUM ORB

CLOSER
☉   CONJUN ♅   0  8 .016
♇   SEMISX XX  0 12 .100
♄   SEMISX E   0 14 .119
☽   QINCNX ⚶   0 25 .211
♄   SEMISX ♆   0 27 .221
♀   TRIOCT ♆   0 34 .285
⚳   SQUARE ♃   0 37 .094
♆   SEXTIL E   0 41 .170
⚶   SEMISX ☊   0 42 .353
⚶   QINCNX ☋   0 45 .377
⚵   SEMISX A   0 49 .406
⚴   OCTILE ⚷   0 54 .451
⚷   TRINE  ♇   0 56 .143
⚶   TRIOCT ⚷   0 59 .492
☉   SQUARE ♂   1  7 .172
☽   TRINE  ☊   1  8 .174
☽   SEXTIL ☋   1 11 .294
♂   SQUARE ♅   1 15 .192
♂   SEXTIL ⚳   1 37 .403
⚶   SEXTIL ♅   1 44 .434
♆   SQUARE XX  1 47 .273
☉   SEXTIL ⚶   1 52 .466
⚴   OPPOSI ⚶   1 53 .236
♆   SEXTIL ♇   1 59 .495
☉   TRINE  ♃   2  7 .327
♃   TRINE  ♅   2 15 .346
♇   SQUARE M   2 16 .349
♅   SQUARE ☊   2 27 .376
♅   SQUARE ☋   2 29 .383
☿   OPPOSI ⚷   2 33 .319
♀   TRINE  ☋   2 34 .394
☉   SQUARE ☊   2 34 .395
☉   SQUARE ☋   2 37 .403
♇   CONJUN E   2 39 .332
♂   OPPOSI ☊   3 41 .461
♂   CONJUN ☋   3 44 .467
☽   OPPOSI ♀   3 44 .468
☽   CONJUN ⚳   4 10 .522

WIDER
♂   QINCNX ♃   1  0 .502
☊   OCTILE M   1  4 .532
☋   TRIOCT M   1  7 .556
⚷   QINCNX XX  1  8 .563
⚴   SEMISX ☋   1  8 .566
♇   OCTILE ☋   1  9 .578
⚴   QINCNX ☊   1 11 .590
♇   TRIOCT ☊   1 12 .602
♀   OCTILE XX  1 13 .604
☿   SEMISX M   1 13 .605
☽   QINCNX ♅   1 19 .657
⚷   QINCNX M   1 20 .671
♅   OCTILE M   1 23 .689
♀   QINCNX ⚴   1 26 .716
☉   QINCNX ☽   1 27 .721
☉   OCTILE M   1 30 .753
☿   OCTILE ⚶   1 34 .784
♄   SEXTIL XX  2 13 .555
XX  SEXTIL M   2 28 .617
☽   SEXTIL ♂   2 34 .640
♀   SEXTIL ☊   2 37 .653
⚷   SEXTIL ♆   2 54 .726
♄   SQUARE ⚷   3 21 .515
☿   SEXTIL ♇   3 29 .870
☽   SQUARE ♃   3 34 .548
⚷   TRINE  E   3 35 .551
⚴   TRINE  ♅   3 37 .557
☉   TRINE  ⚴   3 45 .577
⚶   SEXTIL ♃   3 59 .997
♀   SQUARE A   4 34 .703
♄   TRINE  M   4 41 .721
☿   SQUARE ⚵   4 44 .728
E   SQUARE M   4 56 .758
⚳   TRINE  ☊   5 18 .816
♀   TRINE  ⚵   5 23 .828
☿   TRINE  ♆   5 27 .839
⚳   TRINE  E   5 50 .898
⚴   TRINE  ♃   5 52 .904
☿   SQUARE ♄   5 54 .907
⚵   TRINE  M   5 57 .914
♀   TRINE  ♂   6 18 .969
♃   OPPOSI ♄   6 41 .835
♀   OPPOSI ⚳   7 55 .989
⚵   CONJUN ☋   7 57 .993
⚵   OPPOSI ☊   7 60 .999

MINOR
♃   binovl ⚷   0  2 .029
♂   binovl XX  0  6 .093
☿   bisept ☋   0 11 .183
⚶   bisept ♇   0 14 .230
☽   binovl ♄   0 15 .248
☿   bisept ♃   0 17 .279
⚳   bisept A   0 23 .378
⚵   binovl ♅   0 26 .435
♃   trispt ☋   0 27 .452
⚳   decile ⚴   0 29 .482
☉   binovl ⚵   0 34 .562
♃   qintil M   0 38 .315
☊   bisept XX  0 44 .735
⚳   4novil M   0 46 .762
XX  novile A   0 47 .775
⚴   decile ⚵   0 49 .812
☉   decile ♀   0 49 .817
♂   novile A   0 52 .868
⚵   novile E   0 52 .870
⚶   qintil XX  0 53 .445
♃   4novil ♇   0 54 .897
♀   decile ♅   0 57 .945
♂   qintil ⚷   0 58 .483
♃   biqntl ♆   1  7 .562
☊   biqntl A   1 11 .590
⚳   qintil ⚵   1 18 .647
⚳   biqntl ⚶   1 24 .702
♀   qintil E   1 45 .875
♆   biqntl M   1 45 .877

PLANETS IN ORDER OF ASPECT WEIGHT

MAXIMUM ORB / %
☉    619   ♅    618   ♃    196   ⚷    154   ♂    149   ♇    133   ☊    132
⚳    130   ☽    121   ☋    112   E     95   ⚶     94   ♆     91   ♀     89
XX    82   ⚴     82   M     79   ♄     75   ☿     68   ⚵     54   A     23

TOTAL WEIGHT =   3196

MAXIMUM - ACTUAL ORB
♅   32.5   ☉   32.0   ♂   26.3   ☊   25.2   ♃   25.0   ☽   24.2   ☋   24.2
⚷   23.8   ♇   22.0   ⚶   18.6   ⚳   16.7   ⚴   16.4   ♆   16.3   ♀   16.2
E   16.0   M   15.9   XX  14.0   ♄   12.7   ☿   12.1   ⚵    6.7   A    4.9

TOTAL WEIGHT =    402
```

***Figure 3.15:** A CCRS aspects page.*

The program is not perfect, of course, and doesn't claim to be. The chart comparisons, for example, lack any indication of orb. The program will not calculate timed progressed hits, and the planetary glyphs in the chart wheels are a bit small. But these are small quibbles given the comprehensiveness and largely trouble-free operation of this program. I highly recommend CCRS as a valuable addition to your program library. I wish it were available for Apple and Commodore computers as well as IBM and CP/M machines.

Note: CCRS is sold strictly for personal use, and may not be used to generate charts to sell.

Apple Star Track

AGS Software, $295

Principal Functions
Prints birth charts, aspect/midpoint page, returns, progressed, directed, synastry charts

Types of Calculations
Aspects included: Major plus semisquare, sesquiquadrate, semisextile, inconjunct, and quintile, septile, novile, and sixteenth aspect series

Custom aspects: No

Number of house systems: 7

Heliocentric charts: No

Methods of progression: Secondary, direct/converse

Timed progressed hits: No

Solar and lunar returns: Direct/converse, harmonic returns, prints return charts

Midpoint analysis: No

Chart comparisons: Prints composite, relationship charts, interaspect table

Harmonics: No

Defaults
Preset calculation defaults: No

Preset printout defaults: No

File Management
Batch processing: 50 natal charts (no batch processing of secondary jobs yet)

Saves files: Yes

File access: Good (includes disk space check, file utilities)

Printouts
Glyphs: Yes

Types of wheels: Closed wheel

Quality of printouts: Good

Computers   *Computer required:* Apple II 48K

Other hardware required: One disk drive, printer

Apple Star Track, soon to be called simply Star Track, is a multimodule program for Apple II computers. Since the features of its natal chart module are identical to those of Natal Horoscope 110, read the section on that program to review them.

One difference between the two programs is that Apple Star Track uses glyphs in its chart wheels and tables (see Figures 3.16 and 3.17).

The glyphs are a mixed blessing, however. While they make the printouts more readable, they take much more time to print. It takes at least fifteen minutes to print out one chart wheel with a complete second page using an Epson MX-80 printer, even with a printer buffer. You can reduce the printout time greatly by omitting page two, or by printing page two without midpoints. Still, I wonder whether the added clarity of the glyphs is worth the wait for most people. This program takes a much longer time to print a complete two-page chart than any other program I've examined. On the other hand, no other program includes glyphs in the second page of printout. (The CCRS program uses glyphs in all its output and is therefore slow to print too, but its second page is different from Apple Star Track's, and thus not comparable.)

You can cut printing time in half if you use a Pro/Writer printer instead of an Epson MX-80. However, other astrological and general software may or may not print glyphs or graphics on the Pro/Writer, so find out which printers will work with the software you need before buying a printer. You might also prefer to purchase this program in the version that uses two-letter abbreviations instead of glyphs and thus prints much more speedily.

Apple Star Track is easy to use and creates files usable both by different modules within the program and by other programs. The files are short—105 files can fit on a file disk—and the program has utilities to edit files, to determine how much space is left on a disk (and how many more files can fit), and to create file disks. The program is also easy to customize. You can change the orbs for the aspects used by the

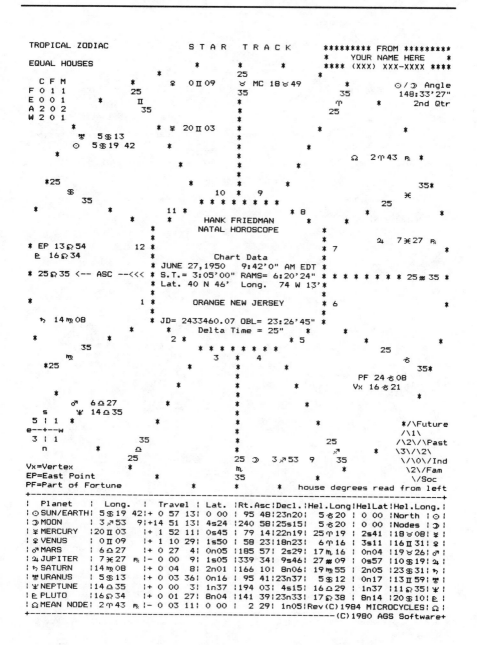

Figure 3.16: An Apple Star Track chart wheel.

HANK FRIEDMAN TROPICAL NATAL HOROSCOPE (C)1980 AGS Software

PLANETS in MODALITIES and ELEMENTS

CARDINAL	☉ ♂ ♅ ♆ ☊ PF Vx	Total = 7	Weighted Score = 8
FIXED	♇ AS MC EP	Total = 4	Weighted Score = 7
MUTABLE	☽ ☿ ♀ ♃ ♄	Total = 5	Weighted Score = 9
FIRE	☽ ♇ ☊ AS EP	Total = 5	Weighted Score = 8
EARTH	♄ MC PF Vx	Total = 4	Weighted Score = 4
AIR	☿ ♀ ♂ ♆	Total = 4	Weighted Score = 7
WATER	☉ ♃ ♅	Total = 3	Weighted Score = 5

Weights Used Above: ☉ ☽ AS MC=3 ☿ ♀ ♂=2 ♃ ♄ ♅ ♆ ♇ ☊=1 PF EP Vx=0

PLANETARY DIGNITIES

Planets in RULERSHIPS ☿ ♃ — there are No Mutual Receptions
Planets in EXALTATIONS ♇
Planets in DETRIMENTS ♂
Planets in FALL

GEOCENTRIC ASPECTS and MIDPOINTS

	☉	☽	☿	♀	♂	♃	♄	♅	♆	♇	☊	AS	MC	PF	EP	
☉	----	19♍	27♊	17♊	20♌	6♉	9♌	5♋	24♌	25♋	19♉	0♌	12♊	14♈	24♋	☉
		36	41	44	53	24	44	16	57	57	01	27	05	44	37	
☽	-⚻-	☽	11♍	2♓	5♏	20♑	24♎	19♍	9♏	10♎	3♒	14♎	26♒	29♐	8♎	☽
	1a27		58	01	10	40	01	33	14	13	18	44	21	01	53	
☿	----	----	☿	10♊	13♌	28♈	2♌	27♊	17♌	18♋	11♉	22♋	4♊	7♈	16♋	☿
				06	15	45	05	38	19	18	23	49	26	05	58	
♀	----	-☍-	----	♀	3♌	18♈	22♋	17♊	7♌	8♋	1♉	12♋	24♉	27♓	7♋	♀
		3s44			18	48	09	41	22	21	26	52	29	09	02	
♂	-□-	-✱-	----	-△-	♂	21♐	25♍	20♌	10♎	11♍	4♑	16♍	27♋	0♐	10♍	♂
	1a07	2a34		6a18		57	18	50	31	30	35	01	38	18	10	
♃	-△-	-□-	7 th-	----	-⚻-	♃	10♐	6♉	26♐	27♉	20♓	1♊	13♈	15♒	25♉	♃
	2a08	3a34	0a16		1a00		48	20	01	01	05	31	08	48	41	
♄	----	9 th-	-□-	7 th-	16 th	-☍-	♄	9♌	29♍	0♍	23♊	4♍	16♋	19♏	29♌	♄
		0a15	5s55	1a08	0a11	6s41		40	21	21	25	51	29	08	01	
♅	-☌-	-⚻-	----	----	-□-	-△-	----	♅	24♌	25♋	18♉	0♌	12♊	14♈	24♋	♅
	0s07	1a19			1s15	2a15			54	53	58	24	01	40	33	
♆	----	----	-△-	-⚼-	----	-±-	-⚺-	----	♆	15♍	8♑	20♍	1♌	4♐	14♍	♆
			5s28	0s35		1s07	0a26			34	39	05	42	21	14	
♇	----	----	-✱-	----	7 th-	9 th-	----	----	-✱-	♇	9♊	21♌	2♋	5♏	15♌	♇
			3s29		1a32	0a54			1s59		38	04	41	21	14	
☊	-□-	-△-	----	-✱-	-☍-	----	----	-□-	----	-⚼-	☊	14♊	25♈	28♒	8♊	☊
	2s37	1s11		2a33	3s45			2s30		1a09		09	46	25	18	
AS	7 th-	----	----	-□-	9 th-	----	----	7 th-	----	----	-±-	AS	7♋	9♏	19♌	AS
	1a11			4a34	0a52			1a04			1a08		12	51	44	
MC	-∠-	----	-⚺-	----	----	-Q-	-△-	-∠-	-±-	-□-	-∠-	-□-	MC	21♓	1♋	MC
	1a30		1a13			0a38	4s41	1a23	1a45	2s16	1s07	6 45		29	22	
PF	9 th-	7 th-	-±-	-△-	----	-∠-	----	9 th-	----	16 th	----	-⚻-	-△-	PF	4♏	PF
	1a11	1a11	1a54	6a01		1s41		1a04		0s05		1 27	5 19		01	
EP	----	----	----	-Q-	7 th-	----	-⚺-	----	-✱-	-☌-	----	----	-□-	9 th-	EP	EP
				1s45	1a08		0a14		0a41	2a40			4 56	0 14		
Vx	----	----	7 th-	-⚼-	----	7 th-	-△-	----	-□-	-⚻-	----	----	-△-	----	----	Vx
			0s36	1s12		0s20	2s13		1s47	0a12			2 28			

2= ☌ CONJUNCT 0 orb 7 — 3= ☍ OPPOSITION 180 orb 7 — 3= ⚼ SESQUISQUARE 135 orb 2
5= ✱ SEXTILE 60 orb 5 — 3= ⚺ SEMISEXTILE 30 orb 2 — 4= ± BIQUINTILE 144 orb 2
11= □ SQUARE 90 orb 7 — 4= ∠ SEMISQUARE 45 orb 2 — 5= ⚻ QUINCUNX 150 orb 2
10= △ TRINE 120 orb 7 — 2= Q QUINTILE 72 orb 2 — 17=# th MINOR HARMONIC # orb 3%
a = applying — s = separating
69= total aspects

Revision (C)1984 MICROCYCLES

Figure 3.17: *Page 2 of an Apple Star Track printout displaying aspects and midpoints.*

program, which are the same as those in the Natal Horoscope program. You can configure the program for your printer interface, add three personal lines (for example, name and address) at the top of the chart without too much difficulty, and set up the program to print out the second page with or without the wheel, with or without midpoints, and with or without interpretation (if you happen to own Deluxe Astroscope or Deluxe Sex-O-Scope).

AGS is now including batch processing via the Multi-Loader module at no extra cost. At this time, the Multi-Loader will only batch process natal-chart jobs (no secondaries, returns, etc.) but the firm will probably change this shortly to permit secondary charts to be part of the batch process. Batch processing with Apple Star Track is highly recommended, because using the Multi-Loader frees you from having to enter delta-T for each chart, allows you to enter latitudes and longitudes without the N, S, E, and W that are required when you enter single charts, and computes (for U.S. time zones) the time-zone number from the letters entered (e.g., computing 5 for EST) so you don't have to enter both. The Multi-Loader also makes it simple to prepare a number of relocation charts for a person: a special command recalls the last birth data entered, allowing you to alter it as you wish and post it as the next job. Thus I can keep recalling the birth data for a person to change the longitude and latitude and post it as another job.

For those who have Apples without lower-case chips, the Multi-Loader can even enter upper- and lower-case letters in person and place names. The only deficiencies I saw in the Multi-Loader are likely to be fixed: the aforementioned lack of batch processing for secondaries, and the fact that you must type the whole chart name over if you want to save a file with its previous name.

Besides processing natal charts, Apple Star Track will also calculate:

secondary progressed charts (with solar arc, Naibod, or Quotidian progressed M. C.);

solar and lunar returns (for a date or to a specific zodiacal point with sidereal, converse, and harmonic options);

composite and relationship charts (between any two chart files, natal or secondary);

solar and Aries Rising charts;

solar-arc directed charts.

It will print a synastry table, including interaspects and the placements of planets in the other chart's houses. The synastry module makes it easy to compare charts on separate file disks, which destinguishes Apple Star Track from most other programs. It has a number of other helpful features, as well:

> by entering a zero, you can back out of almost any part of the program to the previous menu;

> you can display the disk catalog (for either drive) from within the program just before entering the file name (although there is no directory and you have to enter the whole file name);

> you can edit any part of the birth data you enter without starting over;

> and if you make a mistake, the program usually doesn't crash.

Another thing that makes the program pleasant to use is the "handholding" it provides. For example, many programs show you nothing on the screen when the computer is thinking, but this program usually explains (in English) what the computer is doing during most processes.

What makes Apple Star Track less than optimal has more to do with what it does *not* offer than with the routines that are present. First, its high price ($295), puts it in competition with M-65 from Matrix, and in comparison Apple Star Track lacks a great deal. Apple Star Track cannot create harmonic charts (unless you purchase the Harmonics/Arc Transforms module for $50), prepare local-space charts, or calculate progressed or directed hits (that is, it cannot scan a time period and tell when the progressed or directed aspect becomes exact or within orb). Nor can it do sophisticated midpoint analysis (you can purchase an extra midpoint module, #112 Midpoints, for $25, but it doesn't approach the power of M-65's midpoint features).

Furthermore, the program has no research capabilities, while M-65 has an excellent research module, and Apple Star Track has no eclipse module, nor heliocentric or solstice point options. Its effective time range is much shorter than M-65's (1800–2000 compared with 1700–2300 for M-65, and M-65 can do also ancient charts reasonably well), and Apple Star Track has notably fewer options in many other areas (e.g., house systems, types of progressions and directions, methods of customizing, types of chart wheels, etc.) than its Matrix competitor.

Viewed by itself, Apple Star Track is not a bad program, but times have changed and astrologers can get much more for their money now than they could when Apple Star Track first came out in 1980. For years, this was the best astrology program available for the Apple, and it is still easier to use than M-65, but it will have to be enhanced substantially (or made a great deal less expensive) to compete with the programs now on the market for Apple users. Still, for those who don't need more than Apple Star Track offers, the program will provide a simple environment for generating a variety of charts easily and enjoyably.

Apple Star Track Screen-Only Package

AGS Software, $190 ($50 for owners of Apple Star Track)

Principal Functions	Calculates and displays birth charts, aspects, returns, progressed and directed charts
Types of Calculations	*Aspects included:* Major plus semisquare, sesquiquadrate, semisextile, inconjunct, and quintile, septile, novile, and sixteenth aspect series.
	Custom aspects: No
	Number of house systems: 7
	Heliocentric charts: No
	Methods of progression: secondary, direct/converse
	Timed progressed hits: No
	Solar and lunar returns: Prints direct/converse, harmonic return charts
	Midpoint analysis: No
	Chart comparisons: None
	Harmonics: No
Defaults	*Preset calculation defaults:* No
	Preset printout defaults: No
File Management	*Batch processing:* No
	Saves files: Yes
	File access: Fair
Printouts	*None*
	Types of wheels: Displays square wheel
Computers	*Computer required:* Apple II 48K
	Other hardware required: One disk drive.

The screen version of Apple Star Track, also called the Superprogram-Screen version (at $190 alone or $50 to owners of Apple Star Track), does many of the same things as Apple Star Track, but it displays data on the screen instead of printing it out.

Its methods of creating charts, listing planetary information, preparing aspects, listing dignities, and preparing returns and progressions are identical to Apple Star Track's, but without the printouts. It even lets you save the files of the charts you create.

The differences are that the screen version lacks:

batch loading;

customizing of routines;

midpoint listings;

synastry options;

solar-arc charts;

file utilities.

(Regarding the latter, however, the program will let you see the disk catalog so you can look for file names.) Moreover, you have to enter delta-T and N, S, E, W, and the screen wheel is a forty-column square wheel, much like those of Matrix programs.

Since files created in the screen version are completely compatible with those made by other versions of Apple Star Track and vice versa, this program is of great value to those who want to own both programs. However, it is clearly useful by itself for the person who has an Apple but no printer.

The Apple Star Track Add-On Modules

The add-on modules for Apple Star Track work with the files created by Apple Star Track.

The Harmonics/Arc Transforms package prints out harmonic charts with an aspectarian on the second page, and lists 27 harmonics, starting with whichever harmonic you specify. However, it does not highlight harmonic conjunctions, which people usually pay attention to. The module also calculates arc-transform charts (where 360 is divided by the angular separation between two planets and the result is used as the harmonic modulus) and prints out the chart with an optional aspectarian on page two.

The Midpoints Module first calculates and prints a list of the midpoints and then sorts the midpoints (for whichever dial you select). It then prints a sorted list of midpoints with the planets included in the sort.

The Astro-Mapping Module prepares a list with the longitude of each planet on the upper and lower meridian and the latitude of each planet on the zenith and the nadir. It also makes a table for any set of latitudes from −60 to +60 in five-degree increments, showing the longitude where each planet rises and sets. This program corrects for planetary latitude, and therefore uses mundane angles instead of ecliptic ones. The tables it generates could be used effectively in relocation analysis.

Blue Star 7

Matrix Software, $150

Principal Functions	Prints natal, progressed, directed, transit, local space charts; plus a variety of tables
Types of Calculations	*Aspects included:* Majors plus semisquare, sesquiquadrate, inconjunct
	Custom aspects: 15 total
	Number of house systems: 6 plus user-defined ascendant, lists cusps for 10 house systems
	Heliocentric charts: Yes
	Methods of progression: Secondary, tertiary, minor
	Solar and lunar returns: No
	Timed progressed hits: Yes
	Midpoint analysis: Prints list of sorted midpoints, midpoint tree diagrams
	Chart comparisons: Prints interaspect table, composite charts
	Harmonics: Prints harmonic charts
Defaults	*Preset calculation defaults:* House system, zodiac, coordinate system, direct/converse, method of progressed angles
	Preset printout defaults: Page two on/off, type of wheel
File Management	*Batch processing:* 5 jobs
	Saves files: No

Blue Star 7 *(continued)*

Printouts   *Glyphs:* Yes

Types of wheels: Closed, spoke, open, bi-wheel
charts; all with proportionately spaced planets

Quality of printouts: Very good

Computers   *Computer required:* Commodore CBM/PET,
Commodore 64, IBM PC

Other hardware required: One disk drive

Blue Star 10

Matrix Software, $200

Principal Functions	Prints natal, progressed, directed, transit, local-space charts; plus a variety of tables
Types of Calculations	***Aspects included:*** Majors plus semisquare, sesquiquadrate, inconjunct
	Custom aspects: 15 total
	Number of house systems: 6 plus user-defined ascendant, lists cusps for 10 house systems
	Heliocentric charts: Yes
	Methods of progression: Secondary, tertiary, minor
	Solar and lunar returns: No
	Timed progressed hits: Yes
	Midpoint analysis: Prints list of sorted midpoints, midpoint tree diagrams
	Chart comparisons: Prints interaspect table, composite charts
	Harmonics: prints harmonic charts
Defaults	***Preset calculation defaults:*** House system, zodiac, coordinate system, direct/converse, method of progressed angles
	Preset printout defaults: Page two on/off, type of wheel
File Management	***Batch processing:*** 5 jobs
	Saves files: Yes
	File access: Excellent (includes file support disk)

Blue Star 10 *(continued)*

Printouts   *Glyphs:* Yes

Types of wheels: Closed, spoke, open, bi-wheel charts; all with proportionately spaced planets

Quality of printouts: Very good

Computers   *Computer required:* Commodore 64

Other hardware required: One disk drive

Blue Star 7 and 10 are written in machine language, and therefore operate very swiftly. Although the two programs are similar, the difference is worth noting: Blue Star 10 saves chart files that are completely compatible with the M-65 system, the state-of-the art package reviewed in Chapter 6, and includes a file-utility disk (to delete files, prepare file disks, inspect files, etc.), while Blue Star 7 doesn't save files at all. Both programs create chart wheels for the four major house systems (Equal, Koch, Placidus, and Campanus) plus Aries, solar, and user-defined Ascendant houses. They also calculate and print charts for:

secondary, tertiary, minor, and Quotidian progressions;

solar, Naibod, degree/year, Ascendant, vertical, and user-defined arc directions);

transit charts (charts for a second date and place);

converse progressions and directions;

five coordinate systems (geocentric, right ascension, local space, mundoscope, and prime vertical systems.

The programs will produce open-wheel and bi-wheel charts as well as normal chart wheels with an optional second-page aspectarian. They will also:

calculate progressed hits;

draw midpoint trees;

find interaspects;

display planetary patterns;

list house cusps for ten-house systems;

compute angular separations;

and sort midpoints.

The printouts from both programs are similar to those of M-65 (see Figures 6.1, 6.2, and 6.3).

Only Blue Star 7 is available for the IBM PC computer, not Blue Star 10. Note that Blue Star 7 is the only program offered by Matrix for the IBM PC reviewed in this section. Since both programs are written for the Commodore 64 and the prices are not significantly different, the best choice for C-64 owners is Blue Star 10. Only Blue Star 7 is available for the CBM/PET.

As noted, Matrix's M-65 is an established program for professional astrologers reflecting the current state of the art. Blue Star 10 can substitute for M-65-A (the main module of this package) for those who don't need all of M-65-A's options but who want to use M-65's screen module (M-65-C) or research module (M-65-B).

Some of the features of M-65-A not included in Blue Star 10 are:

parallax-corrected Moon positions;

the eclipse/lunation module;

wheels constructed for certain house systems (Regiomontanus, Meridian, Porphyry, Morinus, and Topocentric);

a few local-space options;

the capacity to generate charts outside the twentieth century;

solar and lunar returns;

and relocated charts.

Still, all things considered, Blue Star 10 is faster and easier to use than M-65-A, and calculates Uranian planets. Nonetheless, I think too much has been left out to make the $100 savings over M-65-A worthwhile. Most people who plan to spend this much on a program would prefer M-65-A's added capabilities, even with its increased complexity.

Chapter Four

Transit Programs

Although astrological programming has advanced enough to make possible an excellent transit calculation and printing program, no such program has yet emerged. Some of the transit programs sold today are slower than calculating transits by hand using ephemeris tables, and none notes the planetary stations—that is, the times when planets slow down to a standstill—which can be very important. In fact, the only programs that calculate transits well are parts of transit-interpretation packages, which carry a stiff price tag (at least $300), especially if all you really need to do is calculate transits. (Matrix is completing work on a program called Transit Master that will perform sophisticated transit and progression calculations from files created by the M-65 program discussed in Chapter 6.)

When astrologers prepare transits, for themselves or others, they compare the planetary positions in the sky with planetary positions in the birth chart. To examine the duration of a transit's effect, the astrologer must determine how long the transiting planet is within orb. Therefore, a good transit program should allow the astrologer to select the preferred orb and then calculate when the transit enters the orb, becomes exact, and leaves the orb.

M-14: Complete Transit Search

Matrix Software, $100

Principal functions:	Calculates, displays, and prints out exact transit hits to planets, points, and midpoints

Types of Calculations

Aspects included: Majors plus semisquare, sesquiquadrate, inconjunct

Custom aspects: Can define a very large set of aspects

Number of house systems: 1 (choice of 4 major systems)

Applying and Separating Orbs: No

Specifiable Transit Span: Yes

Heliocentric transits: Yes

Midpoint transits: Yes

Defaults

Preset calculation defaults: No

Preset printout defaults: No

File Management

Batch processing: No

File access: None

Printouts

Quality of printouts: Fair

Computers

Computer required: Commodore 64, PET, Apple II, TRS-80 Models I, III, and 4, IBM PC

Other hardware required: IBM and Apple versions require one disk drive

The only transit-calculation package Matrix now has on the market is M-14, also called Transit Search: Where & When Transits. It costs $100 and is available for Apple, IBM, Commodore, and TRS-80 models I and III computers. M-14 cannot calculate approaching or separating orbs, and some versions of this program (e.g., the Apple version) can take longer than searching for transits by eye, since it takes so much time to select the specific options you want for each choice presented to you. Furthermore, M-14 cannot be permanently customized. This means that although you can select a wide variety of options each time you run the program, you cannot select these options once for repeated use. Rather, you must choose your house system, aspects, and so on, every time you use the program. This repeat-entry requirement is not only time-consuming, it is also counterproductive, since if you inadvertently make a typographical error you must start again from scratch.

The program does have great flexibility: you can select time periods, define the aspects you want, select the degree of precision to which the transits will be calculated (the more precision, the slower the operation). It will calculate transiting and transited points, and midpoint transits, as well as points you define. If you want only exact hits, the program works well. The IBM version is particularly fast. Astrologers who specialize in transits to or from midpoints would enjoy this program considerably. See Figure 4.1 for a sample printout.

You do not need any other programs to use M-14, but this is a mixed blessing. While you are not locked into buying other Matrix programs, M-14 does not create files and cannot batch process or use the files generated by other programs. Therefore, you must re-enter peoples' birth data every time you use the program. I wish M-14 were able to calculate approaching and leaving transit orbs and to read other programs' files. It would also have been easier to use if you could customize it by setting the options you want. At present, the absence of these features greatly reduces the value of the program.

G EOCENTRIC TRANSITS FOR HANK FRIEDMAN

```
DATE=? 06.271950
AM*PM? AM
TIME? 9.42        DECL. RAMC= 46.36
TZ? 4             +17 26   MC= 18TA49
LONG? 74.14       +13 00  ASC= 25LE35
LAT? 40.46        -22 27  VTX= 16CP21
DELTA T? 29       +16 40  EQA= 13LE54

      LONG    LAT      DECL       EQUAL

SU!05CN20 +    00 !+23 20!      1=25LE35
ME!20GE02 -    45 !+22 19!      2=25VI35
VE!00GE09 - 1 50 !+18 23!       3=25LI35
MA!06LI27 +    05 !- 2 29!      4=25SC35
JU!07PI27R- 1 05 !- 9 47!       5=25SA35
SA!14VI08 + 2 01 !+ 8 06!       6=25CP35
UR!05CN12 +    16 !+23 37!      7=25AQ35
NE!14LI35 + 1 37 !- 4 15!       8=25PI35
PL!16LE33 + 8 04 !+23 34!       9=25AR35
MO!03SA55 - 4 24 !-20 56!      10=25TA35
NO!02AR43 +    00 !+ 1 05!     11=25GE35
                               12=25CN35
```

TRANSITS FROM 06.091984 THRU 06.291984

TRANSITS

MM-DD-YY	*GMT*	TRA	ASP	RAD	ZODIAC
6-09-84	2 30	JUP	SES	ASC	10CP35
6-18-84	1 05	NEP	INC	VEN	00CP09

TRANSITS FROM 07.011984 THRU 09.011984

TRANSITS

MM-DD-YY	*GMT*	TRA	ASP	RAD	ZODIAC
7-04-84	15 30	JUP	SXT	JUP	07CP27
7-09-84	11 30	MAR	SXT	SAT	14SC08
7-12-84	10 45	JUP	SQR	MAR	06CP27
7-17-84	7 54	MAR	SXT	VTX	16SC21
7-17-84	23 04	MAR	SQR	PLU	16SC33
7-21-84	10 05	MAR	SES	NOD	17SC43
7-22-84	11 00	JUP	OPP	SUN	05CP20
7-23-84	16 06	JUP	OPP	URA	05CP12
7-24-84	9 30	MAR	OPP	MC	18SC49
7-27-84	13 02	MAR	INC	MER	20SC02
7-27-84	23 15	MAR	SES	URA	20SC12
7-28-84	6 46	MAR	SES	SUN	20SC20
7-30-84	23 53	MAR	SSQ	MAR	21SC27
8-08-84	19 37	JUP	SES	MC	03CP49
8-09-84	1 51	MAR	SQR	ASC	25SC35
8-17-84	56	MAR	SSQ	NEP	29SC35
8-18-84	2 53	MAR	OPP	VEN	00SA09
8-20-84	9 18	MAR	SSQ	VTX	01SA21
8-22-84	20 04	MAR	TRI	NOD	02SA43
8-25-84	18	MAR	CON	MON	03SA55
8-27-84	6 53	MAR	INC	URA	05SA12
8-27-84	12 11	MAR	INC	SUN	05SA20
8-29-84	10 58	MAR	SXT	MAR	06SA27
8-31-84	4 06	MAR	SQR	JUP	07SA27

Figure 4.1: An M-14 printout of transits.

Transit Star

AGS Software, $99

Principal functions: Calculates, displays, and prints out exact harmonic conjunctions to planets, points, and midpoints for a single date at a time

Types of Calculations

Aspects included: conjunctions only (for whatever harmonic selected)

Custom aspects: No

Number of house systems: None

Applying and Separating Orbs: No

Specifiable Transit Span: No

Heliocentric transits: No

Midpoint transits: Yes

Defaults

Preset calculation defaults: No

Preset printout defaults: No

File Management

Batch processing: No

File access: Fair

Printouts

Quality of printouts: Poor

Computers

Computer required: CP/M Apple, TRS-80 Models I, III, and 4, IBM PC, CP/M computers

Other hardware required: Requires one disk drive Requires Astro Star I or II

AGS offers computer astrologers two transit-calculation programs: Transit Star (#420) for CP/M, TRS-80, and IBM computers, to be used as an add-on to Astro Star, and Transit Package (#113) for Apple II series computers. Both programs are ineffective by themselves and must be used with other natal-chart packages. Transit Star requires Astro Star I, while Transit Package requires Apple Star Track or Natal Horoscope Program. The total costs are thus $400 and $225, respectively. The pairing of Transit Package with another program also forces the user to switch disks frequently.

For general use, Transit Star is actually a much poorer program than other transit packages. It cannot print out exact transit hits in chronological order, nor applying and separating orbs. I have spent years looking at a variety of astrological programs and printouts, and the transit printouts from this program are the least intelligible I have seen (see Figure 4.2).

Transit Star, which does run smoothly, generates a screen display or printout that indicates transit hits for a single date. Hits are marked by an asterisk at the right side of the planet's position listing. Not so bad? Well, if you use the first harmonic—i.e., the planets as they appear in the birth chart—the only transits this program catches are conjunctions,

```
STEP =    2: O HARMONIC =    1 DATE, GMT:   6 10 1984   12 00
  -NO  2AR43      -UR  5CN12      -SA 14VIO8     *SA 10SC33     *JU 10CP26
  -MC 25TA35      -SO  5CN20      -MA  6LI27     -MO  3SG53     -JU  7PI27
  -VE  0GE09      -PL 16LE31      -NE 14LI35     *UR 11SG13
  -ME 20GE03      -AS 25LE35     *PL 29LI33     *NE  0CP21
STEP =    2: O HARMONIC =    4 DATE, GMT:   6 12 1984   12 00
  *NE   0 17      -MA   6 27     *SA  40 27      -VE  60 09     -SA  74 08
  -NO   2 43     *JU  10 12      -PL  46 31      -MO  63 53     -ME  80 03
  -UR   5 12      -NE  14 35      -AS  55 35      -JU  67 27
  -SO   5 20     *PL  29 31      -MC  55 35     *UR  71 08
STEP =    2: O HARMONIC =    1 DATE, GMT:   6 14 1984   12 00
  -NO  2AR43      -UR  5CN12      -SA 14VIO8     *SA 10SC21     *JU  9CP58
  -MC 25TA35      -SO  5CN20      -MA  6LI27     -MO  3SG53     -JU  7PI27
  -VE  0GE09      -PL 16LE31      -NE 14LI35     *UR 11SG03
  -ME 20GE03      -AS 25LE35     *PL 29LI29     *NE  0CP14
STEP =    2: O HARMONIC =    1 DATE, GMT:   6 16 1984   12 00
  -NO  2AR43      -UR  5CN12      -SA 14VIO8     *SA 10SC16     *JU  9CP44
  -MC 25TA35      -SO  5CN20      -MA  6LI27     -MO  3SG53     -JU  7PI27
  -VE  0GE09      -PL 16LE31      -NE 14LI35     *UR 10SG58
  -ME 20GE03      -AS 25LE35     *PL 29LI28     *NE  0CP11
STEP =    2: O HARMONIC =    1 DATE, GMT:   6 18 1984   12 00
  -NO  2AR43      -UR  5CN12      -SA 14VIO8     *SA 10SC12     *JU  9CP29
  -MC 25TA35      -SO  5CN20      -MA  6LI27     -MO  3SG53     -JU  7PI27
  -VE  0GE09      -PL 16LE31      -NE 14LI35     *UR 10SG54
  -ME 20GE03      -AS 25LE35     *PL 29LI26     *NE  0CP08
```

Figure 4.2: A printout from Transit Star.

indicated by placing asterisks next to planets that are conjunct another planet, and it is not always obvious which planets are transiting which natal positions.

On the other hand, if you use the fourth harmonic (to catch the squares and oppositions which become conjunctions in the fourth harmonic chart), you can't tell whether the asterisks indicate a square or an opposition until you switch back to the first harmonic display. And things get worse still. The program will not automatically print out a set of these asterisked displays for a specified time period. Instead, you must keep pressing keys to examine each date.

Therefore, the program is really designed for the researcher who wants to step through a range of dates, one at a time, looking for significant hits. Consequently, I recommend this program to only astrologers who want to investigate harmonic transits at their screens, and not to general users.

Transit Package

AGS Software, $100

Principal functions: Calculates, displays, and prints out applying, exact, and separating transit hits to planets, points, and midpoints

Types of Calculations

Aspects included: Majors plus semisquare, sesquiquadrate, inconjunct, semisextile

Custom aspects: Can define 5 harmonic-aspect series

Number of house systems: Only house system present in original chart file

Applying and Separating Orbs: Yes

Specifiable Transit Span: Yes

Heliocentric transits: Yes

Midpoint transits: Yes

Defaults

Preset calculation defaults: Zodiac, precession on/off, coordinate system, outer or complete transits, orbs, level of precision, transited planet selection, transiting and transited midpoints on/off, 5 user-defined harmonic transits, hard and/or soft aspect transits.

Preset printout defaults: No

File Management

Batch processing: No

File access: Fair

Printouts

Quality of printouts: Fair

Computers

Computer required: Apple II

Other hardware required: Two disk drives

Transit Package, in contrast, is significantly better than both M-14 and Transit Star. This program has features one can really appreciate, especially in comparison with the other programs. It could be used by itself if you were willing to enter each birth chart point by point, but it is primarily designed to work with one of the AGS chart programs for the Apple II, as previously indicated.

First, Transit Package is easy to customize. You use the Transit Input Module to specify the planets you want transiting and transited, the aspects, house system, zodiac, coordinates (longitude, latitude, heliocentric longitude, right ascension, etc.), precession correction, applying orbs, separating orbs, days between sweeps, midpoint transits, and harmonic transits. Then, after you have selected the format you wish, you save it and never have to select these features again. You simply ask for your format file. You can have as many format files as you want, for different clients or for different types of transit searches.

This module is one of the easiest customizing programs to use. The only small problem I had with it was in saving the transit format file. The program does not tell you to switch disks at the proper time, so it is easy to save the file onto disk 2 instead of the main transit disk, which means you have to transfer it afterwards.

Transit Package includes an ephemeris-generating program, which enables you to generate text-file ephemerides (some are already generated for you) for additional years of transits. Because this program reads planetary positions from text files instead of calculating them over and over again as M-14 does, it runs much faster than M-14. The one disadvantage of the text-file approach is that its files are large and not many files will fit on a disk. You therefore have to generate ephemerides for each year. Because of its greater speed, however, I prefer this approach to M-14's.

Like most of AGS's programs, Transit Package handles files a bit primitively. You cannot select the chart to be transited from a directory of charts on file. Rather, you must remember the names of the people on your disk file and then enter the entire name of the person whose chart you want. Futhermore, you have to specify which drive holds the client files and which the format file, instead of keeping the client file disk in drive 2, which would be much easier to manage.

When you put the main program in the disk drive and activate the program, nothing happens. As the program stands now, you have to type RUN TRANSIT OUTER (or RUN TRANSIT ALL) to activate the program. It is much easier to work from a menu for easy selection of options, and it would take a minuscule amount of programmming to add a menu. Few programs on sale today lack menus, so hopefully

AGS will correct this deficiency soon. You could do so yourself with a minimum of programming knowledge.

Once you have the program running, all you have to do is select either screen or printer output and the number of days you want transits for, and then the program takes off. For a sample printout, see Figure 4.3.

If you specify entering and leaving orbs when using this program, you *must* keep them the same (e.g., one degree entering and one degree leaving) or you will run into one of two problems: If you set the leaving orb as zero (many astrologers don't use leaving orbs for transits), the program will not register the entering times for retrograde approaches at all;

```
: TRANSITS FOR HANK FRIEDMAN       : BIRTH JUNE 27 1950 AT 9:42:0 AM EDT :
: TRANSITS IN GEO. LONGITUDE       : FORMAT FILE, T, USED.               :
: TROPICAL TRANSITS                : STARTING JUNE 1,1984 FOR 45 DAYS.   :

              TRANSITS                                    COMMENTS


JUNE 1,1984
NE     (E T) SQQ PL     (N) AT 21:46 E.T.


JUNE 9,1984
JU     (X T) SQQ MC     (N) AT  3:46 E.T.
JU     (X T) SQQ AS     (N) AT  3:46 E.T.


JUNE 17,1984
NE     (X T) QNX VE     (N) AT 10:33 E.T.
JU     (E T) SQQ MC     (N) AT 18:23 E.T.
JU     (E T) SQQ AS     (N) AT 18:23 E.T.


JUNE 26,1984
JU     (L T) SXT JU     (N) AT 16:45 E.T.


JULY 4,1984
JU     (X T) SXT JU     (N) AT 12:48 E.T.
JU     (L T) SQU MA     (N) AT 13:57 E.T.


JULY 12,1984
JU     (E T) SXT JU     (N) AT 14:11 E.T.
JU     (X T) SQU MA     (N) AT 15:23 E.T.


JULY 13,1984
JU     (L T) OPP SU     (N) AT 16:08 E.T.

JULY 14,1984
JU     (L T) OPP UR     (N) AT 16:11 E.T.
```

Figure 4.3: A sample printout from Transit Package.

if you set the orbs at different values, the labeling for entering and leaving orbs will not work properly.

Another tiny bug, noticeable only to Equal-House-System users like myself, is that if the chart file is set up for equal houses, both the transited nonagesimal and what is called the M. C. are actually the nonagesimal.

Another feature I disliked in the Transit Package was that you cannot select trines and sextiles without also including semisextile and quincunx transits in the printout. Fortunately, the program does provide a solution: instead of selecting easy aspects (which includes the extra aspects mentioned), you can choose the sixth harmonic transits which are the same as sextiles, and the third harmonic, which equals trines, and get printouts without the semisextile and quincunx.

One final criticism: semisquares are indicated with SSQ and sesquiquadrates with SQQ, instead of SES, which is much easier to distinguish from SSQ.

Transit Package calculates transits only for ephemeris time, so it cannot be set for your local time zone. But AGS is about to correct that. One weakness of this program is that it does not collate transits for you (i.e. list the entering, exact, and leaving dates for a specific transit on one line). In fact, only Matrix's M-91 interpretive package (reviewed in Chapter 5), and its new M-65 Transit Master program (reviewed in Chapter 6) will collate transits.

In summary, Transit Package is the best of the transit-calculation programs presently marketed. I wish it could create charts by itself in addition to reading those in AGS files, but even without this ability the program is fast, accurate, and basically easy to use. I expect the Transit Master program, however, to far surpass the Transit Package once it becomes available.

As I noted earlier, however, you can also use one of the interpretive transit packages to calculate transits, and thus avoid the mislabeling problem of the Transit Package altogether. The Matrix transit-printing package (M-91) will not calculate transits without creating an interpretive printout, whether you want it or not. This isn't bad, but it wastes time and paper if you don't plan to use the interpretation. However, the AGS interpretive transit program (The Daily Astro-Report #590), reviewed in Chapter 5, can print out transits without interpretation.

Chapter Five

Interpretive Software

Both AGS and Matrix sell more interpretive programs than any other type of software. The reason for the great demand for this kind of package is that many people who do not understand astrology can nevertheless learn from and use the printouts generated by interpretive programs. Not only have many people earned a reasonable income marketing the reports, but they serve a public that wants their astrology explained to them.

There are a number of reasons why both newcomers to astrology and astrologers themselves buy interpretive software:

1. To begin learning astrological interpretations.

2. To entertain at parties or show off their computer.

3. To give clients printed reports to supplement the verbal chart reading.

4. To calculate transits as well as interpret them.

5. To set up a business selling charts and interpretations.

6. To get a second opinion about a specific interpretation.

Interpretive software is only as good as the person who prepared the interpretations. Since tastes vary, you should examine the sample pages of text from these programs, illustrated throughout the chapter, before deciding upon a specific program. Computer printouts of astrological interpretations cannot in any way substitute for chart readings by a professional astrologer, because a human can synthesize all of the factors and balance their influences, while a computer simply reproduces the information entered into it for single factors. One of the most common complaints against computer-generated interpretive reports is the degree of contradiction between parts of the report, a consequence of the computer's mechanical regurgitation of the text entered by the person who wrote the program.

All of the programs reviewed in this chapter run well, but the large-scale report packages take a bit of time to print out their reports, so if you plan to go into business selling the reports, you may want to purchase a high-speed printer, a printer buffer, and a fast computer to speed up your work as your business expands.

Matrix and AGS both publish small and large-scale packages for many machines. The small packages are for the home user who does not want to hand out printed reports. In fact, only Astrotalk, the Matrix small package, prints out information, and its printouts are not suitable for marketing. The AGS small packages display their results only on the screen.

The larger packages not only create printouts with better formatting and more information, but will also include transit interpretations, chart comparisons, and—for those who want to range further afield than astrology—numerology, biorhythm, and even lucky number reports. (The latter are not reviewed in this book.)

Astrotalk

Matrix Software, $39.95

Principal Functions	Displays and prints natal-chart data and interpretations of natal charts
Types of Calculations	***Aspects included:*** Major aspects plus semisquare and sesquiquadrate
	Custom aspects: No
	Number of house systems: Koch only
File Management	***Batch processing:*** No
	Saves files: No
Printouts	***Prints wheels:*** No
	Quality of printouts: Fair
	Quality of interpretation: Good
Computers	***Computer required:*** Commodore 64, PET, Apple, IBM PC and PC*jr*
	Other hardware required: One disk drive; IBM version requires 128K

Astroscope, Screen Version

AGS Software, $30

Principal Functions	Displays natal data, aspect list, and interpretations of natal chart
Types of Calculations	*Aspects included:* Major aspects
	Custom aspects: No
	Number of house systems: Placidus only
File Management	*Batch processing:* No
	Saves files: No
Printouts	*Prints wheels:* No
	Quality of printouts: No printouts
	Quality of interpretation: Very good
Computers	*Computer required:* Apple, TRS-80 Models I, III, and 4, IBM PC, CP/M
	Other hardware required: One disk drive for Apple version, two drives for TRS-80 version

Three small astrological interpretation packages are currently available: Astrotalk from Matrix (for Apple II, Commodore, and IBM PC computers; forthcoming for CP/M) at $40; and screen versions of Astroscope and Sex-O-Scope from AGS (for Apple II, TRS-80, CP/M, and IBM computers) at $30 each. These packages simply interpret natal charts.

Only Astrotalk can print out the screen display, while only the AGS programs display a list of aspects before interpreting them. Astrotalk is accurate for the 20th century, while the AGS programs are accurate for the 19th and 20th centuries. While these programs are sufficiently accurate for their purposes, serious astrological work requires greater accuracy. With Astrotalk you can select a specific planet in a sign, aspect, or house, and see the interpretation on the screen (in addition to examining a person's birth chart), while the AGS programs limit you to going through the planets in order as they appear in a specific birth chart. For this reason, students of astrology might prefer the Astrotalk program.

The only significant bug I found in any of the programs was that the AGS versions left out interpretations for a number of aspects for the outer planets. This is a problem because you cannot examine individual aspect interpretations with the AGS programs. You cannot, for example, ask to see Sun trine Jupiter, but have to go through the entire set of interpretations in order. Nonetheless, I was impressed with the content of the AGS Astroscope program and suggest that you look at the sample output from these programs in Figures 5.1 and 5.2 before making a decision.

In summary, Astrotalk by Matrix is a useful program for students of astrology. It runs smoothly, and you can either enter just the birth date (if that alone is known or if you want a solar chart—where the Ascendant is at the same position as the Sun); or the birthdate and time; or the birthdate, time and geographical coordinates. The program uses the major aspects plus the semisquare and sesquiquadrate (with the latter two given the same interpretation as the square), Koch houses, and gives you a choice of tropical, sidereal, or heliocentric planetary positions. The documentation is more readable and easy to use than any other documentation I have seen in the astrology field, and includes a convenient longitude and latitude table for about 200 U.S. and major foreign cities.

Astroscope, from AGS, is much like Astrotalk in its basic functioning. You get only tropical planetary positions, cannot inspect individual planetary meanings (e.g. go to Venus in Aquarius or Mars trine Sun), cannot specify solar charts, and have to fill in time zones, longitude and latitude (even if the birthplace is unknown). However, Astroscope gives you more information on each position it interprets than does Astrotalk, and the interpretations are very well written indeed. While the documentation is more detailed and harder to read and use than Astrotalk's, the program itself is easy to use. In addition, the booklet packaged with Astroscope includes a great deal of additional useful information, such as:

how to construct a chart;

how to gather birth data;

detailed information on U.S. time zone changes;

an international time-zone table and map;

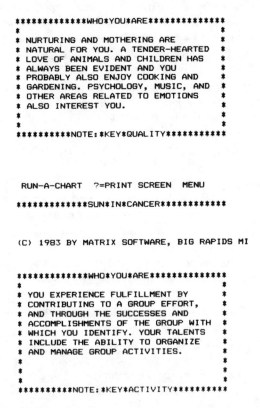

Figure 5.1: Astrotalk output.

```
              ASCENDANT IN LEO
         YOU LIKE TO BE A CENTER OF AT-

         TENTION & WANT TO APPEAR TO BE

         STRONG, CONFIDENT & DOMINANT.

         PROUD EVEN TO VANITY. WHEN ALL

         IS FALLING APART, YOU LOOK LIKE

         A MILLION BUCKS! DIGNIFIED AND

         HONORABLE. YOU LIKE THE POWER &

         PRIVILEGE, IF NOT THE RESPONSI-
    TYPE 'O' TO STOP, ANY OTHER TO CONT..
```

```
         BILITY, THAT COMES WITH LEADER-

         SHIP. STUBBORN & IDEALISTIC.

         OTHERS IMPRESS YOU ONLY IF THEY

         HAVE INTEGRITY. A PREFERENCE

         FOR RICH, ELEGANT SURROUNDINGS

         & POSSESSIONS. A SHOW-OFF. PHY-

         SICALLY IMPRESSIVE. A REGAL,

         CHARISMATIC DEMEANOR & BEARING!
         TYPE 'O' TO STOP, ANY OTHER TO CONT..
```

```
              SUN IN CANCER
         EMOTIONAL & SENSITIVE, AWARE OF

         'VIBES', GENEROUS, GIVING, LOV-

         ING & CARING WHEN NEEDS FOR E-

         MOTIONAL SUPPORT, LOVE & SECU-

         RITY ARE MET. IF NOT MET, YOU

         TEND TO WITHDRAW INTO YOUR-

         SELF & BE VERY INSECURE & SEL-

         FISH. HOME & FAMILY (ESPECIALLY
         TYPE 'O' TO STOP, ANY OTHER TO CONT..
```

Figure 5.2: Astroscope (screen version) output.

THE MOTHER) REPRESENT SECURITY
& ARE VERY IMPORTANT. EXTREMELY
SENTIMENTAL, VIVID MEMORIES OF
THE PAST. YOU WILL ALWAYS NEED
A SECRET QUIET PLACE OF YOUR
OWN. FEEDING OTHERS GIVES GREAT
PLEASURE, YOU LOVE BEING PART
OF A LARGE FAMILY. DOMESTICITY!
TYPE 'O' TO STOP, ANY OTHER TO CONT..

SUN IN HOUSE ELEVEN
VERY SOCIAL, YOU LIKE BEING
WITH YOUR FRIENDS. YOU CAN SUB-
ORDINATE YOUR INDIVIDUAL NEEDS
TO THE NEEDS OF A GROUP. AN
IDEALIST. A TEAM PLAYER, YOU
CAN EITHER LEAD OR FOLLOW. UN-
SELFISH, A STRONG SENSE OF
JUSTICE, FAIR AND IMPARTIAL.
TYPE 'O' TO STOP, ANY OTHER TO CONT..

SUN SQUARE MARS
(+) AGGRESSIVENESS. A STRONG
WILL. COMPETITIVE. A BATTLER.
PHYSICAL ACTIVITY IS A MUST. A
GOOD LEADER. COURAGE. ACTION!
(-) EGOTISTIC. MUST LEARN TO
LOSE GRACEFULLY. QUARRELSOME.
RASH & IMPULSIVE. HOT-TEMPERED.
STUBBORN & VERY PROVOCATIVE!
TYPE 'O' TO STOP, ANY OTHER TO CONT..

Figure 5.2: (continued)

a table of cities in the U.S. and the world that includes local standard time as well as longitude and latitude;

a useful glossary;

information on how to synthesize the various parts of the chart interpretation;

keywords for the planets, signs, houses, and aspects;

a short list of famous people's birth data;

and a bibliography.

In summary, the care taken with the booklet, and the high quality of the interpretations, make up for both the lack of printed interpretations and the fact that some aspects appear in the initial aspect listing but not in the interpretive part of the program. Therefore, I would recommend this program at least as highly as Astrotalk.

Sex-O-Scope, Screen Version

AGS Software, $30

Principal Functions	Displays natal data, aspect list, and interpretations of natal chart
Types of Calculations	***Aspects included:*** Major aspects ***Custom aspects:*** No ***Number of house systems:*** Placidus only
File Management	***Batch processing:*** No ***Saves files:*** No
Printouts	***Prints wheels:*** No ***Quality of printouts:*** No printouts ***Quality of interpretation:*** Very good
Computers	***Computer required:*** Apple, TRS-80 Models I, III, and 4 ***Other hardware required:*** One disk drive for Apple version, two disk drives for TRS-80 version

Sex-O-Scope includes the same high-quality booklet packaged with Astroscope, and operates similarly. I was puzzled that while Astroscope is up and running once you boot it (place it in the disk drive and turn the system on), to run Sex-O-Scope you have to type RUN SEXO-SCOPE. The programs are so similar that even the errors are identical: the programs skip the interpretation for the same aspects. This program's interpretations are well-thought-out and well-written, and yet quite personal and not as superficial as you would want if you were to show this at a party (see Figure 5.3). Of course, the topic is exclusively

```
            MOON SEXTILE MARS
     (+) SUPERACTIVE, RESPONSIVE.

     A SMALL SUGGESTION BRINGS ON

     ORGASM. A HIGH SPEED LOVER

     WITH NO THOUGHT FOR TOMORROW.

     (-) IMPULSIVE. CHANGES OF MOOD.

     COMES TOO SOON OR TOO LATE.

     PICKS FIGHTS WHEN SEX IS WHAT

     IS REALLY NEEDED. COMBATIVE.

     TYPE '0' TO STOP, ANY OTHER TO CONT..
```

```
            MOON SQUARE JUPITER
     (+) BOUNTIFUL BREADBASKET OF A

     LOVER. LOVE FEEDS LOVE, OPENS

     NEW REALMS OF FEELING, EMOTION-

     AL EXPRESSION -- IT'S ALL OK.

     (-) OVERREACTS, MAY OVERWHELM

     LOVER WITH RESPONSE, NEEDS TO

     KNOW WHEN TO QUIT, GO AHEAD.

     TOO MUCH OR TOO LITTLE SEX.

     TYPE '0' TO STOP, ANY OTHER TO CONT..
```

Figure 5.3: Sex-O-Scope (screen version) output.

your sexual habits, preferences, and style and is not in any way a general interpretation program. Every chart factor is related to sex, which can get monotonous for some people, yet may provide valuable insight for others.

I would suggest leaving people alone with this program to study the interpretations for their own chart, and not even look over their shoulder. For what it does, the program is quite good. Contradictions between separate portions of the interpretation (e.g., Saturn parts vs. Mars parts) need to be carefully synthesized by the reader, but nonetheless, a surprising amount of the interpretation strikes close to home. This is definitely a program for adults.

Large-Scale Interpretive Report Programs

This category includes birth-chart interpretation programs, a variety of predictive programs, and some synastry programs. Since these programs are designed for those who intend to sell the printouts to others, the programs will put your name and address on the printouts to personalize them.

It takes quite a while to print out a single report. While all of the AGS programs in this category offer batch processing, some of the Matrix programs don't. With those that lack batch processing you must return to the computer to enter the next job after a report is printed.

Anyone who intends to prepare a number of reports daily should have a printer buffer. Such a device speeds up processing greatly, lets you print multiple copies easily, and returns the computer to you long before the printing is completed.

M-90 Natal Chart Interpreter

Matrix Software, $300

Principal Functions	Prints report interpreting natal chart
Types of Calculations	***Aspects included:*** Major aspects plus semisquare
	Custom aspects: 15 aspects
	Number of house systems: 9 plus solar, Aries, and user-defined Ascendant houses
File Management	***Batch processing:*** Yes
	Saves files: No
Printouts	***Prints wheels:*** No
	Quality of printouts: Good
	Quality of interpretation: Good
Computers	***Computer required:*** Commodore 64, PET, Apple, TRS-80 Models I, III, and 4, IBM PC
	Other hardware required: Printer, one disk drive; TRS-80 and IBM versions require two disk drives

Deluxe Astroscope

AGS Software, $350

Principal Functions	Prints natal-chart wheel, aspect page, and multiple pages of natal chart interpretation
Types of Calculations	**Aspects included:** Major aspects
	Custom aspects: No
	Number of house systems: 4 (omits Equal House System)
File Management	**Batch processing:** Yes
	Saves files: No
	File access: Very good (uses Apple Star Track files)
Printouts	**Prints wheels:** Yes
	Quality of printouts: Very good
	Quality of interpretation: Very good
Computers	**Computer required:** Apple, IBM PC, TRS-80 Models III and IV, CP/M
	Other hardware required: Two disk drives

The programs reviewed in this section are designed to interpret birth charts for the novice and the beginning student of astrology.

Matrix's offering is M-90 Natal Chart Interpreter (for Commodore, Apple II, TRS-80, and IBM PC computers) at $300, while AGS publishes a printing version of Astroscope (for the TRS-80) at $150-$200, and a version called Deluxe Astroscope that generates larger reports and has batch processing (for IBM, Apple II, and CP/M computers) at $350. AGS also markets analogous Sex-O-Scope and Deluxe Sex-O-Scope programs with similar features and prices, while Matrix publishes M-94 Relating Potential for Commodore and Apple computers at $300.

Both M-90 and Deluxe Astroscope are available for Apple and IBM computers, and are aimed at the same market. Both programs are easy to use, and both generate reports for distribution to others.

Of course, each program has some features the other lacks. M-90, for example, gives you a choice of the nine most popular house systems, will create Aries and solar charts, and lets you specify the Ascendant. Deluxe Astroscope, on the other hand, offers only four house systems, and omits the Equal House System while including Regiomontanus. I find this strange, as I know of no astrologers who use Regiomontanus, while the Equal House System is the most popular house system in Great Britain and India, and is becoming increasingly popular mong American astrologers. Unfortunately, many AGS interpretive programs lack the Equal House System.

To start Deluxe Astroscope you have to type RUN DELINPUT. You also have to figure out for yourself that you must type RUN CONFIG to run the program that configures the main program for your printer card, and type RUN AGSTITLE to design your name and address title. It would have been simple to include a tiny menu program to do this for you. Certainly no mass-market program should be this primitive. I assume that the documentation will be improved (and maybe they'll add a menu?).

M-90, on the other hand, has a routine to customize your report with your name and address, but it is slow and hard to use—at least in the Apple version. Matrix should have fixed this quite a while ago, as their chart generation programs have a much better routine. When I made an error using this routine (I tried to use the right and left arrows instead of the control characters to move around the screen), I could not get out, because Matrix's protection scheme froze the program. I had to turn off the computer and start over.

M-90 works adequately if you follow the directions in the documentation, but it doesn't flow intuitively in a number of places. You *have* to refer to the documentation to figure some things out. For instance, in the batch process mode, after entering the first chart the screen displays the message <RETURN> = PROCESS ANOTHER CHART with the <RETURN> highlighted in inverse video and a flashing cursor on the A in ANOTHER. What you are supposed to do is hit Return if you want to *stop* entering charts and the A key if you want to enter another chart. Once you read the instructions, things like this are clear, but not when you first look at them on the screen. Another case in point is the Key Print option. With this option, you can include astrological keywords (like MO-4TH-HSE and MO-INC-JUP) in the printout. The keywords are abbreviated in a way that might confuse the novice who wants to begin learning a little astrology (and yet the reports are to be handed out to the novice), and the program is set up so that the keywords are omitted unless you select the option, instead of encouraging their usage. (I also couldn't figure out how to turn on the keyword option until I studied the documentation.) However, once you have read the instructions and are familiar with M-90's quirks, things progress smoothly.

The M-90 printout looks more finished than the Deluxe Astroscope reports. It is the type of report that you could easily market. Each page is well organized, with general guidelines for understanding the printout (see Figure 5.4), the stronger aspects are highlighted, and each page of interpretation is devoted to a single planet (see Figure 5.5). On the other hand, there is no discussion of the Midheaven, and all of the aspect interpretations appear twice (e.g., the Moon square Jupiter the interpretation appears on both the Moon page and the Jupiter page). Nevertheless, there are several very nice features to this program. You can easily change the text of the interpretations to suit your needs, even rewriting all the interpretations, and you can change any or all of the aspects and orbs, as well as the highlighting of aspects, and add additional aspects to the program, up to 15 total. Since the program does include the semi-square aspect but not the sesquiquadrate aspect, most people would want to add at least this aspect. You can save your additions and changes, and they thereafter become part of the program.

Although you cannot change either the aspects or the interpretations in Deluxe Astroscope, it does have many nice features. It emphasizes elements and modalities, and interprets the Midheaven. It prints a list of the five major aspects that is quite easy to read. Its interpretations for each planet in its sign are longer than M-90's and they seem (to me) a little more informative and balanced than M-90's.

Deluxe Astroscope prints out a full-page chart wheel with each report, which M-90 does not, but the printouts don't have M-90's "report look." The strong aspects are not highlighted, and the keywords cannot be removed. However, the keywords are clearly presented as full words (e.g. Venus trine Jupiter), which is much easier to understand than M-90's VE-TRI-JU. The clients' name is printed at the top of each page (not so in M-90), and the text is printed in both upper- and lower-case letters, while M-90's is all uppercase. As a result, Deluxe As⌄roscope's printouts are easier to read.

```
THE POSITIONS OF THE PLANETS AND HOUSES CUSPS AT THE TIME OF
YOUR BIRTH ARE GIVEN BELOW. THE INTERPRETATION OF THIS ASTRO-
LOGICAL DATA IS DIVIDED INTO TEN CHAPTERS AS FOLLOWS:

I.      GENERAL CHARACTERISTICS & LIFE PATTERNS
II.     DOMESTIC MATTERS * PERSONAL FEELINGS * WOMEN
III.    LOCAL CONTACTS * COMMUNICATION * MENTAL
IV.     AFFECTIONS * SOCIABILITY * PLEASURES * BEAUTY
V.      ENERGY * PURPOSE * SPORTS
VI.     ENTHUSIASMS * PRODUCTIVITY * LUCK
VII.    WORK * DUTIES * DISCIPLIINES
VIII.   INDEPENDANCE * THE UNEXPECTED * UNUSUALNESS
IX.     IMAGINATION * EMOTIONS * INSIGHTS
X.      PSYCHOLOGICAL NEEDS * CURIOSITY * SECRETS


            G E N E R A L   G U I D E L I N E S

* SOME OF THE INTERPRETATIONS GIVEN IN THE 'CHAPTER HIGH-
  LIGHTS' SECTION MAY APPEAR IN TWO CHAPTERS BECAUSE THESE
  PARTICULAR INTERPRETATIONS ARE APPROPRIATE FOR BOTH CHAPTERS.
  IT DOES NOT DENOTE GREATER STRENGTH OF THIS INTERPRETATION.

* IF YOU FIND THE SAME THEME SHOWING UP REPEATEDLY IN THE
  INTERPRETATIONS, THEN THIS FACTOR IS PARTICULARLY STRONG.

* INTERPRETATIONS GIVEN IN THE 'CHAPTER HIGHLIGHTS' SECTION OF
  EACH CHAPTER ARE ORDERED WITH STRONGEST INFLUENCES FIRST.
  YOU MAY HAVE ASTERISKS PRECEEDING SOME INTERPRETATIONS TO
  INDICATE AN UNUSUALLY STRONG FACTOR - THE GREATER THE NUMBER
  OF ASTERISKS, THE GREATER THE STRENGTH OF THE INFLUENCE.

* IF TWO INTERPRETATIONS SOUND CONTRADICTORY, THEN THIS SIMPLY
  MEANS THAT YOU EXPRESS OPPOSITE QUALITIES AT DIFFERENT TIMES
  AND IN DIFFERENT SITUATIONS.

* REMEMBER THAT YOUR HOROSCOPE IS A BLUEPRINT OF YOUR POTENTIALS
  YOU CAN RESPOND TO YOUR PATTERN OF PLANETS, HOUSES AND SIGNS
  IN A MATURE OR IMMATURE WAY -- IT'S UP TO YOU!


    PLANET POSITIONS AND EQUA HOUSE CUSPS FOR THIS HOROSCOPE
        THIS CHART IS TROPICAL GEOCENTRIC
*PLANET**IN*SIGN*******DDSGMM***PLANET**IN*SIGN*******DDSGMM***HOUSE CUSPS
*SUN      IN CANCER    *05CA20* *SATURN  IN VIRGO    *14VI08* * 1=25LE35 *
*MOON     IN SAGITARIUS*04SA05* *URANUS  IN CANCER   *05CA12* * 2=25VI35 *
*MERCURY  IN GEMINI    *20GE02* *NEPTUNE IN LIBRA    *14LI35* * 3=25LI35 *
*VENUS    IN GEMINI    *00GE09* *PLUTO   IN LEO      *16LE34* * 4=25SC35 *
*MARS     IN LIBRA     *06LI27* *ASCEND  IN LEO      *25LE35* * 5=25SA35 *
*JUPITER  IN PISCES    *07PI27* *MIDHEAV IN TAURUS   *18TA49* * 6=25CP35 *
************************************************************************
  PROGRAM CALCULATIONS BY MATRIX SOFTWARE, BIG RAPIDS MICH
```

Figure 5.4: M-90 introductory page

In addition, you can edit entered birth data on the screen, you can rerun a job without reentering the birth data, and you can take advange of batch processing, which is easy to use. Finally, I like the quality of the interpretations enough to recommend Deluxe Astroscope. You can compare for yourself the appearance and quality of the interpretations from both programs in Figures 5.4–5.6.

```
****************************************************************************
*                                                                        *
*                                                                        *
*   CHAPTER I           GENERAL CHARACTERISTICS * LIFE PATTERNS           *
*                                                                        *
*                                                                        *
****************************************************************************

   A P P R O A C H ,     A T T I T U D E
     YOU'RE GENEROUS, GOOD-HUMORED, DRAMATIC AND LOVE TO BE THE KING
   OR QUEEN.   EITHER CHILDREN, LOVE AFFAIRS, GAMES, CREATIVITY OR
   THEATRICAL INTERESTS ARE IMPORTANT AND YOU FIND TIME FOR THEM IN
   YOUR PERSONAL LIFE. YOU WITHDRAW WHEN NOT ADMIRED.          ASC-LEO
   K E Y     Q U A L I T Y
     YOU'RE SENSITIVE, INTUITIVE AND CAN BE POSSESSIVE, EMOTIONAL
   AT TIMES. YOU'LL DO ANYTHING FOR FAMILY OR THOSE UNDER YOUR
   CARE.   YOU'RE SYMPATHETIC, EVEN SENTIMENTAL, BUT YET ARE GOOD AT
   BUSINESS, SENSING IN ADVANCE WHAT THE PUBLIC WILL WANT.    SUN-CAN
   K E Y     A C T I V I T Y
     THE VITAL MEN YOU KNOW CONSIDER YOU THEIR FRIEND.   IN FACT YOU
   HAVE SPECIAL TALENTS FOR FRIENDSHIP AND GROUP PARTICIPATION,
   ESPECIALLY IF THEY PURSUE WORTHY AIMS.   YOU ARE CONCERNED WITH
   IMPROVEMENTS FOR THE GOOD OF ALL.                      SU-11TH-HSE


                   C H A P T E R     H I G H L I G H T S

****   YOU MAY BE WILLFUL, INDEPENDENT AND RESTLESS.  EAGER TO DO YOUR
       OWN THING AT ALL COSTS, YOU MAY STEP ON A FEW TOES.  EITHER YOU
       OR MEN YOU MEET ARE INDIVIDUALISTIC, UNCONVENTIONAL, EXCITING
       BUT UNPREDICTABLE AND OFTEN REBELLIOUS. YOU LIKE VARIETY.   SU-CJN-UR

   *   YOU MAY PUSH TOO HARD, STRAIN YOURSELF OR BE ACCIDENT PRONE.
       GETTING ALONG WITH MEN MAY BE DIFFICULT DUE TO ARGUMENTS AND
       COMPETITIVENESS.   YOU ALWAYS WANT MORE AND BETTER ACCOMPLISH-
       MENTS AND MAY CONFLICT WITH AUTHORITIES.            SU-SQR-MA

   *   RELATIONSHIPS WITH THE OPPOSITE SEX ARE VERY IMPORTANT TO YOU
       ALTHOUGH ACCOMPANIED BY PERSONAL TENSIONS AND PROBLEMS.  WHILE
       YOU BENEFIT THROUGH PARTNERS, CONTACT WITH OTHERS, THERE CAN BE
       DIFFERENCES BETWEEN YOU WHICH OFTEN SEEM HARD TO RESOLVE.   SU-INC-MO

   *   YOU RISE TO THE TOP OF SOME CAREER OR PUBLIC ACTIVITY BUT NOT
       WITHOUT SOME OBSTACLES.  CONFLICT, PROBLEMS INVOLVING IMPORTANT
       MEN COULD PRESENT DIFFICULTIES OR THOSE IN AUTHORITATIVE POSI-
       TIONS MAY BE UNWILLING TO COOPERATE AT TIMES.        SU-SSQ-MI

   *   YOU COULD OFTEN BE JUST PLAIN LUCKY!  YOU HAVE MANY OPPORTUNI-
       TIES TO EXPAND YOUR MENTAL HORIZONS AND EMOTIONAL SELF-EXPRESS-
       ION.   DEALING WITH CHILDREN, BEING THE GENEROUS BENEFACTOR ARE
       JOYOUS EXPERIENCES FOR YOU.   YOU GAIN THROUGH PRESTIGIOUS MEN.SU-TRI-JU
```

Figure 5.5: M-90 sample output

ASTROSCOPE FOR HANK FRIEDMAN

ASCENDANT IN LEO

You like to be a center of attention and want to appear to be
strong, confident and dominant. Proud even to vanity. When all
is falling apart, you look like a million bucks! Dignified and
honorable. You like power & privilege, but not the responsibi-
lities, that come with leadership. Stubborn and idealistic.
Others impress you only if they have integrity. A preference
for rich, elegant surroundings & possessions. A show-off. Phy-
sically impressive. A regal, charismatic demeanor and bearing!

MIDHEAVEN IN TAURUS

Your need to find security in life may become your dominant
life goal. You are worried about the here & now, about making
sure that your progression forward in life does not upset what
you have spent a lifetime developing. Very cautious and very
conservative. You tend to get stuck in ruts that you have created. Your lack of ability to tolerate change tends to make
you fussy and particular and difficult to please. Generally
good at professions dealing with $, because you're cautious.

SUN IN CANCER

Emotional, sensitive, aware of "vibes". Generous, giving, lov-
ing & caring when needs for emotional support, love and security are met. If not met, you tend to withdraw into yourself
and be very insecure and selfish. Home and family (especially
the mother) represent security & are very important. Extremely
sentimental, vivid memories of the past. You will always need
a secret quiet place of your own. Feeding others gives great
pleasure, you love being part of a large family. Domesticity!

SUN IN HOUSE ELEVEN

Very social, you like being with your friends. You can sub-
ordinate your individual needs to the needs of a group. An
idealist. A team player, you can either lead or follow. Un-
selfish, a strong sense of justice, fair and impartial.

Figure 5.6: Deluxe Astroscope printout

M-94: Relating Potential

Matrix Software, $300

Principal Functions	Prints report interpreting natal chart with respect to psychological factors
Types of Calculations	**Aspects included:** Major aspects plus semisquare
	Custom aspects: 15 aspects
	Number of house systems: 9 plus solar, Aries, and user-defined Ascendant houses
File Management	**Batch processing:** Yes
	Saves files: No
Printouts	**Prints wheels:** No
	Quality of printouts: Good
	Quality of interpretation: Good
Computers	**Computer required:** Commodore 64, PET, Apple, IBM PC
	Other hardware required: Printer, one disk drive; IBM versions require two disk drives

Deluxe Sex-O-Scope

AGS Software, $300

Principal Functions

Prints natal-chart wheel, aspect page, and multiple pages of natal-chart interpretation with respect to sexual and emotional patterns

Types of Calculations

Aspects included: Major aspects

Custom aspects: No

Number of house systems: 4 (omits Equal House System)

File Management

Batch processing: Yes

Saves files: No

File access: Very good (works with Apple Star Track files)

Printouts

Prints wheels: Yes

Quality of printouts: Very good

Quality of interpretation: Good

Computers

Computer required: Apple, IBM PC, TRS-80 Models III and 4, CP/M

Other hardware required: Two disk drives

Whereas M-90 and Astroscope focus upon the individual's chart in general, both Matrix's M-94 Relating Potential and AGS's Sex-O-Scope printing version (and Deluxe Sex-O-Scope) are designed to examine an individual's chart with respect to sexual and relationship patterns. Both are otherwise virtually identical in operation and style of output to M-90 and Astroscope respectively, except that M-94 will do batch processing.

Sex-O-Scope and Deluxe Sex-O-Scope focus specifically on the client's sex life, with interpretations similar to those in the screen version of Sex-O-Scope. M-94 Relating Potential is much more general, describing the person in terms of their emotional patterns, social style, and general temperment. In fact, unless you were told the report was specifically about relating potential, you might find it simply a more psychologically oriented version of M-90. M-94 will offend virtually no one, and does not broach topics that are too personal, while Sex-O-Scope goes into intimate sexual and emotional details.

If you are interested in purchasing one of these programs, review the sections on M-90 and Astroscope, and look at the sample printouts from M-94 and Sex-O-Scope in Figures 5.7 and 5.8. If you are considering M-90 or Deluxe Astroscope, you might decide instead to buy M-94 Relating Potential, as the latter has good psychological interpretations, and the same format as M-90.

SEX-O-SCOPE for Hank Friedman

Ascendant in Leo

Playful, outgoing, full of fun and very much in the moment,
with little immediate need for commitment. Sex is play, happy
amusement to please the body, emotions & commitment are separate, come later, depending. Radiant, sunny disposition may
belie other needs underneath, but physical sex drive is likely strong & needs satisfaction before inner self can be examined. Open and honest. Looks more for affection than technique. The spirit of the thing is what counts, not details.

Midheaven in Taurus

Known for staying power on the one hand, stolidity on the
other. Reputation for going all the way, pursuing the full
course, may be a)hard to fulfill, b)undesirable to try to, or
c)just the thing a potential partner ought to believe.

Sun in Cancer

Intense, private, hard to reach at first. Wants long-range love
to go with sex, but willing to give anything once a lover is
decided upon. Sex is a back-to-the-womb, nurturing experience.
Can be clinging, devoted, possessive. Not the freewheeling
type, but pays off triple in sheer passion once aroused. Not
kinky, but will go along with lover's needs to keep affair a-
live. Non-verbal, touching, emotional, but careful of love
commitments. It's too important a game to gamble on too freely.

Sun in House Eleven

Natural attraction & desirability. Must live up to image: not
always easy. Treasures intimate friends. May be hard to get to
know at first, but once there is committed. Likes socializing
but the inner person is the inner sanctum -- a rich treasure.

Sun Square Mars

(+) High energy, unflagging motivation. Strong stamina with
good pacing. Gives just enough and keeps right on delivering.
(-) Sporadic push, may over- or underdo, sex drive desultory
but may run to either extreme. Needs to learn easier pacing.

Figure 5.7: Sex-O-Scope printout.

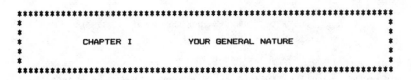

```
***********************************************************************
*                                                                     *
*                                                                     *
*              CHAPTER I              YOUR GENERAL NATURE              *
*                                                                     *
*                                                                     *
***********************************************************************
```

A P P R O A C H ,   A T T I T U D E
  YOUR SUNNY, CHEERFUL OUTWARD PROJECTION ATTRACTS THOSE WHO NEED
WARMTH AND AFFECTION THEY LACK. YOUR EASYGOING PRESENCE MAY DRAW
TO YOU MORE THAN YOU WANT TO TAKE FULL RESPONSIBILITY FOR, SO DO
NOT MAKE COMMITMENTS ASKED OF YOU UNLESS YOU CAN GIVE YOUR ALLASC-LEO
K E Y   Q U A L I T Y
  YOU ARE VERY PROTECTIVE OF YOURSELF AND OF OTHERS CLOSE TO YOU,
MAKING YOU A STAUNCH FRIEND. YOU NEED TO BALANCE YOUR OWN NEED
FOR CLOSENESS WITH YOUR PARTNER'S NEED FOR FREEDOM, OR YOUR LOVE
CAN BECOME RESTRICTING AND CAUSE HURT TO YOURSELF AND OTHERS. SUN-CAN
K E Y   A C T I V I T Y
  YOU MAY FIND YOURSELF TO BE MORE SOCIALLY SELF-CONSCIOUS (AND
COMPETENT) THAN OTHERS, WHICH CAN BE ADVANTAGEOUS AS LONG AS YOU
DO NOT EXPECT THEM TO FOLLOW SUIT ALL THE TIME. BE GRACIOUS, BUT
NEVER CONDESCENDING, AND YOUR RELATIONSHIPS WILL FLOWER.   SU-11TH-HSE

                   C H A P T E R   H I G H L I G H T S

**** YOUR EXTREMELY INSISTENT INDIVIDUALISTIC STYLE MAY BRING ADMIRA-
      TION OR ANNOYANCE OR BOTH, BUT WILL NOT GO UNNOTICED. THERE ARE
      TIMES, HOWEVER, WHEN A LITTLE SOCIAL CAMOUFLAGE IS ESSENTIAL,
      SO YOU WOULD DO WELL TO DEVELOP IT TO GET WHAT YOU WANT.   SU-CJN-UR

   * IT MAY BE QUITE DIFFICULT TO STOP YOURSELF FROM FLYING OFF THE
      HANDLE AND GETTING INTO ARGUMENTS THAT IN THE END GO NOWHERE.
      THE LIFE LESSON IS TO WALK AWAY, AND THE REWARDS ARE IMMEDIATE
      IN SHEER ENERGY SAVED. WHEN IN DOUBT, DON'T.   SU-SQR-MA

   * BORN UNDER A FULL MOON, YOU TEND TO SWING TO EMOTIONAL EXTREMES,
      FIRST JUBILANT, THEN IN DESPAIR, AND BACK AGAIN. BEFORE JUDGING
      YOURSELF OR ANOTHER, GIVE YOURSELF TIME FOR A SECOND THOUGHT ON
      THE MATTER TO AVOID OVER OR UNDERREACTION TO A PARTNER.   SU-INC-MO

   * YOUR PERSONALITY MAY NOT SEEM TO DIRECTLY SUGGEST THE REPUTATION
      YOU WOULD LIKE TO ACHIEVE, SO YOU MAY HAVE TO CALL ON OTHERS TO
      DO THE PUBLIC RELATIONS NECESSARY TO GET IT WHERE YOU WANT IT.
      IN ANY CASE, YOU SHOULD AVOID BEING YOUR OWN P.R. PERSON. SU-SSQ-MI

   * YOU HAVE A NICE EASY, BROAD SENSE OF PERSONAL PACING THAT ALLOWS
      YOU TO COVER A LOT OF GROUND WITHOUT APPEARING TO, WITH LARGE,
      RELAXED SWEEPS. YOU WILL BE ABLE TO GENTLY OPEN UP MORE INTRO-
      VERTED TYPES AND BROADEN THEIR WORLD, OPEN THEIR HEARTS.   SU-TRI-JU
```

*Figure 5.8: M-94 Relationship Potential printout.*
```

Predictive Report Packages

Predictive report packages are programs that interpret the future for individuals, using any of a variety of astrological predictive methods. Both AGS and Matrix publish predictive transit programs (as well as biorhythm and numerology programs), and AGS also offers a Monthly Astro-Report program based upon lunar returns.

AGS plans to release several additional predictive report packages this year, including:

Yearly Astro-Report, based upon Solar Returns;

Progressed Astro-Report, using secondary progressions;

Life Astro-Report, which interprets outer planet transits;

Hourly Astro-Report, based on the angularity of the planets.

Matrix's predictive report transit program is the $500 M-91 Transit Writer, for Commodore CBM/PET and C-64, Apple II series, TRS-80 models I & III, and IBM PC computers. AGS's program of the same type is Daily Astro-Report (for CP/M and IBM PC computers), at $350. Each transit program has advantages that the other lacks, as shown in Table 5.1.

	M-91 *Transit Report*	*Daily* *Astro-Report*
Lunar Transits	No	Yes
Prints complete report	Yes	No
Sky-to-sky transits	No	Yes
Prints natal chart	No	Yes
Accuracy	To the nearest day	To the minute
Handles stations	Somewhat	No
Indicates duration	Yes	No
Files included	10 years	None
File generation	None	200-year range
Highlights of year	Yes	No
Monthly format	Yes	No
Customizing	No	Excellent
Option for no text	No	Yes
Precession option	No	Yes
Batch processing	No	Yes

Table 5.1: M-91 Transit Report Compared to Daily Astro-Report

M-91: Transit Writer

Matrix Software, $500

Principal Functions
Prints transit reports

Types of Calculations
Aspects included: Major aspects

Custom aspects: No

Number of house systems: 9 plus solar, Aries, and user-defined Ascendant houses

File Management
Batch processing: No

Saves files: No

Printouts
Prints wheels: No

Quality of printouts: Good

Quality of interpretation: Very good

Computers
Computer required: Commodore 64, PET, Apple, IBM PC, TRS-80 Models I, III, and 4

Other hardware required: Printer, two disk drives

M-91 includes all the data needed to prepare transits for the period from 1980 through 1989, and you can purchase the data for additional periods from Matrix at a nominal cost. Although M-91 will not print out the chart, each report does list the position of the planets, Ascendant, Midheaven, and house cusps (you may choose from among nine house systems, as well as Aries or solar chart options).

The documentation is very brief but adequate, except for the section on including a name-and-address label. I had a hard time getting my name and address to look right, because the screen display is 40 columns and the printout is 80 columns, and I got confused by the carriage return symbols. This is one of the times that better explanations with examples would have helped a great deal. I did find it easy to change the transit interpretations themselves, although the routines are a bit slow on the Apple, and could use updating.

The program itself is easy to run, and it operates efficiently. You may choose between a three month, half year, or yearly report, and can specify all of the transiting planets (except the Moon), or a group of them (e.g., Jupiter through Pluto). You can customize the approaching and separating transit orb for each planet individually. This option is listed without explanation in the documentation, but is still easy to use.

There is one serious weakness in M-91—and *all* transit programs—which results from its method of calculating orbs and indicating the duration of a particular transit. As most astrologers know, because planets circle the Sun instead of vice versa, planets viewed from the Earth periodically appear to slow down, stand still, move backward (retrograde), stand still again, and then move forward. No transit program presently on the market comes close to handling this pattern effectively. Most simply ignore this cycle, which is unfortunate, because at the time of station (planetary standstill) the transit is often most powerful. Those programs that do allow applying and separating orbs only note when the transiting planet is at the distance specified (usually one degree away from the planet on either side). Therefore, if Saturn, for instance, approaches a person's Sun, crosses the one degree orb line (and is noted by the program) and then slows down and stops near but not on the Sun, most transit programs (including AGS's Daily Astro-Report) will ignore this important station and only indicate when Saturn has again returned to the one degree orb line. M-91 *will* list the time of station in this situation, but as an exact transit and not as a station. *No* transit program notes the station that occurs when Saturn has crossed over the Sun and then stations before reaching the first degree away from the Sun. The only way you might notice anything unusual about the transit is that the time between orb hits is larger than usual. This is unsatisfactory at best.

Matrix's M-91 is the only program that even attempts to list transits with their beginning, ending, and exact hit dates, and deserves acclaim for the effort. However, because the program doesn't list any stations after exact hit (which is not extremely common but common enough), it ends up listing transit periods with long durations and some inaccurate dates. For example, in one report, M-91 listed Saturn opposed Uranus the first time as occuring from May 22 to August 31 with exact hit on June 8. Later in the same report a second swing of the transit is described as occurring from May 22 to August 31 with exact hit on August 16. What actually happened was that Saturn did apply on May 22, and became exact on June 8, but then stood still on July 13, which should have been listed as the final date for the first set of transits (instead of August 31) and as the beginning date (instead of May 22) of the second transit swing. However, the program did accurately list the first applying and exact hit dates, the second exact hit, and the final date for the second swing. It is a shame for a client to get a report that is confusing with respect to the duration of a transit. As I said, in most yearly reports, this will happen at most twice, but even once is too much.

Nevertheless, M-91 is the *only* transit program available that generates reports suitable for distributing to the general public. It dares to list durations, even with the occasional problem, and does a very good job of presenting and interpreting transits, as Figure 5.9 shows. I wish it could be made to print transit listings without interpretations, and wish it also would allow the user to specify the time zone for which the transit should be calculated. Because time zone cannot be specified, the dates listed are accurate only to plus or minus one day.

A feature I like about the program is its "Highlights for the Year," which lists the most important transits of the year in chronological order (with interpretations). Not every swing of a transit is always listed in this overview, however.

```
               JUNE   1984
                                 (BEGINNING DATE - JUN  1, 1984)   VE-TRI-MA<
          JUN  1  OPPORTUNITIES TO HARMONIZE WITH THE OPPOSITE SEX MAY ARISE. YOU
                  COULD ALSO PURSUE ARTISTIC, GRATIFYING CREATIVE INTERESTS

                                 (BEGINNING DATE - JUN  1, 1984)   ME-CON-MC<
                  PUBLIC TALKS, PUBLICITY, BUSINESS DISCUSSIONS OR NEWS ARE SPOT-
                  LIGHTED.  YOU CAN GET IDEAS ACROSS TO HIGHERUPS, SIGN PAPERS.

                                 (BEGINNING DATE - JUN  2, 1984)   VE-SQR-JU
                  YOU COULD BE EXTRAVAGANT, LAVISH.  AVOID SPENDING ON HOME,
                  FAMILY OR BUSINESS MORE THAN YOU CAN AFFORD.

                                 (BEGINNING DATE - JUN  4, 1984)   ME 9
                  EDUCATION, FAR-OFF COMMUNICATIONS, PUBLISHING, LEGAL, TRAVEL,
            *     POLITICAL, RELIGIOUS INTERESTS OR IN-LAWS OCCUPY YOUR THOUGHTS.

                                 (BEGINNING DATE - JUN  4, 1984)   MA-SXT-SA<
                  YOU COULD HAVE A WONDERFUL SENSE OF ACCOMPLISHMENT BECAUSE OF
            *     FOLLOWING THROUGH ON A JOB WELL DONE.  MAKE BUSINESS DECISIONS.

                                 (BEGINNING DATE - JUN 16, 1984)   SU 10
                  AMBITIONS, CAREER, BUSINESS AND DEALINGS WITH AUTHORITIES OR
          ***     PARENTS SEEM EMPHASIZED. IMPORTANT MEN MAY DOMINATE THE SCENE.

                                 (BEGINNING DATE - JUN 16, 1984)   VE 10
                  ATTEND PUBLIC SOCIAL EVENTS, ENTERTAIN HIGHERUPS, USE LOOKS,
          ***     SALES ABILITY TO FURTHER GOALS.  PLEASURE AND BUSINESS MIX.

                                 (BEGINNING DATE - AUG  8, 1984)   MA 3
                  YOU COULD GET AROUND LOCALLY, CONTACT RELATIVES, WRITE, STUDY OR
        *******   TALK TO MORE PEOPLE DURING THIS TIME.  AVOID BEING ABRUPT, CURT.

                                    (JUN  3 - JUN  5)   SU-SQR-SA
          JUN  4  INTERFERENCE WITH YOUR VENTURES CAN BE FRUSTRATING.  PROBLEMS
                  WITH OR FOR MEN REQUIRE PATIENCE.  THE BRAKES ARE ON JUST NOW.

                                    (JUN  3 - JUN  5)   SU-TRI-NE
                  SOMEONE'S IN A ROMANTIC MOOD.  INSPIRATION COMES EASILY THROUGH
                  ONE WHO SEEMS INTUITIVE.  ENJOY A MOVIE, MUSIC, THE ARTS.

                                    (JUN  4 - JUN  5)   ME-SQR-AS
                  YOU MAY GET UNWANTED NEWS OR BE DISTRACTED BY A TALKER.  MAKING
                  UP YOUR MIND, CHOOSING ONE IDEA TO STICK TO SEEMS HARD.

                                    (JUN  4 - JUN 19)   ME 10
                  BUSINESS TALKS, PAPERS, CONTACTS WITH AUTHORITIES ARE FAVORED.
          ***     DISCUSS GOALS WITH PARENTS, HIGHERUPS WHO CAN PROMOTE OR HELP.

                                    (JUN  5 - JUN  7)   SU-SXT-PL
          JUN  6  DEEPSEATED EMOTIONAL BONDS CAN BE MOST REASSURING.  RESEARCH,
                  SUBTLENESS, SOLVING MYSTERIES ARE ALL FAVORED NOW.

                                    (JUN  5 - JUN  7)   VE-SQR-SA
                  YOU MAY HAVE TO FOREGO PLEASURES FOR MORE SERIOUS OBLIGATION,
                  NECESSITIES OF LIFE.  LOVE, SOCIAL LIFE, BEAUTY IS BLOCKED.
```

Figure 5.9: M-91 transit output

Daily Astro-Report

AGS Software, $350

Principal Functions Prints chronological list of transits including dates for applying and separating orbs with interpretations for date of exact contact

Types of Calculations *Aspects included:* Major aspects

Custom aspects: 15 aspects

Number of house systems: 8 house systems

File Management *Batch processing:* Yes
Saves files: No

Printouts *Prints wheels:* Yes

Quality of printouts: Good

Quality of interpretation: Good

Computers *Computer required:* IBM PC, some CP/M computers

Other hardware required: Two disk drives

The Daily Astro-Report program from AGS, on the other hand, gives interpretations only on the date of exact transit, and if you specify applying and separating orbs, they are not listed with any interpretation, nor are they listed adjacent to the exact hit, but elsewhere in the printout (see Figure 5.10). In other words, this program does not prepare a report per se, but presents interpretations only at exact hit. To use the Daily Astro-Report, you have to collect the applying dates, separating dates, and exact dates and collate them yourself.

On the other hand, it *will* print transits without interpretations, for the astrologer who wants to use this program only as a calculation package, it times transits precisely, and will, if you wish, include many additional aspects, and transits by the Moon.

The documentation neglects to mention that you have to have your DYS (interpretation) files on disk 2 if you want to print out interpretations (and gives no error message if you make the mistake of putting them on disk 1 as the instructions tell you to). The documentation also forgets to tell you that it takes about an hour to generate two months of ephemeris files, and the program includes no such files. Of course, the files only have to be generated once, but it takes eight hours of computer time for each year you want to examine. It would have been much friendlier to the user if AGS had included a year or two of files with the program. On the other hand, the reason it takes so long is the program's notable accuracy. The big advantage, however, of having the program calculate ephemeris files for you, is that it is not limited (as is M-91) to a brief time span of transit search. You can generate files for any time in a 200 year period.

I admire the strengths of Daily Astro-Report, including its wide range of options and its ease of operation, and yet for all of its power, it doesn't deal with planetary stations by transit (as mentioned above) at all. I *would* recommend this program to astrologers who watch transits hour by hour and want the precision, range of time period, and transit and aspect options, but do not intend to market the results. It is not really a report generation program. The quality of the interpretations is adequate, but the format is not acceptable for presentation to a layman. As a sophisticated transit-calculation package, for both transit-to-transit and transit-to-natal calculations, the program is very worthwhile, and would meet the needs of many astrologers.

Daily transits for kathi friedman, 5/18/1984 - 7/18/1984   Page 1

5/18/1984

2:45 AM PDT   Trans. Mars 18Sc17 R square Natal Ascendant   Entering orb

6:38 AM PDT   Trans. Mercury 2Ta28 semisqua Natal Moon   Exact

> You may have problems getting ideas across due to emotional
> clouding. Talks and communications may involve females.

2:33 PM PDT   Trans. Sun 28Ta06 square Natal Mars   Leaving orb

2:37 PM PDT   Trans. Mercury 2Ta46 semisqua Natal Uranus   Exact

> Your ideas now may surprise others. You want intellectual
> freedom. Transport and communication matters are erratic.

7:17 PM PDT   Trans. Sun 28Ta17 opposed Natal Jupiter   Leaving orb

7:34 PM PDT   Trans. Mercury 2Ta57 square Natal Saturn   Exact

> You have problems to solve and delays to contend with. Your
> mind may be blocked and transport may be a source of worry.

7:42 PM PDT   Trans. Moon 17Cp18 enters Sixth House   Exact

> Duty, responsibility and scheduling are emphasized now. You
> may have to make changes or adjustments in schedule but should
> find yourself to be adaptable and flexible.   You may also be
> concerned about health and the need for rest.

11:56 PM PDT   Trans. Mercury 3Ta07 conjunct Natal Midheaven   Entering orb

5/19/1984

8:35 AM PDT   Trans. Mercury 3Ta28 semisqua Natal Moon   Leaving orb

4:00 PM PDT   Trans. Mercury 3Ta46 semisqua Natal Uranus   Leaving orb

7:33 PM PDT   Trans. Venus 22Ta02 sextile Natal Mercury   Entering orb

8:44 PM PDT   Trans. Mercury 3Ta57 square Natal Saturn   Leaving orb

5/20/1984

0:56 AM PDT   Trans. Mercury 4Ta07 conjunct Natal Midheaven   Exact

> You tend to communicate well now, particularly regarding your
> personal goals. You find traveling to be appropriate.
>   or if negative
> You may be busy and active now for practical purposes. Ad-
> justments in schedule require calls & transport arrangements.

Daily Astro-Report, 5/20/1984   Copyright (C) 1983 AGS Software

Figure 5.10: *Printout from Daily Astro-Report.*

Monthly Astro-Report

AGS Software, $350

Principal Functions	Prints interpretations of lunar returns based on planets crossing the angles
Types of Calculations	*Aspects included:* Conjunctions to angles, parans *Number of house systems:* 8 house systems
File Management	*Batch processing:* Yes *Saves files:* No
Printouts	*Prints wheels:* Yes *Quality of printouts:* Very good *Quality of interpretation:* Very good
Computers	*Computer required:* IBM PC, some CP/M computers *Other hardware required:* Two disk drives

This very versatile program for those interested in looking at lunar returns is at present available for the IBM PC computer at $365, and CP/M computers at $350. As usual in its interpretive series, AGS has given the user control over almost all the options, enabling you to tailor the program to your needs. You can print out a natal chart as well as the lunar return chart if you wish, and interpretive paragraphs are also optional.

The program is exceptionally powerful, giving you the choice of eight house systems, relocated returns, harmonic returns, multiple returns, precession correction, and tropical or sidereal returns. The interpretations are of excellent quality, and include interpretations of both planet-to-planet transits and planet-to-angle transits, and are shown in Figure 5.11.

It is important to go into some detail about what planet-to-angle transits are, and how this program enables you to look at them in great detail. When a planet is close to an angle, its influence increases significantly. Astrologers have often used two very different types of angles in their work, the mundane angles of the actual horizon and meridian, and the ecliptic angles of the Ascendant and Midheaven. (If you work with Equal Houses and ecliptic angles, you get the Ascendant and nonagesimal angles, with the nonagesimal 90 degrees from the Ascendant. If you select Meridian Houses with ecliptic angles, the M. C., I. C., and points square to them will be the angles the program employs.) Most astrologers don't realize that a planet can be well below the Ascendant (into the First or Second House) by longitude while it is still above the horizon, due to its latitude. Using mundane angles places planets appropriately above or below the horizon. Monthly Astro-Report allows you to choose the type of angles you want to use, and to specify how many degrees a planet can be from an angle and still be considered angular.

In addition, you can also select parans if you choose mundane angles. A paran occurs when two planets are both angular at the same time, whether or not they are in aspect. The program lets you specify the orb for parans, and will of course interpret parans.

I cannot but respect AGS for producing such a complete package, and highly recommend it to students of lunar returns.

AGS's Other Predictive Astro-Reports

By the late fall of 1984, AGS plans to release the other predictive report packages mentioned at the beginning of this section. The Yearly Astro-Report, which bases predictions upon solar returns, progresses the angles in order to give predictions for the entire year. The Progressed

Lunar cycle chart preceding July 21, 1984
Interpretation for hank friedman
Type 1/1

Natal Sun rising

At this time you are likely to feel a heightened sense of your
own self worth. This inner sense of self-confidence will
assist you in becoming more influential among your peers than
usual. If the SUN is on the MC or ASC, increased vitality.

Natal Saturn at lower merid.

At this time, you are likely to feel naked and vulnerable --
with all your weaknesses exposed to others. An excellent time
to take care of unpleasant details in your life, to face the
"facts" of your situation, to correct your faults.

Natal Uranus rising

You will feel more inclined to act more erratically than is
normal for you -- to do the unexpected. You will prefer to
indulge your curiosity by exploring untrodden paths rather
than continuing in your regular workaday routine.

Transiting Jupiter setting

You are likely to feel much more appreciated by those around
you.   They will show their respect for you by going out of
their way to give you praise.   You may also receive a gift or
honor as a token of the esteem of others.

Transiting Neptune setting

Those with whom you have to deal are likely to appear to be
vague and uncertain, thus causing you to be confused and
unsure of where you stand.   The unclear general conditions
around you necessitate caution in making major decisions.

Natal Sun rises as natal Saturn crosses lower merid.

During this period of time, you will be capable of working
extremely hard. Indeed, circumstances will probably force you
to perform this hard and disagreeable labor. You will do this
out of a sense of duty, not for the sheer love of it.

Natal Sun rises as natal Uranus rises

Your attitude at this time is totally one-pointed and certain.
You will not compromise with any one or any thing now.   Your
independent way of thinking and acting could upset daily habit
patterns and living conditions.

page 1

Figure 5.11: Monthly Astro-Report.

Astro-Report employs progressed lunar aspects (both to other planets in the progressed chart and to planets in the natal chart), and sign changes of the progressed planets, in interpreting the secondary progressions. The Life Astro-Report focuses on the long-term transits of the outer planets in preparing its interpretations, while the Hourly Astro-Report, which will be released both in business and home-use versions, concentrates on parans, the angularity of planets in the sky, and the relationship of the transiting angles to the natal chart. It uses whatever locality you wish.

Synastry Report Programs

AGS publishes two synastry report programs: Contact Astro-Report and the Composite Astro-Report (both at $350 for CP/M, and $365 for IBM PC computers). Matrix is about to release a Synastry Report Writer program, but it was not ready for review in time for this book. Check with Matrix for sample report pages and more details on the program.

Since many features of the two AGS synastry programs are similar, I will show what they have in common first. Neither can prepare Equal House charts, incorporating instead the Regiomontanus, Koch, Campanus, and Placidus house systems. This is a foolish decision on AGS's part, as there are literally thousands of times more users of the Equal House System than of Regiomontanus. Both require the user to enter longitudes and latitudes with a letter (N, S, E, W) between the degrees and minutes, which slows down data entry.

On the other hand, the programs are very well constructed, with excellent documentation, fine data editing routines, and batch processing. Both can be restarted if something goes wrong and can add three name and address lines to the top right of each chart wheel. The reports generated by the programs have a relaxed feel about them, but they could be marketed, especially if you placed them in some type of binder.

Composite Astro-Report

AGS Software, $350

Principal Functions

Prints natal and composite charts and interpretation of composite chart

Types of Calculations

Aspects included: Major aspects

Custom aspects: None

Number of house systems: 4 (omits Equal House System)

File Management

Batch processing: Yes

Saves files: No

Printouts

Prints wheels: Yes

Quality of printouts: Very good

Quality of interpretation: Very good

Computers

Computer required: IBM PC, some CP/M computers

Other hardware required: Two disk drives

The Composite Astro-Report constructs composite charts for a pair of individuals. The theory behind composite charts is that, by constructing a chart from the midpoints of planetary pairs (e.g. the midpoint between person A's Sun and person B's Sun, which is called the Sun in a composite chart), you can find accurate and useful information about the relationship between the two people. While the technique was not accepted by many astrologers upon its introduction, it is gradually coming into favor in the astrological community.

The program itself is quite good. It can print out both natal charts, the composite chart wheel, a page that lists composite chart aspects and orbs, and an interpretive report of roughly nine pages. I really like the quality of the interpretations given by the Composite Astro-Report. They are among the best interpretations I've seen, and they are exceptionally easy to read because of their open spacing and the use of both lower- and uppercase letters. See Figure 5.12 for an example. You can derive house cusps either from the midpoints of each cusp, or from the midpoint of the M. C.

The program's only fault is that it cannot customize your aspect set (and nowhere in the documentation is there a list of the aspects used, with their orbs).

Even though I am not personally sold on the value of composite charts (especially when compared to the value of looking at the interaspects between two charts), I am charmed by the quality of this program and highly recommend it.

COMPOSITE ASTRO-REPORT for hank friedman and kathi friedman.

Sun Trine Moon

No matter what kind of relationship you are in, you are good
friends. You enjoy a rare compatibility on both an emotional
and an intellectual level. In a sexual relationship this compatibility extends to the physical level as well. You approach
each other as equals. Neither one of you wants to always play
the active or passive role so you switch frequently. You are
very accepting of one another. This allows you to be relaxed.
You feel more complete together than apart.

Sun Conjunct Mercury

The two of you have an excellent mental rapport. You each have
an easy time understanding the way the other thinks. You love
to talk about everything, and frequently do. Communicating
verbally comes easy to the two of you, but you may get hung up
when it comes to communicating on an emotional level. You may
have to put extra effort into this part of your relationship.
You may travel together. At least you will do different things
and have new ideas. You excite each other's curiosity.

Sun Square Pluto

There are some very real dangers with this aspect, the main
one being power struggles between you. There's also the chance
that the two of you will have power struggles with the world,
but it is more likely that one or both of you will try to
change the other. You WILL change each other, very deeply,
just by being together. Conscious attempts to force change
will result in fierce opposition from the one being manipu-
lated. Try to help rather than dominate each other.

Sun Conjunct Midheaven

This will probably be one of your more important relationships
in terms of overall effect on your lives. It will especially
affect your life directions, career goals, and the way you relate to the world in general. You both feel stronger as a result of being together. You attribute a greater ease in public
self-expression to knowing each other. Together you have the
ability to attract attention and to accomplish a great deal as
long as you avoid arrogance. You work well together.

Figure 5.12: Composite Astro-Report output.

Contact Astro-Report

AGS Software, $350

Principal Functions Prints natal charts, interaspect page, and interpretation of inter-chart factors

Types of Calculations

Aspects included: Major aspects

Custom aspects: None, but can change aspect orbs

Number of house systems: 4 (omits Equal House System)

File Management

Batch processing: Yes

Saves files: No

Printouts

Prints wheels: Yes

Quality of printouts: Very good

Quality of interpretation: Fair

Computers

Computer required: IBM PC, some CP/M computers

Other hardware required: Two disk drives

Contact Astro-Report also functions very well, and has several special features. You can do multiple comparisons with a given individual's chart without entering the first person's data over again each time. The program uses the five major aspects only, and you cannot add aspects, but you can choose different aspect *orbs*. You can print out either natal relationship potentials for both charts, or the chart comparison interpretation, or both, and you can get multiple prinouts of any of these reports.

The natal relationship potentials report interprets each person's:

Sun sign and house;

Moon sign and house;

rising sign;

balance of elements and modes;

planet ruling the Fifth, Seventh, and Eighth Houses;

planets within the Fifth, Seventh, and Eighth Houses;

signs of the Fifth, Seventh, and Eighth Houses.

Unfortunately, I found the quality of the interpretations in this section spotty, as did other astrologers to whom I showed the output. One of the primary problems is common to all interpretation programs: they print out only fixed paragraphs for each position, and cannot synthesize the effects of the various attributes (signs, houses, planets). Consequently, they not only often contradict themselves, but come up with erroneous information. Because of both the complexity involved in describing a person's relationship potential and the lack of artistry on the part of the author of the Contact Astro-Report's interpretations, the weakness is more noticeable here than in some other interpretation programs.

The chart-comparison interpretation section looks at the locations of each person's planets in the houses of the other person's chart. The positions are first listed conveniently on one page, and then an interpretation for each is printed. This section also determines which hemisphere of each chart is emphasized by the other's planetary placements, then lists interaspects with orbs, and interprets them.

The quality of the interpretations again is highly variable. The interpretations of the planets of one chart in the houses of the other are adequate, but the writing in the interaspect section is relatively poor (see Figure 5.13). The program prints out each person's birth chart as part of its output.

I really like all of the routines the program performs, but find the quality of the interpretations too inadequate to recommend. I hope AGS improves the quality of the interpretation, as the rest of the program is optimal.

---

              hank's Sun Sextile kathi's M.C..

You are a couple who will be actively involved with the
world. You can be dynamic together, but if your direction is
not the same, success could be undermined. So combine
energies in projects that can give recognition to you both.

              hank's Moon Trine kathi's Saturn.

This combination indicates that emotions should be controlled,
or at least understood. If either of you is inhibited in ex-
pressing feelings, clarify the situation with the partner.
Feeling secure in the relationship can also ease restrictions.

              hank's Mars Trine kathi's Node.

You and your partner will be actively involved with others,
possibly often directing activities. If you want to
concentrate your efforts elsewhere, remember that someone else
can run the show and you can still be lively participants.

              hank's Jupiter Square kathi's Node.

You and your partner will probably share relationships with a
great number of people, and together will enjoy the company
of others. But in order to sustain a partnership there has to
be more than just popularity with the populace.

              hank's Uranus Sextile kathi's M.C..

One of you can help the other to be more creative and original
in career, or more independent in interaction with the world.
The affect may be sporadic, and some ideas may be too eccen-
tric, but at least the contact will be very stimulating.

              hank's Pluto Sextile kathi's Moon.

Your feelings for each other can run very deeply, as though a
strong force were holding you together. But this combination
can also lead to subconscious manipulation. If this seems to
be happening, remember that two can play at that game.

Copyright (C) 1983, Astro-Graphics Services Inc.

Figure 5.13: Contact Astro-Report.

Chapter Six

State-of-the-Art Software

The 1980s are a fortunate time for astrologers of the world. By using computers and the latest astrological software, astrologers today can explore wide ranges of astrological territory, test their theories with much greater ease than ever before, and examine charts for many centuries and from many planes of reference. A few years ago, neither of the software packages discussed in this chapter were available. A few years from now, the same software may exist, but will probably have been revised many times. As new computers emerge on the scene, the power of astrological software will continue to grow, but even the programs available now have more power than most contemporary astrologers need.

The two packages that represent the state of the art are M-65 from Matrix and Nova from AGS. M-65 is available for the Commodore 64 and CBM/PET, the Apple II series, the IBM PC, and TRS-80 computers. A CP/M version is in the works. Because so few astrologers now own TRS-80 computers, Matrix no longer supports M-65 on these computers and will not release any additional modules for those machines. AGS is adapting Nova for IBM PC and CP/M computers. In most cases, those owning MS-DOS computers will be able to use either M-65 or Nova.

Since M-65 has been out for more than three years, I have had the opportunity to use it for some time. Nova, on the other hand, is not yet available to the general public and I will review a prerelease version supplied to me by Rob Hand.

M-65-A

Matrix Software, $300

Principal Functions
Prints a wide variety of charts and tables, generates files for use by many other programs.

Types of Calculations
Aspects included: Major aspects plus semisquare, sesquiquadrate, inconjunct

Custom aspects: 15 aspects with orbs

Number of house systems: 11 plus user-defined Ascendant

Heliocentric charts: Yes

Methods of progression: Secondary, tertiary, and minor progressions

Methods of direction: Solar, Naibod, degree/year, user-defined arc

Solar and lunar returns: Calculates and prints solar and lunar return wheels including demi-returns, incremental returns, returns to any point in the Zodiac

Timed progressed hits: Yes

Midpoint analysis: Prints midpoint structures and midpoint sorts for any dial

Chart comparisons: Prints interaspects, bi-wheels, composite and relationship charts

Harmonics: Prints tables of harmonics and harmonic charts

Defaults
Preset calculation defaults: House system, parallax Moon on/off, geocentric or geographic latitude, mean or true node

Preset printout defaults: Type of wheel, harmonic, aspect table on/off, wheel on/off, tables on/off, choice of many tables, planetary pictures on/off

M-65 *(continued)*

File Management	***Batch processing:*** 40 jobs
	Saves files: Yes
	File access: Excellent (includes file utilities)
Printouts	***Glyphs:*** Yes
	Types of wheels: Closed, open, bi-wheel
	Quality of printouts: Very good
Computers	***Computer required:*** Apple II series, Commodore 64, PET, TRS-80 model 3, IBM and MS-DOS computers
	Other hardware required: One drive for Commodore 64, two drives for other versions, printer.

M-65 comes in several modules. M-65-A is the main module. For convenience I'll refer to it simply as M-65 from this point on. M-65 is the main program, which creates, files, analyzes, and prints out charts and astrological data. M-65-B is the research module. You can use it to ask questions of your files—that is, to search your files for aspects, planets in houses, and so on. M-65-C is a screen module, useful if you want to sit at the computer and look at various files and their interactions without printing them out. M-65-D is a Uranian module, which calculates and creates files and prints charts complete with Uranian planets. The analysis sections of M-65-D do not employ the Uranian positions, but could be programmed by the user to do so. Additional modules are being prepared as of this writing, and will also be discussed.

M-65 has both incredible strengths and weaknesses. No other program for the Apple II and Commodore line comes close to the power of this program. On the other hand, there are still some routines that do not work properly, and the documentation for the program is very extensive, and somewhat hard to read.

What M-65 Can Do

M-65 is first and foremost a file-based chart-service program. It was designed for easy access to files, batch processing of multiple jobs, and creating a variety of printouts.

Files

M-65 generates the most complete and compact files of any program I've looked at. The files contain not only birth data and the longitude of the planets and major points (M.C. and Ascendant), but also latitude, declination, daily motion, right ascension, house cusps, planetary distance, heliocentric coordinates, true node, and parallax Moon. For the novice, such features don't mean much, but once you start to do research on your files, the presence of so many pieces of information in each file allows you to ask complex questions (such as who has a fast Moon square a Fourth House Mars) and get the answers quickly and easily. In addition, even the beginner can take advantage of the Inspect File routine, to look at any of the information contained in the files.

An advantage of the file structure is that you can store many files on a single disk (about 180 for an Apple, 300 for IBM), and you can gain access to the files within the program via an alphabetical directory, which you can begin searching at any letter of the alphabet. The files were designed to be transportable from one type of computer to another (e.g., Apple to IBM to C-64), and Matrix plans to distribute file disks of famous people and others for research purposes. File access is easy, quick, and accurate, so you can use the same files repeatedly for different jobs.

After entering a person's birth data you can easily at any time not only print out the chart, but also request progressions, returns, comparisons, and tables. The only time you have to re-enter birth data is when you want to create a relocation chart or to switch to a different zodiac. Since relocation is a popular technique and many people want relocated charts for several areas, it is a shame that M-65 makes you re-enter the birth data for each location, and doesn't allow you to keep all the charts concerning one person in a single file. Matrix is just about to release a new menu module called Blue Star (initially for the IBM/MS-DOS machines only) that will allow you to do several relocations for the same person more easily, and store all the files under one name.

Furthermore, M-65 cannot compare files on separate disks or transfer individual files from one disk to another. As a result, if you want to compare two or more people whose files are on separate file disks, you have to re-enter the data so that it is all on one file disk. I wrote a small routine to compare files on separate disks, which can be done without too much knowledge of programming.

Finally, because M-65's file system is different from anyone else's, you cannot use the files the program creates with other programs. You must use the utility provided in M-65 to prepare and copy file disks, and you cannot recover a "crashed" disk the way you can with normal files (using a disk-recovery program). Since the information on the files is carefully packed, so that the greatest amount of data possible can occupy the smallest space, the file disks are sensitive, and are more likely to be wiped out (or made into gibberish) than regular files in the event of an accident. Therefore, it is essential that you back up your file disks, and update the backups regularly as you add new people to your disks, so you don't lose your work. Still, with careful handling your file disks can go undamaged for years.

The M-65 package now includes an Inspect-A-File module, which you can use to scan files easily, to examine on the screen daily motions, latitudes, heliocentric positions, and the like, and to delete whole files or just secondary files (e.g., a progressed chart) from your file disks.

Chart Wheels and Glyphs

Matrix has put a great deal of effort into the design of their chart wheels, and as a result, their wheels are superior to those generated by most AGS programs. First, the planets are proportionately spaced around the circle, much as they are in the real sky. Second, M-65 can print three types of chart wheels. The normal closed wheel (Figure 6.1) has divisions for the twelve houses, and is used for preparing regular charts. The open-wheel charts (Figure 6.2) have nothing in the center, and are favored by heliocentric and midpoint astrologers, as well as by those who like to draw in the aspect lines. The bi-wheel charts, on the other hand, have one person's data printed inside the chart wheel and a second set of data outside the wheel, and are quite useful for chart comparisons and for placing present (or progressed) planetary positions around a person's birth chart (see Figure 6.3).

Matrix programs will print glyphs on many printers (check with Matrix regarding the correct combination of printer and interface for your computer). Note in my example of a bi-wheel chart that where the planets are near an angle (on the outside of the bi-wheel) the minutes of arc are deleted, as are retrograde symbols for the planets outside the rim. Fortunately, the table at the bottom of the bi-wheel contains this data. The one thing I don't like about M-65's wheels is that the person's last name is given first in the label for the chart wheel.

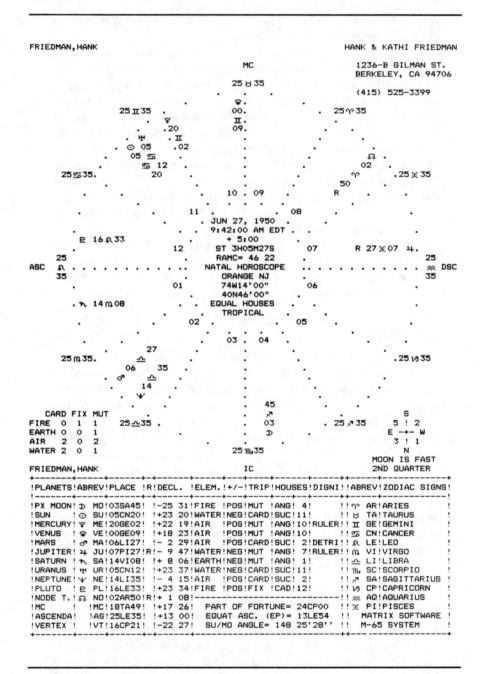

FRIEDMAN, HANK

Figure 6.1: A standard M-65 chart wheel.

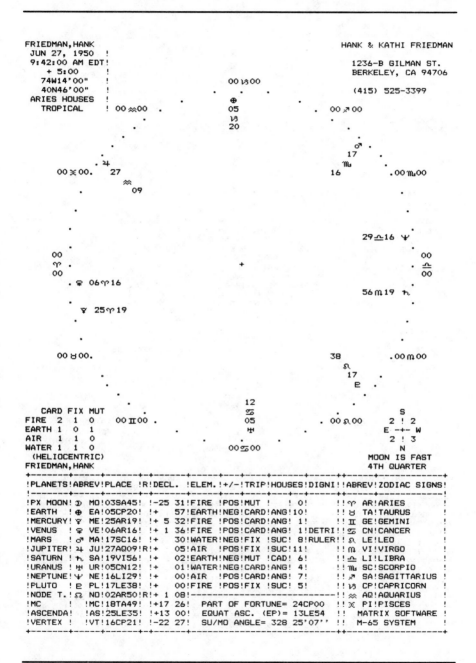

```
FRIEDMAN,HANK                                          HANK & KATHI FRIEDMAN
  JUN 27, 1950  !
  9:42:00 AM EDT!                                          1236-B GILMAN ST.
     + 5:00      !                                         BERKELEY, CA 94706
   74W14'00"     !                      00 ♑00
   40N46'00"     !                 .         .             (415) 525-3399
 ARIES HOUSES    !                       ⊕
    TROPICAL     ! 00 ♒00   .          05           .   00 ♐00
                         .  ♒        ♑                     .
                                     20
                               .

                                                          ♂
                                                          17    .
              ♃                                           ♏
        00 ♓00.     27                                   16        .00 ♏00
                   ♒                                                   .
                   09
                  .                                                      .

          .                                                                .
                                                               29♎16  ♆
        00                           +                               00
        ♈  .                                                         ♎
        00                                                       .   00
           .  ♀ 06♈16                                      56 ♏19  ♄

          ♄  25♈19
             .

        00 ♉00.                                        38        .00 ♍00
                 .                                      ♌
                                                        17   .
                                                        ♇
          .                          12
                                      ♋                         S
    CARD FIX MUT          .           05          .            2 ! 2
  FIRE  2  1  0   00 ♊00 .            ♅                .  00 ♌00   E -+- W
  EARTH 1  0  1                                                2 ! 3
  AIR   1  1  0                                                   N
  WATER 1  1  0             .        00 ♋00    .   .       MOON IS FAST
   (HELIOCENTRIC)                                          4TH QUARTER
  FRIEDMAN,HANK
```

PLANETS	ABREV	PLACE	R	DECL.	ELEM.	+/-	TRIP	HOUSES	DIGNI	ABREV	ZODIAC SIGNS
PX MOON	☽ MO	03SA45		-25 31	FIRE	POS	MUT		0	♈ AR	ARIES
EARTH	⊕ EA	05CP20		+ 57	EARTH	NEG	CARD	ANG	10	♉ TA	TAURUS
MERCURY	☿ ME	25AR19		+ 5 32	FIRE	POS	CARD	ANG	1	♊ GE	GEMINI
VENUS	♀ VE	06AR16		+ 1 36	FIRE	POS	CARD	ANG	1	DETRI	♋ CN	CANCER
MARS	♂ MA	17SC16		+	30	WATER	NEG	FIX	SUC	8	RULER	♌ LE	LEO
JUPITER	♃ JU	27AQ09	R	+	05	AIR	POS	FIX	SUC	11	♍ VI	VIRGO
SATURN	♄ SA	19VI56		+	02	EARTH	NEG	MUT	CAD	6	♎ LI	LIBRA
URANUS	♅ UR	05CN12		+	01	WATER	NEG	CARD	ANG	4	♏ SC	SCORPIO
NEPTUNE	♆ NE	16LI29		+	00	AIR	POS	CARD	ANG	7	♐ SA	SAGITTARIUS
PLUTO	♇ PL	17LE38		+	00	FIRE	POS	FIX	SUC	5	♑ CP	CAPRICORN
NODE T.	☊ NO	02AR50	R	+ 1	08					♒ AQ	AQUARIUS
MC	MC	18TA49		+17 26	PART OF FORTUNE= 24CP00					♓ PI	PISCES
ASCENDA	AS	25LE35		+13 00	EQUAT ASC. (EP)= 13LE54						MATRIX SOFTWARE
VERTEX	VT	16CP21		-22 27	SU/MO ANGLE= 328 25'07''						M-65 SYSTEM

Figure 6.2: *An open M-65 chart wheel.*

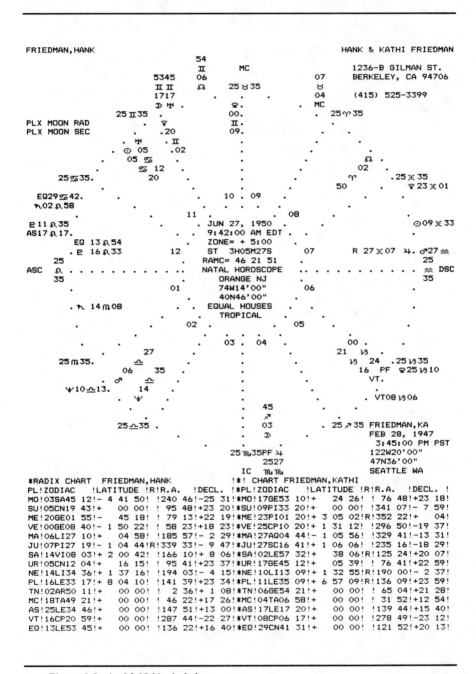

Customizing Features

You can customize M-65 in a number of ways. First, you can set up a default configuration tailored to your needs. This means that the program will run with your choice of house system, geographic or geocentric latitude, parallax-corrected or uncorrected Moon, and mean or true node. A custom-aspect routine lets you select your own set of aspects and orbs (up to fifteen aspects total), and a set of custom-output routines will tailor the printouts to your specifications. In addition, its routine for creating your own name-and-address label on the chart wheel is easy to use.

The custom-output routines let you select any of several styles of printout as automatic options. The strength of this customizing feature is that you can choose the type of information you want in each printout. You can specify as many as seven different sets of printouts (called *auto-options*) for each of three modules (the analyze module, the printwheel module, and the bi-wheel module).

For example, in customizing the printwheel module, you could set auto-option 1 to give you a closed wheel, an aspect page, no planetary patterns, and no notes attached to the chart, and auto-option 2 to print an open wheel for a second harmonic chart containing planetary patterns but not aspects, and so on. The instructions for customizing each module are brief but sufficient, provided you are not scared by computers or by a multiplicity of choices.

The customizing routines could have been easier to use if they had presented one question at a time, rather than all the features for each auto-option at once. The documentation could have walked the user through the process more carefully by giving a step-by-step example of customizing.

A deficiency of this customizing method is that you have to keep your own records of what each auto-option does, because once you save the set of options you have chosen and start using the program, the program asks you which of the auto-options you want only by number (1, 2, 3, 4, 5, 6, or 7), without indicating what each one does. Matrix does supply M-65 with the more commonly requested auto-options built in for those who are afraid to approach the customizing routine, but to use these built-in auto-options you have to search through the documentation to find out what they do (page C-225 in the M-65 Users' Notes).

In the update of M-65 I evaluated, Matrix forgot to include the preset auto-options in the printwheel module. If you receive a copy that lacks preset options, send it back to Matrix and they will fix it.

It would have been a bit easier to use the auto-option feature if Matrix had designed the program to show on the screen what each auto-option prints, either by labeling the choice in English (e.g., normal printwheel, with aspects, no patterns), or by letting you label it yourself. Admittedly, such a routine would have taken up a lot of memory and might have slowed the program down a little, but it would have been a big help in making this feature more usable. Nevertheless, M-65 includes everything necessary to tailor itself to your own needs.

Matrix is working on correcting these deficiencies, and in the new Blue Star Menu (which is included automatically with the IBM/MS-DOS version of M-65), you are no longer limited to a few auto-options, but can choose any printing options for each job and review what you've selected at any time (with a list of what you've chosen displayed clearly on the screen).

The custom-aspect routine is a little slow and confusing to use in the beginning. Nonetheless, it allows you to define aspects, orbs, and three-letter names for each aspect.

Batch Processing

M-65 can handle as many as forty jobs at one time, and keeps track for you (on the screen) of the number of jobs you have already programmed. This is a nice feature, but it is easier than you might think to reach the forty-job limit, since it takes two jobs, not one, to create and then print a chart. With the new Blue Star Menu that comes with the IBM version the number of jobs you can process in a batch is limited only by disk space. Still, the batch processing works very smoothly, and functions well even if you have to re-enter a job a second time (because you made typing errors, for example), keeping track of the exact number of jobs entered.

The batch processing method was well conceived. M-65 saves a lot of time in processing multiple jobs by first calculating the Sun and the Moon positions for all the jobs and then loading the next module, which calculates the planetary positions for all the jobs, and so on, instead of processing each job completely and then reloading each module for subsequent jobs.

Additional Printouts

Besides giving the user a number of types of chart-wheel printouts to choose from, this program will also print out many types of tables:

1. the interaspects between two charts;

2. the house cusps as derived by ten different house systems;

3. timed progressed hits including entering and leaving orbs;

4. several types of sorted midpoints, with planets inserted;

5. midpoint trees with conjunctions and oppositions accented;

6. sorted harmonics with conjunctions accented;

7. aspects sorted by orb;

8. angular separations (sorted) for the planets;

9. solstice-point calculation and sort;

10. planetary-patterns diagrams (e.g., grand trines, T-squares).

These tables are exceptionally useful, as they enable you to examine in depth many areas of astrology. They are easy to read and well designed. For examples of these tables, see Figures 6.4 through 6.12.

The planetary-patterns routine (Figure 6.4) does not work as it should at this time. It compares only the interaspects between one planet (e.g., the Moon) and the rest without looking at the angles between the remaining planets to determine whether they are within orb. M-65 will regard a group of planets as being in a T-square formation when one pair of the planets is not in aspect within the orb specified. For example, if the Moon correctly square Jupiter (5-degree orb) and the Moon is opposed Venus (6-degree orb) but Venus is not square Jupiter (10 degrees from square, out of orb), M-65 will label the group a T-square. I expect that Matrix will fix this problem at some point.

Alternate Types of Charts

Along with the natal charts, which are very accurate within the years 1700–2300 and less accurate but still usable from 4713 B.C., M-65 will calculate charts using a variety of local space-coordinate systems. These local space charts are often used in relocation work, and view the sky from a point of reference other than the ecliptic. M-65 will also create composite charts, relationship charts (midpoint in time and space between the two dates), a variety of sidereal charts, heliocentric charts, many types of progressed charts, harmonic charts (unfortunately with Aries rising, instead of the harmonic Ascendant, but the latter is listed in the table at the bottom of the page), and solar- and lunar-return charts (including precessed returns, demireturns, and returns to a specific point in the sky).

I should warn you that I am not a sidereal astrologer (one who uses a Zodiac based on star positions instead of the Sun's orbit), and have not extensively tested the sidereal routines, such as enneads, anlunars, pssrs, and Quotidians. I also lack experience with the large variety of progressed techniques offered in both M-65 and Nova.

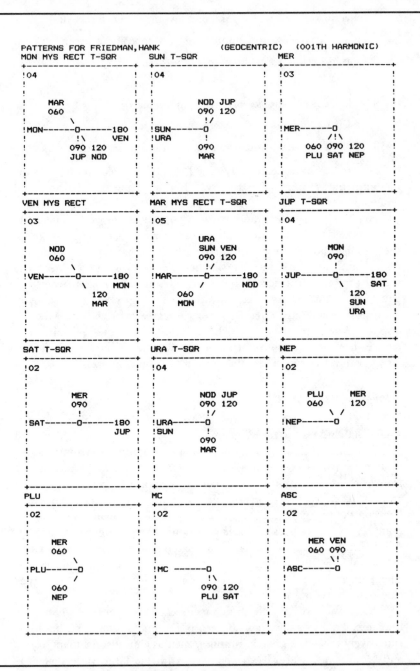

```
PATTERNS FOR FRIEDMAN,HANK          (GEOCENTRIC)  (001TH HARMONIC)
MON MYS RECT T-SQR        SUN T-SQR                MER
+-----------------------+ +-----------------------+ +-----------------------+
!04                    ! !04                    ! !03                    !
!                      ! !                      ! !                      !
!     MAR              ! !     NOD JUP          ! !                      !
!     060              ! !     090 120          ! !                      !
!       \              ! !       !/             ! !                      !
!MON-----O------180    ! !SUN-----O             ! !MER-----O             !
!       !\     VEN     ! !URA     !             ! !        /!\           !
!     090 120          ! !        090           ! !     060 090 120      !
!     JUP NOD          ! !        MAR           ! !     PLU SAT NEP      !
!                      ! !                      ! !                      !
!                      ! !                      ! !                      !
+-----------------------+ +-----------------------+ +-----------------------+
VEN MYS RECT              MAR MYS RECT T-SQR       JUP T-SQR
+-----------------------+ +-----------------------+ +-----------------------+
!03                    ! !05                    ! !04                    !
!                      ! !     URA              ! !                      !
!     NOD              ! !     SUN VEN          ! !     MON              !
!     060              ! !     090 120          ! !     090              !
!       \              ! !       !/             ! !       !              !
!VEN-----O------180    ! !MAR-----O------180    ! !JUP-----O------180    !
!        \     MON     ! !        /     NOD     ! !        \     SAT     !
!        120           ! !     060              ! !        120           !
!        MAR           ! !     MON              ! !        SUN           !
!                      ! !                      ! !        URA           !
!                      ! !                      ! !                      !
+-----------------------+ +-----------------------+ +-----------------------+
SAT T-SQR                URA T-SQR                NEP
+-----------------------+ +-----------------------+ +-----------------------+
!02                    ! !04                    ! !02                    !
!                      ! !                      ! !                      !
!     MER              ! !     NOD JUP          ! !     PLU     MER      !
!     090              ! !     090 120          ! !     060     120      !
!       !              ! !       !/             ! !       \ /            !
!SAT-----O------180    ! !URA-----O             ! !NEP-----O             !
!              JUP     ! !SUN     !             ! !                      !
!                      ! !        090           ! !                      !
!                      ! !        MAR           ! !                      !
!                      ! !                      ! !                      !
!                      ! !                      ! !                      !
+-----------------------+ +-----------------------+ +-----------------------+
PLU                      MC                       ASC
+-----------------------+ +-----------------------+ +-----------------------+
!02                    ! !02                    ! !02                    !
!                      ! !                      ! !                      !
!     MER              ! !                      ! !     MER VEN          !
!     060              ! !                      ! !     060 090          !
!       \              ! !                      ! !       \!             !
!PLU-----O             ! !MC -----O             ! !ASC-----O             !
!        /             ! !        !\            ! !                      !
!     060              ! !     090 120          ! !                      !
!     NEP              ! !     PLU SAT          ! !                      !
!                      ! !                      ! !                      !
!                      ! !                      ! !                      !
+-----------------------+ +-----------------------+ +-----------------------+
```

Figure 6.4: An M-65 planetary-picture output.

```
ASPECTS & 360 MIDPOINTS FOR FRIEDMAN,HANK               (GEOCENTRIC)

   MO !  SU  !  ME  !  VE  !  MA  !  JU  !  SA  !  UR  !  NE  !  PL  !  NO  !
03SA45!05CN20!20GE02!00GE09!06LI27!07PI27!14VI08!05CN12!14LI35!16LE33!02AR50!
------+------+------+------+------+------+------+------+------+------+------!
--MO--! *INC*!163 43! *OPP*! *SXT*! *SQR*! 79 37! *INC*! 49 11!107 12! *TRI*!
      ! 1 35A!      ! 3 37S! 2 42A! 3 42A!      ! 1 27A!      !      !   55S!
19VI32!--SU--! 15 18! 35 11! *SQR*! *TRI*! 68 48! *CJN*! 99 15! 41 14! *SQR*!
      !      !      !      ! 1 07A! 2 08A!      !  OBS!      !      ! 2 30S!
11VI54!27GE41!--ME--! 19 53!106 25!102 35! *SQR*! 15 10! *TRI*! *SXT*! 77 12!
      !      !      !      !      !      ! 5 54S!      ! 5 27S! 3 29S!      !
01PI57!17GE44!10GE05!--VE--! *TRI*! 82 41!103 59! 35 03! *SES*! 76 25! *SQR*!
      !      !      !      ! 6 19A!      !      !      !  34S!      ! 2 42A!
05SC06!20LE53!13LE15!03LE18!--MA--! *INC*! 22 19! *SQR*!  8 07! 49 54! *OPP*!
      !      !      !      !      ! 1 00A!      ! 1 15S!      !      ! 3 37S!
20CP36!06TA24!28AR45!18AR48!21SA57!--JU--! *OPP*! *TRI*!142 53!159 06! 25 23!
      !      !      !      !      !      ! 6 41S! 2 15A!      !      !      !
23LI57!09LE44!02LE05!22CN08!25VI18!10SA48!--SA--! 68 56! 30 27! 27 35!161 18!
19VI29!05CN16!27GE37!17GE40!20LE50!06TA20!09LE40!--UR--! 99 23! 41 21! *SQR*!
      !      !      !      !      !      !      !      !      !      ! 2 22S!
09SC10!24LE57!17LE18!07LE22!10LI31!26SA01!29VI21!24LE53!--NE--! *SXT*!168 16!
      !      !      !      !      !      !      !      !      ! 1 59S!      !
10LI09!25CN57!18CN18!08CN21!11VI30!27TA00!00VI21!25CN53!15VI34!--PL--! *SES*!
      !      !      !      !      !      !      !      !      !      ! 1 17A!
03AQ18!19TA05!11TA26!01TA29!04CP39!20PI09!23GE29!19TA01!08CP42!09GE42!--NO--!
--MC--
165 04! *SSQ*! 31 13! 11 19! *SES*! 71 22! *TRI*! *SSQ*!145 45! *SQR*! *SSQ*!
      ! 1 30A!      !      ! 2 38A!      ! 4 41S! 1 23A!      ! 2 16S!   59S!
26AQ17!12GE05!04GE26!24TA29!27CN38!13AR08!16CN29!12GE01!01LE42!02CN41!25AR50!
--AS--
 98 10! 50 15! 65 33! *SQR*! 40 52!168 07! 18 33! 50 23! 49 00!  9 01!142 45!
      !      !      ! 4 34A!      !      !      !      !      !      !      !
14LI40!00LE27!22CN48!12CN52!16VI01!01GE31!04VI51!00LE23!20VI05!21LE04!14GE12!
------+------+------+------+------+------+------+------+------+------+------!
   MO !  SU  !  ME  !  VE  !  MA  !  JU  !  SA  !  UR  !  NE  !  PL  !  NO  !
03SA45!05CN20!20GE02!00GE09!06LI27!07PI27!14VI08!05CN12!14LI35!16LE33!02AR50!
```

```
CHART DATA-SCOPE FOR FRIEDMAN,HANK
+-------------------------+    +------------------------+    +------------+
! ASPECTS PER PLANET    ! !    !   ASPECT ANALYSIS    ! !    !  HOUSES    !
!--+------+-+---------+--!    !--+--+-+--------+------!    !------------!
!CO!PLANET! ! DAILY   ! !    ! !NA ! ASPECT  !       !    ! PLANETS    !
!DE!  NAME!R! MOTION  !# !    ! #! ME!   ARC  ! ORB   !    ! PER HOUSE  !
!--+------+-+---------+--!    !--+--+-+--------+------!    !------------!
!PX!03SA45! ! 15 02 14! 6!    ! 1!CJN!   00'  ! 7 00' !    !01=25LE35! 1!
!SU!05CN20! !    57 13! 6!    ! 3!OPP! 180 00'! 7 00' !    !02=25VI35! 2!
!ME!20GE02! ! 1 52 11! 3!    ! 6!TRI! 120 00'! 7 00' !    !03=25LI35! 0!
!VE!00GE09! ! 1 10 29! 5!    ! 8!SQR!  90 00'! 7 00' !    !04=25SC35! 1!
!MA!06LI27! !    27 03! 7!    ! 4!SXT!  60 00'! 5 00' !    !05=25SA35! 0!
!JU!07PI27!R!    00 07! 5!    ! 3!SSQ!  45 00'! 3 00' !    !06=25CP35! 0!
!SA!14VI08! !    04 09! 3!    ! 3!SES! 135 00'! 3 00' !    !07=25AQ35! 1!
!UR!05CN12! !    03 36! 6!    ! 3!INC! 150 00'! 3 00' !    !08=25PI35! 1!
!NE!14LI35! !    00 02! 3!    ! !   !        !       !    !09=25AR35! 0!
!PL!16LE35! !    01 27! 4!    ! !   !        !       !    !10=25TA35! 2!
!NO!02AR50!R!    00 00! 7!    ! !------------------!    !11=25GE35! 2!
!MC!18TA49! !    00 00! 6!    ! ! COPYRIGHT (C)  1982  !    !12=25CN35! 1!
!AS!25LE35! !    00 00! 1!    ! !   MATRIX SOFTWARE    !    !           !
+--+------+-+---------+--+    +--+------------------+-+    +---------+--+
```

Figure 6.5: An M-65 aspect page with midpoints. Note that midpoints are not optional.

ANALYSIS FOR FRIEDMAN,HANK   (GEOCENTRIC)   SORTED BY ANGULAR SEPARATION

360 MP	ZOD MD	PAIR	ANGSEP	ORB	ASP
145 35	25LE35	ASCEN			
243 45	03SA45	MOON			
95 20	05CN20	SUN			
80 02	20GE02	MERCU			
60 09	00GE09	VENUS			
186 27	06LI27	MARS			
337 27	07PI27	JUPIT			
164 08	14VI08	SATUR			
95 12	05CN12	URANU			
194 35	14LI35	NEPTU			
136 33	16LE33	PLUTO			
2 50	02AR50	NODE			
48 49	18TA49	MIDHE			
286 21	16CP21	VERTE			
133 54	13LE54	EQU A			
294 00	24CP00	PAR F			
95 16	05CN16	SU/UR	08	08S	CJN
135 14	15LE14	PL/EQ	2 40	2 40A	CJN
190 31	10LI31	MA/NE	8 07		
141 04	21LE04	PL/AS	9 01		
54 29	24TA29	VE/MC	11 19		
139 44	19LE44	AS/EQ	11 41		
87 37	27GE37	ME/UR	15 10		
87 41	27GE41	SU/UR	15 18		
154 51	04VI51	SA/AS	18 33		
70 05	10GE05	ME/VE	19 53		
175 18	25VI18	MA/SA	22 19		
350 09	20PI09	JU/NO	25 23		
150 21	00VI21	SA/PL	27 35		
149 01	29LE01	SA/EQ	30 14		
179 21	29VI21	SA/NE	30 27		
64 26	04GE26	ME/MC	31 13		
77 40	17GE40	VE/UR	35 03		
77 44	17GE44	SU/VE	35 11		
114 37	24CN37	SU/EQ	38 34		
114 33	24CN33	UR/EQ	38 42		
166 01	16VI01	MA/AS	40 52		
115 57	25CN57	SU/PL	41 14		
115 53	25CN53	UR/PL	41 21		
265 03	25SA03	MO/VT	42 36	2 24A	SSQ
25 50	25AR50	NO/MC	45 59	59S	SSQ
72 01	12GE01	UR/MC	46 23	1 23A	SSQ
72 05	12GE05	SU/MC	46 30	1 30A	SSQ
170 05	20VI05	NE/AS	49 00		
219 10	09SC10	MO/NE	49 11		
161 30	11VI30	ME/VE	49 54		
120 27	00LE27	SU/AS	50 15		
120 23	00LE23	UR/AS	50 23		
311 54	11AQ54	JU/EQ	51 06		
160 10	10VI10	MA/EQ	52 33		
106 58	16CN58	ME/EQ	53 52		
108 18	18CN18	ME/NE	56 31	3 29S	SXT
215 06	05SC06	MO/MA	57 18	2 42A	SXT
31 29	01TA29	VE/NO	57 18	2 42A	SXT
165 34	15VI34	NE/PL	58 01	1 59S	SXT
164 14	14VI14	NE/EQ	60 41	41A	SXT
112 48	22CN48	ME/AS	65 33		
129 44	09LE44	SU/SA	68 48		
129 40	09LE40	SA/UR	68 56		
13 08	13AR08	JU/MC	71 22		
97 01	07CN01	VE/EQ	73 45		
98 21	08CN21	VE/PL	76 25		
324 36	24AQ36	NO/VT	76 29		
41 26	11TA26	ME/NO	77 12		
203 57	23LI57	MO/SA	79 37		
18 48	18AR48	VE/JU	82 41	6 19A	TRI
122 05	02LE05	ME/SA	84 06	5 54S	SQR
91 22	01CN22	MC/EQ	85 04	4 56S	SQR
102 52	12CN52	VE/AS	85 26	4 34A	SQR
92 41	02CN41	PL/MC	87 44	2 16S	SQR
140 53	20LE53	SU/MA	91 07	1 07A	SQR
140 50	20LE50	MA/UR	91 15	1 15S	SQR
240 28	00SA28	NE/VT	91 46	1 46S	SQR
49 01	19TA01	UR/NO	92 22	2 22S	SQR
49 05	19TA05	SU/NO	92 30	2 30S	SQR
290 36	20CP36	MO/JU	93 42	3 42A	SQR
97 12	07CN12	MC/AS	96 45	6 45A	SQR
194 40	14LI40	MO/AS	98 10		
144 57	24LE57	SU/NE	99 15		
144 53	24LE53	UR/NE	99 23		
236 24	26SC24	MA/VT	99 54		
28 45	28AR45	ME/JU	102 35		
112 08	22CN08	VE/SA	103 59		
133 15	13LE15	ME/MA	106 25		
190 09	10LI09	MO/PL	107 12		
188 49	08LI49	MO/EQ	109 51		
137 18	17LE18	ME/NE	114 33	5 27S	TRI
106 29	16CN29	SA/MC	115 19	4 41S	TRI
36 20	06TA20	JU/UR	117 45	2 15A	TRI
36 24	06TA24	SU/JU	117 52	2 08A	TRI
303 18	03AQ18	MO/NO	119 05	55S	TRI
225 15	15SC15	SA/VT	122 13	2 13S	TRI
347 35	17PI35	MC/VT	122 28	2 28A	TRI
123 18	03LE18	VE/MA	126 19	6 19A	TRI
68 22	08GE22	NO/EQ	131 04		
69 42	09GE42	PL/NO	133 43	1 17A	SES
353 15	23PI15	VE/VT	133 48	1 12S	SES
127 22	07LE22	VE/ME	134 26	34S	SES
117 38	27CN38	MA/MC	137 38	2 38A	SES
215 58	05SC58	AS/VT	140 46		
74 12	14GE12	NO/AS	142 45		
266 01	26SA01	JU/NE	142 53		
121 42	01LE42	NE/MC	145 45		
169 32	19VI32	MO/SU	148 25	1 35A	INC
169 29	19VI29	MO/UR	148 33	1 27A	INC
211 27	01SC27	PL/VT	149 48	12A	INC
261 57	21SA57	MA/JU	151 00	1 00A	INC
210 07	00SC07	VT/EQ	152 27	2 27A	INC
3 11	03AR11	ME/VT	153 41		
55 41	25TA41	JU/EQ	156 26		
57 00	27TA00	JU/PL	159 06		
213 57	03SC57	EQ/PF	160 06		
83 29	23GE29	SA/NO	161 18		
161 54	11VI54	MO/ME	163 43		
326 17	26AQ17	MO/MC	165 04		
61 31	01GE31	JU/AS	168 07		
278 42	08CP42	NE/NO	168 16		
10 47	10AR47	UR/VT	168 51		
10 50	10AR50	SU/VT	168 59		
250 48	10SA48	JU/SA	173 19	6 41S	OPP
274 39	04CP39	MA/NO	176 23	3 37S	OPP
331 57	01PI57	MO/VE	176 23	3 37S	OPP

Figure 6.6: An M-65 angular separation-sort output.

```
45 DEGREE TREE DIAGRAMS FOR FRIEDMAN,HANK              (GEOCENTRIC)
+---------------++---------------++---------------++---------------++---------------+
!   PL    D  '!!   NO    D  '!!   MC    D  '!!   UR    D  '!!   SU    D  '!
!            !!!MC-+-EQ  1 28!!PL-+-MC  1 08!!UR-+-NO  1 11!!UR-+-NO  1 19!
!            !!!ME-+-NE    32!!ME-+-VT    38!!SA-+-PF  1 08!!SA-+-PF  1 16!
!            !!!PL-+-MC    09!!UR-+-NO*   12!!SU-+-NO  1 07!!SU-+-NO  1 15!
!            !!!ME-+-VT*   21!!SA-+-PF*   15!!MA-+-NO*   33!!MA-+-NO*   41!
!            !!!UR-+-NO  1 11!!SU-+-NO*   16!!AS-+-EQ    28!!AS-+-EQ    36!
!            !!!SA-+-PF  1 14!!MA-+-NO    50!!SU-+-UR*   04!!SU-+-UR*   04!
!            !!!SU-+-NO  1 15!!AS-+-EQ    55!!MA-+-UR    38!!MA-+-UR    30!
!            !!         !!!SU-+-UR  1 27!!SU-+-MA    41!!SU-+-MA    33!
!            !!         !!         !!!PL-+-AS    52!!PL-+-AS    44!
+---------------++---------------++---------------++---------------++---------------+
!   MA    D  '!!   AS    D  '!!   NE    D  '!!   VE    D  '!!   VT    D  '!
!SU-+-UR  1 11!!VE-+-MC  1 06!!JU-+-MC* 1 27!!SA-+-EQ  1 08!!MA-+-PF  1 07!
!MA-+-UR    37!!NO-+-VT*   59!!NO-+-PF  1 10!!UR-+-PF    33!!SA-+-PL  1 00!
!SU-+-MA    34!!UR-+-NE*   42!!SA-+-EQ    34!!MO-+-AS    29!!NE-+-VT    53!
!PL-+-AS    23!!SU-+-NE*   38!!UR-+-PF*   01!!SU-+-PF    29!!SA-+-MC*   08!
!ME-+-PF*   34!!MO-+-PL    26!!MO-+-AS*   05!!MA-+-PF*   05!!JU-+-AS    10!
!VE-+-EQ    34!!MA-+-NE    04!!SU-+-PF*   05!!SA-+-PL    12!!MO-+-VE    36!
!MC-+-AS    45!!JU-+-EQ    06!!MA-+-PF    39!!NE-+-VT*   19!!ME-+-EQ*   37!
!            !!!UR-+-PF    12!!SA-+-PL    46!!SA-+-MC  1 20!!         !
!            !!!SU-+-VT    15!!NE-+-VT    53!!JU-+-AS* 1 22!!         !
!            !!!MO-+-MC*   42!!         !!         !!         !
!            !!!MA-+-VT    49!!         !!         !!         !
!            !!!JU-+-PL  1 25!!         !!         !!         !
+---------------++---------------++---------------++---------------++---------------+
!   MO    D  '!!   JU    D  '!!   PF    D  '!!   SA    D  '!!   ME    D  '!
!ME-+-PL    27!!VE-+-SA    19!!ME-+-AS* 1 12!!ME-+-JU    23!!EQ-+-PF  1 05!
!VE-+-JU    03!!ME-+-AS    21!!NO-+-EQ    38!!NO-+-AS    04!!MO-+-UR    33!
!NE-+-PF*   32!!NO-+-EQ    55!!MO-+-SA    03!!NE-+-EQ*   06!!MO-+-SU    30!
!ME-+-MC*   41!!MO-+-SA  1 30!!UR-+-EQ*   33!!VT-+-EQ    59!!NE-+-AS    03!
!SA-+-AS  1 06!!         !!!SU-+-EQ*   37!!UR-+-AS  1 15!!MO-+-MA    04!
!VT-+-PF  1 26!!         !!!PL-+-NO    42!!SU-+-AS  1 19!!JU-+-NO    07!
!            !!         !!!ME-+-VE  1 05!!NE-+-PL* 1 26!!PL-+-PF    15!
!            !!         !!!MA-+-EQ  1 10!!         !!!AS-+-VT    56!
!            !!         !!         !!         !!!JU-+-UR  1 18!
!            !!         !!         !!         !!!SU-+-JU  1 22!
!            !!         !!         !!         !!!MC-+-PF  1 23!
+---------------++---------------++---------------++---------------++---------------+
!   EQ    D  '!   '*'=CONJUNCTIONS & OPPOSITIONS
!ME-+-UR  1 17!
!SU-+-ME  1 13!
!ME-+-MA*   39!
!MO-+-PF    01!
!SA-+-NE    27!
+-------------+
```

Figure 6.7: M-65 midpoint trees. Asterisks indicate conjunctions and oppositions to midpoints in the natal chart.

90 DEGREE MIDPOINTS FOR FRIEDMAN,HANK   (GEOCENTRIC)

```
+----------------------------------------------------------------------------------+
! 1 22=MC/EQ    16 58=ME/EQ    35 58=AS/VT    54 53=UR/NE    72 01=UR/MC  !
! 2 41=PL/MC    18 18=ME/PL    36 20=JU/UR    54 57=SU/NE    72 05=SU/MC  !
! 2 50=NO***    18 48=VE/JU    36 24=SU/JU    55 35=AS***    74 08=SA***  !
! 3 11=ME/VT    20 11=VT/PF    37 22=VE/NE    55 41=JU/EQ    74 12=NO/AS  !
! 4 39=MA/NO    20 36=MO/JU    39 10=MO/NE    56 17=MO/MC    74 14=NE/EQ  !
! 5 12=UR***    22 08=VE/SA    39 40=SA/UR    56 24=MA/VT    75 34=NE/PL  !
! 5 16=SU/UR    22 48=ME/AS    39 44=SU/SA    57 00=JU/PL    76 01=MA/AS  !
! 5 20=SU***    23 57=MO/SA    39 48=AS/PF    58 25=NO/PF    77 35=MC/VT  !
! 6 27=MA***    24 33=UR/EQ    41 26=ME/NO    59 01=SA/EQ    77 40=VE/UR  !
! 7 01=ME/PF    24 37=SU/EQ    41 54=JU/VT    60 09=VE***    77 44=SU/VE  !
! 7 01=VE/EQ    25 50=NO/MC    43 15=ME/MA    60 14=MA/PF    79 29=MO/UR  !
! 7 12=MC/AS    25 53=UR/PL    43 54=EQ***    60 21=SA/PL    79 32=MO/SU  !
! 8 21=VE/PL    25 57=SU/PL    45 14=PL/EQ    60 28=NE/VT    80 02=ME***  !
! 8 42=NE/NO    27 38=MA/MC    45 15=SA/VT    61 31=JU/AS    80 05=NE/AS  !
! 8 49=MO/EQ    28 45=ME/JU    45 44=JU/PF    61 57=MO/VE    80 09=JU/NO  !
!10 09=MO/PL    30 07=VT/EQ    46 33=PL***    63 45=MO***    81 25=MC/PF  !
!10 31=MA/NE    30 23=UR/AS    47 18=ME/NE    64 17=NE/PF    81 57=MA/JU  !
!10 47=UR/VT    30 27=SU/AS    48 49=MC***    64 26=ME/MC    83 15=VE/VT  !
!10 50=SU/VT    31 27=PL/VT    49 01=UR/NO    64 51=SA/AS    83 29=SA/NO  !
!12 52=VE/AS    31 29=VE/NO    49 04=SA/PF    67 27=JU***    85 03=MO/VT  !
!13 08=JU/MC    31 42=NE/MC    49 05=SU/NO    68 22=NO/EQ    85 18=MA/SA  !
!14 35=NE***    32 05=ME/SA    49 44=AS/EQ    69 42=PL/NO    86 01=JU/ME  !
!14 36=UR/PF    33 18=VE/MA    50 50=MA/UR    70 05=ME/VE    87 04=VE/PF  !
!14 40=SU/PF    33 18=MO/NO    50 53=SU/MA    70 10=MA/EQ    87 37=ME/UR  !
!14 40=MO/AS    33 57=EQ/PF    51 04=PL/AS    70 48=JU/SA    87 41=SU/ME  !
!16 21=VT***    35 06=MO/MA    54 29=VE/MC    71 30=MA/PL    88 53=MO/PF  !
!16 29=SA/MC    35 17=PL/PF    54 36=NO/VT    71 54=MO/ME    89 21=SA/NE  !
+----------------------------------------------------------------------------------+
```

45 DEGREE MIDPOINTS FOR FRIEDMAN,HANK   (GEOCENTRIC)

```
+----------------------------------------------------------------------------------+
!   14=PL/EQ     8 49=MO/EQ    16 29=SA/MC    26 54=MO/ME    35 06=MO/MA  !
!   15=SA/VT     9 29=VE/MC    16 31=JU/AS    27 01=UR/MC    35 09=JU/NO  !
!   44=JU/PF     9 36=NO/VT    16 57=MO/VE    27 05=SU/MC    35 17=PL/PF  !
! 1 22=MC/EQ     9 53=UR/NE    16 58=ME/EQ    27 38=MA/MC    35 58=AS/VT  !
! 1 33=PL***     9 57=SU/NE    18 18=ME/PL    28 45=ME/JU    36 20=JU/UR  !
! 2 18=ME/PL    10 09=MO/PL    18 45=MO***    29 08=SA***    36 24=SU/JU  !
! 2 41=PL/MC    10 31=MA/NE    18 48=VE/JU    29 12=NO/AS    36 25=MC/PF  !
! 2 50=NO***    10 35=AS***    19 17=NE/PF    29 14=NE/EQ    36 57=MA/JU  !
! 3 11=ME/VT    10 41=JU/EQ    19 26=ME/MC    30 07=VT/EQ    37 22=VE/NE  !
! 3 49=MC***    10 47=UR/VT    19 51=SA/AS    30 23=UR/AS    38 15=VE/VT  !
! 4 01=UR/NO    10 50=SU/VT    20 11=VT/PF    30 27=SU/AS    38 29=SA/NO  !
! 4 04=SA/PF    11 17=MO/MC    20 36=MO/JU    30 34=NE/PL    39 10=MO/NE  !
! 4 05=SU/NO    11 24=MA/VT    22 08=VE/SA    31 01=MA/AS    39 40=SA/UR  !
! 4 39=MA/NO    12 00=JU/PL    22 27=JU***    31 27=PL/VT    39 44=SU/SA  !
! 4 44=AS/EQ    12 52=VE/AS    22 48=ME/AS    31 29=VE/NO    39 48=AS/PF  !
! 5 12=UR***    13 08=JU/MC    23 22=NO/EQ    31 42=NE/MC    40 03=MO/VT  !
! 5 16=SU/UR    13 25=NO/PF    23 57=MO/PF    32 05=ME/SA    40 18=MA/SA  !
! 5 20=SU***    14 01=SA/EQ    24 33=UR/EQ    32 35=MC/VT    41 01=JU/ME  !
! 5 50=MA/UR    14 35=NE***    24 37=SU/EQ    32 40=VE/UR    41 26=ME/NO  !
! 5 53=SU/MA    14 36=UR/PF    24 42=PL/NO    32 44=SU/VE    41 54=JU/VT  !
! 6 04=PL/AS    14 40=MO/AS    25 05=ME/VE    33 18=VE/MA    42 04=VE/PF  !
! 6 27=MA***    14 40=SU/PF    25 10=MA/EQ    33 18=MO/NO    42 37=ME/UR  !
! 7 01=ME/PF    15 09=VE***    25 48=JU/SA    33 57=EQ/PF    42 41=SU/ME  !
! 7 01=VE/EQ    15 14=MA/PF    25 50=NO/MC    34 29=MO/UR    43 15=ME/MA  !
! 7 12=MC/AS    15 21=SA/PL    25 53=UR/PL    34 32=MO/SU    43 53=MO/PF  !
! 8 21=VE/PL    15 28=NE/VT    25 57=SU/PL    35 02=ME***    43 54=EQ***  !
! 8 42=NE/NO    16 21=VT***    26 30=MA/PL    35 05=NE/AS    44 21=SA/NE  !
+----------------------------------------------------------------------------------+
```

Figure 6.8: M-65 midpoints.

```
ALTERNATE HOUSE CUSPS FOR FRIEDMAN,HANK              (GEOCENTRIC)
+---------------------------------------------------------------------------+
!                                                                           !
!       MERI HSE        REGI HSE        PORP HSE        EQUA HSE        MORI HSE  !
!       1=13LE54        1=25LE35        1=25LE35        1=25LE35        1=18LE49  !
!       2=15VI11        2=18VI47        2=23VI20        2=25VI35        2=17VI27  !
!       3=17LI45        3=15LI00        3=21LI04        3=25LI35        3=15LI05  !
!       4=18SC49        4=18SC49        4=18SC49        4=25SC35        4=13SC54  !
!       5=17SA27        5=27SA22        5=21SA04        5=25SA35        5=15SA11  !
!       6=15CP05        6=00AQ04        6=23CP20        6=25CP35        6=17CP45  !
!                                                                           !
!       KOCH HSE        TOPO HSE        CAMP HSE        PLAC HSE        SOLR HSE  !
!       1=25LE35        1=25LE35        1=25LE35        1=25LE35        1=05CN20  !
!       2=23VI20        2=18VI07        2=24VI42        2=18VI07        2=05LE20  !
!       3=21LI14        3=15LI49        3=21LI28        3=15LI49        3=05VI20  !
!       4=18SC49        4=18SC49        4=18SC49        4=18SC49        4=05LI20  !
!       5=28SA01        5=24SA01        5=19SA21        5=24SA10        5=05SC20  !
!       6=27CP56        6=26CP55        6=22CP54        6=27CP02        6=05SA20  !
!                                                                           !
+---------------------------------------------------------------------------+
```

Figure 6.9: An M-65 alternate-house cusps table.

```
HARMONIC SORT FOR FRIEDMAN,HANK                 (GEOCENTRIC)
! HAR=001   ! HAR=002   ! HAR=003   ! HAR=004   ! HAR=005   ! HAR=006   ! HAR=007   !
!02AR50=NO !05AR40=NO !08AR31=NO*!11AR21=NO !07AR54=AS !00AR52=VE !19AR51=NO !
!18TA49=MC !12AR54=MA !11AR16=MO*!20AR48=UR*!14AR11=NO !17AR01=NO !01GE01=VE !
!00GE09=VE !29AR09=NE !11TA41=EQ !21AR19=SU*!00TA01=PF !22AR31=MO !08GE56=SA !
!20GE02=ME !07CN39=MC !19TA40=PL !25AR49=MA*!10TA10=ME !08TA43=MA !20LI13=ME*!
!05CN12=UR*!00LE17=VE !16GE44=AS !28TA18=NE !10CN40=SA !23GE23=EQ*!22LI11=JU*!
!05CN20=SU*!07LE30=MO !12LE24=SA !05GE24=VT !26CN00=UR*!27GE28=NE*!07SC16=EQ !
!13LE54=EQ*!10VI04=ME !19LE03=VT !06CN01=PF !26CN39=SU*!09CN20=PL !15SC10=MA !
!16LE33=PL*!10LI24=UR*!26LE28=MC !25VI35=EQ !18LE46=MO !00LE12=ME !18SA02=PF !
!25LE35=AS !10LI39=SU*!12VI01=PF !06LI13=PL !02SC16=MA !03VI29=AS !26SA16=MO !
!14VI08=SA !02SC42=VT !00LI26=VE !15LI17=MC !04SA07=MC*!01SC12=UR*!12CP02=NE !
!06LI27=MA !18SC00=PF !19LI21=MA !12SC19=AS !07SA17=JU*!01SC58=SU*!29CP03=AS !
!14LI35=NE !27SA48=EQ !13SC44=NE !00SA35=VE !12SA53=NE !14SC44=JU !06AQ24=UR*!
!03SA45=MO !03CP07=PL !00SA06=ME !15SA01=MO !00AQ43=VE !24SA48=SA !07AQ18=SU*!
!16CP21=VT !21CP10=AS !15CP36=UR*!29SA49=JU !09AQ29=EQ !08CP06=VT !11PI45=MC !
!24CP00=PF !14AQ55=JU !15CP59=SU*!26CP32=SA !22AQ46=PL !22CP56=MC !
!07PI27=JU !28AQ16=SA !22CP22=JU !20AQ08=ME !21PI45=VT !24AQ01=PF !

HARMONIC SORT FOR FRIEDMAN,HANK                 (GEOCENTRIC)
! HAR=008   ! HAR=009   ! HAR=010   ! HAR=011   ! HAR=012   ! HAR=013   ! HAR=014   !
!12AR26=PL !00AR17=ME !15AR48=AS !05AR29=SA !01AR44=VE !09AR30=NE !09TA43=NO*!
!22AR41=NO !25AR32=NO !28AR22=NO !01TA12=NO*!04TA02=NO !06TA52=NO !10TA27=ME*!
!00TA35=MC !03TA47=MO*!00GE02=PF*!02TA51=EQ*!15TA02=MO !01GE53=VE !14TA22=JU*!
!11TA36=UR*!07TA12=SA*!04GE32=MA*!02GE06=PL !02GE25=UR*!06GE55=JU !18TA54=VT*!
!12TA38=SU*!27TA09=VT !20GE19=ME !22CN00=JU !03GE57=SU*!02CN32=AS !14GE33=EQ !
!21TA37=MA !19GE24=MC !08LE14=MC !10VI21=ME*!17GE26=MA !02LE33=VT !00CN20=MA !
!24GE38=AS !05LE04=EQ*!14LE33=JU !11VI17=MO*!29GE28=JU !07VI37=UR*!21CN46=PL !
!26CN37=NE*!06LE02=PF*!25LE46=NE !11VI22=AS*!16VI45=EQ*!09VI16=SU*!02LE0=VE !
!01CN09=VE*!16LE49=UR*!16LE49=UR*!21LI21=SA !27VI03=MC !19VI37=SA*!17LE53=SA !
!10LE48=VT !17LE58=SU*!22SC01=UR*!10SA59=MA !24VI55=NE !23SA53=MA !06VI03=PF !
!00VI02=MO !29LE00=PL !23SC17=SU*!29SA51=VT !16LI12=VT*!04CP42=MC !22VI33=MO !
!29VI39=JU !07VI06=JU !01AQ35=VE !01AQ35=VE !18LI39=PL*!18CP48=MO !24LI04=NE !
!12LI02=PF !01LI18=VE !18SA58=EQ !27AQ13=UR*!15SC52=MC !00AQ39=EQ !28SC07=AS !
!23SC04=SA !20SC13=AS !07CP32=MO !28AQ37=SU*!00SA23=ME !20AQ25=ME !12SA49=UR*!
!10CP15=ME !28SC04=MA !15CP33=PL !10PI21=NE !18CP03=PF !03PI45=SA*!14SA36=SU*!
!21PI10=EQ !11AQ11=NE !13PI30=VT !24PI03=PF !06AQ57=AS !05PI13=PL*!23AQ31=MC !
```

Figure 6.10: An M-65 harmonic sort. Asterisks indicate harmonic conjunctions.

```
#ASPECTS SCAN FOR FRIEDMAN,HANK          /SECONDARY      JUN27 83
+---+---+---+---+----+    +---+---+---+---+----+    +---+---+---+---+----+
!PL1!ASP!PL2!CHT!ORBS!    !PL1!ASP!PL2!CHT!ORBS!    !PL1!ASP!PL2!CHT!ORBS!
!---+---+---+---+----!    !---+---+---+---+----!    !---+---+---+---+----!
!MON!INC!SUN!RAD!1 35!    !MON!OPP!MER!SEC!  52!    !MON!TRI!MER!S>R!4 57!
!MON!OPP!VEN!RAD!3 37!    !MON!SES!VEN!SEC!  36!    !MON!SQR!VEN!S>R!5 10!
!MON!SXT!MAR!RAD!2 42!    !MON!TRI!MAR!SEC!1 30!    !MON!SQR!JUP!RAD!3 42!
!MON!INC!URA!RAD!1 27!    !MON!SES!URA!SEC!2 52!    !MON!TRI!TNO!RAD!  55!
!MON!TRI!MC !SEC!4 41!    !MON!SQR!MC !S>R!6 10!    !MON!OPP!ASC!S>R!  36!
!MON!SSQ!VTX!RAD!2 24!    !MON!SSQ!PFO!SEC!  11!    !SUN!TRI!MON!S>R!3 04!
!SUN!SSQ!MER!S>R!1 47!    !SUN!SQR!MAR!SEC!1 07!    !SUN!SXT!MAR!S>R!  22!
!SUN!TRI!JUP!RAD!2 08!    !SUN!INC!JUP!SEC!1 06!    !SUN!INC!JUP!S>R!  39!
!SUN!CJN!URA!RAD!  08!    !SUN!PAR!URA!RAD!  17!    !SUN!SQR!TNO!RAD!2 30!
!SUN!TRI!TNO!S>R!3 59!    !SUN!SSQ!MC !RAD!1 30!    !SUN!SSQ!MC !SEC!1 30!
!SUN!SSQ!ASC!SEC!  11!    !SUN!INC!VTX!SEC!  37!    !SUN!TRI!PFO!SEC!3 00!
!MER!SSQ!VEN!SEC!1 27!    !MER!SQR!VEN!S>R!4 18!    !MER!SXT!MAR!SEC!2 22!
!MER!SQR!SAT!RAD!5 54!    !MER!TRI!NEP!RAD!5 27!    !MER!SXT!PLU!RAD!3 29!
!MER!CJN!ASC!S>R!  16!    !MER!SES!PFO!SEC!1 02!    !MER!INC!PFO!S>R!1 51!
!VEN!CJN!SUN!S>R!4 04!    !VEN!PAR!SUN!S>R!  43!    !VEN!TRI!MAR!RAD!6 19!
!VEN!SSQ!MAR!S>R!2 56!    !VEN!TRI!JUP!SEC!3 41!    !VEN!TRI!JUP!S>R!1 56!
!VEN!SXT!SAT!S>R!4 45!    !VEN!CJN!URA!SEC!2 16!    !VEN!PAR!URA!SEC!  55!
!VEN!CJN!URA!S>R!4 11!    !VEN!PAR!URA!S>R!1 00!    !VEN!SES!NEP!RAD!  34!
!VEN!CJN!NEP!SEC!5 30!    !VEN!SQR!NEP!S>R!5 11!    !VEN!SXT!TNO!RAD!2 42!
!VEN!SQR!TNO!S>R!6 33!    !VEN!SQR!ASC!RAD!4 34!    !VEN!SSQ!ASC!S>R!1 11!
!VEN!SES!VTX!RAD!1 12!    !VEN!TRI!VTX!SEC!1 58!    !VEN!OPP!VTX!S>R!6 57!
!VEN!TRI!PFO!RAD!6 08!    !VEN!SQR!PFO!SEC!  25!    !MAR!TRI!MER!S>R!3 27!
!MAR!INC!JUP!RAD!1 00!    !MAR!SES!JUP!SEC!2 46!    !MAR!PAR!JUP!SEC!  57!
!MAR!SES!JUP!S>R!1 01!    !MAR!PAR!JUP!S>R!  10!    !MAR!SQR!URA!RAD!1 15!
!MAR!OPP!TNO!RAD!3 37!    !MAR!SES!MC !RAD!2 38!    !MAR!TRI!MC !SEC!3 10!
!MAR!SXT!ASC!S>R!2 06!    !MAR!SES!VTX!SEC!1 03!    !MAR!PAR!VTX!SEC!  50!
!MAR!SQR!PFO!S>R!  32!    !JUP!TRI!SUN!S>R!1 57!    !JUP!TRI!SUN!S>R!  23!
!JUP!SQR!VEN!S>R!5 34!    !JUP!INC!MAR!S>R!  45!    !JUP!CJN!JUP!S>R!1 45!
!JUP!PAR!JUP!S>R!  47!    !JUP!OPP!SAT!RAD!6 41!    !JUP!CJN!VTX!SEC!1 43!
!JUP!TRI!URA!SEC!1 25!    !JUP!TRI!URA!S>R!  31!    !SAT!CJN!SAT!S>R!2 55!
!JUP!SSQ!PFO!RAD!1 33!    !SAT!SQR!MER!S>R!2 59!    !SAT!TRI!MC !S>R!1 46!
!SAT!TRI!MC !RAD!4 41!    !SAT!SQR!MC !SEC!3 15!    !SAT!TRI!VTX!S>R!  42!
!SAT!CJN!ASC!SEC!4 35!    !SAT!TRI!VTX!RAD!1 57!    !URA!CJN!SUN!S>R!1 47!
!SAT!CJN!EQA!SEC!1 28!    !SAT!TRI!PFO!S>R!6 57!    !URA!TRI!JUP!S>R!  20!
!URA!PAR!SUN!S>R!  12!    !URA!SQR!MAR!S>R!  40!    !URA!SQR!TNO!RAD!2 22!
!URA!CJN!URA!S>R!1 55!    !URA!PAR!URA!S>R!  05!    !URA!TRI!VTX!SEC!  19!
!URA!SQR!TNO!S>R!4 17!    !URA!SSQ!MC !RAD!1 23!    !NEP!SES!VEN!S>R!  15!
!URA!SQR!PFO!SEC!2 41!    !NEP!TRI!MER!S>R!5 09!    !NEP!SXT!PLU!RAD!1 59!
!NEP!CJN!NEP!S>R!  19!    !NEP!PAR!NEP!S>R!  09!    !NEP!TRI!MC !SEC!5 25!
!NEP!SXT!PLU!SEC!2 35!    !NEP!SXT!PLU!S>R!1 40!    !NEP!SXT!EQA!RAD!  41!
!NEP!SQR!VTX!RAD!1 46!    !NEP!SQR!VTX!S>R!1 28!    !PLU!SSQ!SUN!S>R!2 51!
!NEP!SXT!EQA!S>R!  59!    !NEP!OPP!PFO!SEC!5 05!    !PLU!PAR!MER!S>R!  56!
!PLU!PAR!SUN!S>R!  05!    !PLU!SXT!MER!S>R!2 34!    !PLU!SXT!NEP!S>R!2 54!
!PLU!SSQ!URA!S>R!2 44!    !PLU!PAR!URA!S>R!  21!    !PLU!SES!TNO!RAD!1 17!
!PLU!CJN!PLU!S>R!  55!    !PLU!PAR!PLU!S>R!  18!    !PLU!SQR!MC !RAD!2 16!
!PLU!SES!TNO!SEC!2 55!    !PLU!SES!TNO!S>R!  22!    !PLU!SQR!MC !S>R!1 21!
!PLU!SXT!MC !SEC!2 50!    !PLU!PAR!MC !SEC!  10!    !PLU!CJN!EQA!RAD!2 40!
!PLU!INC!VTX!RAD!  12!    !PLU!INC!VTX!S>R!1 07!    !TNO!SQR!SUN!S>R!5 46!
!PLU!CJN!EQA!S>R!3 35!    !TNO!TRI!MON!S>R!4 12!    !TNO!SQR!URA!S>R!5 39!
!TNO!SXT!VEN!S>R!  35!    !TNO!OPP!MAR!S>R!6 54!
+---+---+---+---+----+    +---+---+---+---+----+    +---+---+---+---+----+
    PL1=ASPECTING PLANET PL2=ASPECTED PLANET ASP=ASPECT CHT=CHART (PDECL)
```

Figure 6.11: An M-65 progressed aspect table. Aspects labeled S>R are progressed-to-natal; aspects labeled SEC are within the progressed chart; aspects labeled NAD are natal-chart aspects.

In addition to the more familiar secondary progressions and solar arc directions, M-65 offers tertiary progressions, minor progressions, user-specified arc progressions, true arc progressions, primary directions, and converse progressions. Users who wish to evaluate the accuracy of these techniques should compare the results from either M-65 or Nova with the results from charts of the same type by Astro Computing Services (ACS), or calculate their own charts by hand to compare with the computer output. This doublechecking might be worthwhile because these programs use so many routines that a few of the more unusual techniques might contain errors. If you find inconsistencies, you might talk to either or both firms to resolve the differences.

```
*ASPECTS SCAN FOR FRIEDMAN,HANK          /FRIEDMAN,KATHI

+---+---+---+---+----+    +---+---+---+---+----+    +---+---+---+---+----+
!PL1!ASP!PL2!CHT!ORBS!    !PL1!ASP!PL2!CHT!ORBS!    !PL1!ASP!PL2!CHT!ORBS!
!---+---+---+---+----!    !---+---+---+---+----!    !---+---+---+---+----!
!MON!CJN!MER!S>R!2 09!    !MON!PAR!MER!S>R!  59!    !MON!SQR!SAT!S>R!3 45!
!MON!TRI!NEP!S>R!3 19!    !MON!SXT!PLU!S>R!1 20!    !MON!PAR!PLU!S>R!  16!
!MON!INC!VTX!S>R!1 32!    !MON!SXT!EQA!S>R!3 59!    !SUN!SQR!MON!S>R!5 48!
!SUN!TRI!SUN!S>R!4 14!    !SUN!CJN!JUP!S>R!2 06!    !SUN!OPP!SAT!S>R!4 35!
!SUN!TRI!URA!S>R!4 21!    !SUN!SSQ!PFO!S>R!  33!    !MER!SQR!MER!S>R!2 59!
!MER!SXT!MC !S>R!4 12!    !MER!INC!ASC!S>R!2 33!    !MER!SXT!PFO!S>R!  59!
!VEN!TRI!VEN!S>R!4 58!    !VEN!SSQ!JUP!S>R!2 43!    !VEN!TRI!MC !S>R!6 21!
!VEN!INC!ASC!S>R!  24!    !VEN!CJN!PFO!S>R!1 10!    !MAR!SQR!MON!S>R!6 40!
!MAR!SQR!VEN!S>R!3 04!    !MAR!SES!NEP!S>R!2 30!    !MAR!OPP!ASC!S>R!1 30!
!JUP!CJN!MON!S>R!6 29!    !JUP!OPP!VEN!S>R!2 52!    !JUP!SSQ!NEP!S>R!2 18!
!JUP!TRI!TNO!S>R!5 34!    !JUP!SQR!ASC!S>R!1 42!    !JUP!SXT!PFO!S>R!3 16!
!SAT!TRI!MON!S>R!  48!    !SAT!SSQ!MER!S>R!2 04!    !SAT!SXT!VEN!S>R!2 49!
!SAT!SXT!MAR!S>R!3 30!    !SAT!TRI!TNO!S>R!  07!    !URA!CJN!MER!S>R!2 17!
!URA!PAR!MER!S>R!  39!    !URA!SQR!SAT!S>R!3 37!    !URA!TRI!NEP!S>R!3 11!
!URA!SXT!PLU!S>R!1 12!    !URA!PAR!PLU!S>R!  35!    !URA!INC!VTX!S>R!1 24!
!URA!SXT!EQA!S>R!4 53!    !NEP!SQR!SUN!S>R!4 53!    !NEP!CJN!MAR!S>R!3 46!
!NEP!PAR!MAR!S>R!  08!    !NEP!INC!JUP!S>R!2 46!    !NEP!SQR!URA!S>R!5 01!
!NEP!CJN!NEP!S>R!4 21!    !NEP!SSQ!ASC!S>R!  22!    !NEP!SQR!VTX!S>R!6 08!
!NEP!SXT!EQA!S>R!3 17!    !PLU!SXT!NEP!S>R!2 59!    !PLU!CJN!PLU!S>R!4 58!
!PLU!PAR!PLU!S>R!  25!    !PLU!CJN!EQA!S>R!2 19!    !TNO!OPP!MON!S>R!3 09!
!TNO!CJN!VEN!S>R!6 46!    !TNO!TRI!MAR!S>R!  27!    !TNO!SQR!JUP!S>R!  33!
!TNO!SXT!TNO!S>R!4 04!    !TNO!SES!PFO!S>R!2 06!    !MC !INC!MON!S>R!  22!
!MC !SXT!SUN!S>R!1 13!    !MC !SSQ!MER!S>R!  55!    !MC !INC!MAR!S>R!2 20!
!MC !SXT!JUP!S>R!3 20!    !MC !SXT!URA!S>R!1 05!    !ASC!SXT!MER!S>R!2 45!
!ASC!SSQ!URA!S>R!2 55!    !ASC!SXT!NEP!S>R!2 43!    !ASC!CJN!PLU!S>R!  44!
!ASC!SES!TNO!S>R!  33!    !ASC!SQR!MC !S>R!1 32!    !ASC!INC!VTX!S>R!  56!
!ASC!CJN!EQA!S>R!3 24!    !VTX!OPP!SUN!S>R!2 47!    !VTX!SXT!MAR!S>R!1 39!
!VTX!SXT!JUP!S>R!  39!    !VTX!TRI!SAT!S>R!6 02!    !VTX!OPP!URA!S>R!2 54!
!VTX!SQR!NEP!S>R!6 28!    !VTX!SQR!TNO!S>R!5 16!    !VTX!SES!ASC!S>R!2 28!
!EQA!TRI!MON!S>R!4 04!    !EQA!SXT!VEN!S>R!  27!    !EQA!SSQ!SAT!S>R!  33!
!EQA!TRI!TNO!S>R!3 09!    !EQA!OPP!PFO!S>R!5 41!    !PFO!OPP!VEN!S>R!2 54!
!PFO!OPP!MC !S>R!6 48!    !PFO!SQR!ASC!S>R!  02!    !PFO!SXT!PFO!S>R!1 37!
+---+---+---+---+----+    +---+---+---+---+----+    +---+---+---+---+----+

PL1=ASPECTING PLANET PL2=ASPECTED PLANET ASP=ASPECT CHT=CHART (PDECL)
```

Figure 6.12: An M-65 interaspects table, used for chart comparisons.

A problem I noticed was that if you set the default for parallax Moon (i.e., customize the program so that it always runs with the parallax option on), the Moon position in solar returns is occasionally wrong. Matrix is working on this problem.

Special Features

M-65 is the only program now available that will calculate and use either the parallax-corrected Moon position or the geocentric Moon position. Most astrologers do not realize that the Moon they use in their birth charts is measured from the center of the Earth instead of the Earth's surface. Parallax correction gives you the Moon's position as actually observed from the surface of the Earth. Since the two positions often vary as much as a whole degree, the Moon sign may change in a number of charts. In my own research on the parallax Moon, I have found that the corrected position (for the surface of the Earth) is indeed more accurate than the uncorrected position in describing the person, the strength of his or her aspects, and the like. I suggest you test a group of charts on your own, paying particular attention to the charts wherein the Moon sign changes (as such a difference is clearly noticeable).

Another of M-65's special features is the capacity to look for lunations (full Moon, half Moon, new Moon) and eclipses for a specific period. This eclipse module not only accurately indicates eclipses and lunations, but also gives the exact longitude of the event, the type of eclipse (e.g., annular, penumbral, etc.), whether the eclipse is visible from the Earth (and in which hemisphere), and, for lunar eclipses, details on the duration.

For the astrologer who wants to attach comments, addresses, phone numbers, or other information to the charts calculated with M-65, Matrix has provided two routines for adding text to any file. One routine lets you add only a few words per file, while the other (called the Add Notes routine) enables you to add more than two hundred characters to the end of your file. M-65 can also insert up to eight extra points in each file (e.g., Chiron, asteroids, sensitive points) complete with longitude, latitude, and daily motion, although you have to hand-enter every point you want to add. You can then use these points in the research module.

M-65-B: The Research Module

In designing M-65, Matrix realized that doing research on a set of charts using only 8-bit computers (Commodore, Apple II, TRS-80) would be painfully slow unless the files could be very quickly scanned and the needed data were already present in the files. The firm spent a great deal of time designing the file structure to suit this need, and succeeded in creating a set of files and a research system that enable astrologers to receive answers to questions about their files in a minimum of time. Unfortunately, the instructions for using the research system are difficult to understand. Though I am quite experienced at deciphering software documentation, I still had some difficulty using the research system. (I couldn't figure out how to print out the results of my search, which was partially the fault of the ambiguous screen display, and I wasn't sure how to pose two questions at the same time, since more than one method seemed plausible.) The documentation for M-65-B thoughtfully provides you with many sample questions, and the firm is improving its documentation (and has published a useful pamphlet, *M65 Made Easy*, for M-65-A). I hope a more accessible introduction to the research system will be issued at some point.

It is important to review what M-65-B is and is not designed to do. It is designed to allow you to find out which people among those on file fulfill the requirements you set up. You can pose simple questions, such as, who has the Moon in Aries? or who has any planet at 29 degrees? You can ask more extensive questions, such as who has the ruler of the Eighth House in the Fourth House and square to Mars? or who has more than four planets in a water sign? You can even make multiple queries, such as who has planets in the Eighth House or in Scorpio? or who has Mars in Aries and the Moon in an Earth sign? You can also compare information from clients regarding matters such as career field with information in the birth charts you have on file. After you have found all the charts that satisfy the requirements of your search command (e.g., find the charts with Moon in Aries), you can then ask the program to direct all further questions to this subgroup of charts. You can also define your own rulerships for each planet if you want to.

M-65-B will keep track of the number of people on file who fulfill search-phrase requirements. You can easily get a count of how many people on your file disk have the Sun in each sign (or house): you simply enter the search phrase THE SIGN OF THE SUN and turn the count feature on. Or you could ask how many people have their Mars at each degree of the zodiac. Or you might even tabulate a list of all of the Mars/Jupiter aspects people have, with an accurate count of how many have each aspect. You could then use a statistical package (Matrix offers one) to determine whether the distribution you've tallied is significantly different from a random distribution.

M-65-B gives you a generous language with which to pose questions, though it takes some effort to understand it. You can create questions concerning rulerships, waxing and waning aspects, house placements, the four elements and three modalities, angular/succedent/cadent positions, midpoints, Arabian parts, retrogradation, aspects with orbs, house cusps, applying and separating aspects, lunar phase, phase angle and angular separation, dispositors, and harmonics. You can ask if any of the points (and you can specify "any" to include only the planets, the planets plus the M.C. and Ascendant, or even Uranian or optional points) meet the requirements of the question, and you can splice questions together with *and* or *or* to generate quite sophisticated queries. You can use either heliocentric or geocentric positions in the search.

The main purpose of M-65-B, then, is to allow you to test your ideas about astrology (for example, Does Venus square Neptune really mean illusions in your love life?) and to find themes (or the absence of themes) in common for all the people you know with a planet in a specific sign, house, aspect, and so on. This can be exceptionally useful in dispelling the misconceptions about astrological meanings, as well as revealing connections that might never have been made otherwise.

The research module of M-65 is being used by several astrologers for scientific research. As Geoffrey Dean points out in his *Recent Advances in Natal Astrology,* however, you have to be extremely careful in doing scientific work of this sort in astrology, for it is all too easy to think you have significant results when you do not. Not only must you use control groups, but even when a difference appears significant it may not be if your sample (group of files) is too small or if the planetary distributions vary more naturally than you realize. See Dean's book for more details.

My guess is that only a small fraction of astrologers take the time to enter the thousands of charts necessary to get statistical significance in their astrological studies, and that, given the choice, most of them would enter charts on a mini- or mainframe computer system hooked up to a mass storage device (a type of drive that can store thousands of files on one disk) rather than using a microcomputer.

The Limitations of M-65

For all the power and versatility inherent in M-65-A, there are certain deficiencies as well. At the time of its release, M-65 contained quite a few bugs, because Matrix was impatient to get the program on the market. At present, most of the bugs have been fixed, and Matrix offers updates of M-65 for the cost of new disks plus mailing fees to those who want the continually improved program. Any problems brought to Matrix's attention are handled as quickly as possible. I hope that Matrix will continue to improve its communication with users, alert them when an inaccurate routine is discovered, and continue to offer updates at cost.

M-65 is complex, and you have to learn how to go about doing each process (creating a chart, printing a chart, customizing the program, and so on). Once you have gotten over the hurdles and are familiar with the way the program works, you can use M-65 relatively easily, but learning the program takes a bit of time and concentration.

The documentation lacks the instructions for entering a standard-time birth in the daylight time/war time/ . . . section. The answer is simply to hit Return. This oversight is confusing to users, and should have been caught before the documentation went out.

Because Matrix decided that users should enter the source of the birth information and the relative accuracy of the birth time, you have to go through two screens concerning these factors every time you enter a birth chart, even if you couldn't care less about them and just want to get on with entering charts. Making these screens mandatory was inconsiderate to the user. Of course, you can simply hit Return and go on to the next screen. Still, Matrix should have left it to the individual to decide whether to enter information about the source of the birth data and its accuracy.

By the way, if you are entering charts for Hawaii or other areas with fractional time zones, you must enter, for example, 10.30, not 10.5 for a 10.5-hour time zone. (Matrix mentions this in the documentation, but since this entry method is inconsistent with that used by all other Matrix programs, it's worth emphasizing here.)

Another irritation in using the versions of the program that I tested is the difficulty of correcting erroneous entries. They do not include on-screen editing to allow you to correct any part of the birth data entered (e.g., the first name, longitude, etc.) once you have finished the whole entry. Nor can you start the entry routine again as soon as you make a mistake. Instead, you have to keep filling in the rest of the birth data until you reach the end, and then hit the re-enter key. If you enter many charts, you may find it a waste of time to have to go through everything, even if you make a typing error at the very beginning. Matrix has just improved the editing routine to correct this weakness in the version for IBM computers but at this writing has not yet sent out the update.

I would like Matrix to take more time to test and debug its software before it sends programs out (even if people have to wait a few more months), and to give examples in the documentation for all its complex routines. Matrix would benefit by these changes, because the firm would have to handle fewer phone calls from customers needing guidance.

In spite of the problems noted here, M-65 is a grand effort. For the past three years, it has offered users more than any other program out today, and it will undoubtedly have a long future. More modules (e.g., a powerful transit module) are in development currently, and those who wish to can purchase detailed line-by-line listings of the main program, to modify M-65 to their specific needs. No other company has taken the time to write a program with such a wide astrological scope for small computers.

New Additions to M-65

Matrix is completely committed to the M-65 system, and is now releasing several additional modules for the program.

The Blue Star Menu

Matrix is now completing work on the Blue Star Menu for the IBM/ MSDOS version of M-65. This menu will allow complete on-screen editing, allow you to set defaults (that is, select certain astrological choices such as the method of progression you usually use), and give you access to the full range of options for every job you enter. It will also let you inspect any of the jobs you've entered and change them easily.

With the Blue Star Menu, you'll be able to define ten sets of commonly used longitudes and latitudes and have the computer enter them for any charts you wish. The new menu uses the extra memory in MS DOS computers as a RAMdisk, which speeds up processing considerably, because the program does not have to go to disk to process jobs. As an extra gift, the program will interface with all Matrix's interpretation programs; it will even have a built-in astroclock that will display, and continuously update the present position for the Ascendant and Midheaven.

The new menu will greatly simplify using M-65. The complex auto-option routine will be gone, relocations will become simple to do, data will be alterable at any point in the entry process, and all the options will be on screen. Anyone who already owns M-65 can purchase the Blue Star upgrade for $25, and all new purchasers of M-65 will receive the module as part of the program at no additional cost.

M-65 Time Change Atlas

Another module for M-65 nearly ready for release is the M-65 Time Change Atlas. It will be released first for the IBM at $50 and later for the C-64 and the Apple II. This program interfaces with the Blue Star Menu and will insert the correct time zone, longitude, and latitude for 1200 cities in charts that you enter. Not only does the Time Change Atlas insert accurate time changes and geographic coordinates for the cities in which 80 percent of the U.S. population is born (and for 60 international cities as well), but it also includes a simple routine to add cities of your choice to the tables. The tables are accurate for the entire twentieth century. This module is more accurate than any other method of entry, and eliminates the need to look up all the information in books.

M-65-C

Matrix Software, $100

Principal Functions	Displays wide range of tables, data, lists, and charts for analysis and inspection.
Types of Calculations	***Aspects included:*** Major aspects plus semisquare, sesquiquadrate, inconjunct
	Custom aspects: 15 aspects with orbs
	Number of house systems: Displays cusps for nine house systems
	Heliocentric charts: Yes
	Methods of progression: None, but will work with secondary files
	Solar and lunar returns: None, but will work with return files
	Timed progressed hits: No
	Midpoint analysis: Displays midpoint lists for any dial for one or two charts; lists can be sorted by orb, aspect, points; midpoint picture analysis
	Chart comparisons: Displays interaspects, planets in other's houses
	Harmonics: Displays tables of harmonics
File Management	***File access:*** Excellent
Screen Displays:	Square wheels, tables, lists; easy to read
Computers	***Computer required:*** Apple II series, Commodore 64, PET
	Other hardware required: Two disk drives

One module of M-65 that has already been released is a screen-oriented version of M-65 for Commodore 64, PET, and Apple computers at $100, called M-65-C. It allows you to examine and use the files generated by M-65-A on your television or monitor screen, so you don't have to depend upon printouts. Besides inspecting files with M-65-C, you can perform many of the functions of M-65-A, including:

   determining planetary patterns;

   selecting a new aspect set;

   viewing house cusps for nine house systems;

   examining solstice points;

   making harmonic charts with sorting and emphasis on conjunctions;

   performing sophisticated midpoint analysis.

M-65-C also includes some new routines, among them the ability to put a (square) chart wheel on the screen and rotate it by specifying any Ascendant for the chart. This feature can be of great value in rectification work, where birth time is uncertain, and you want to determine a more precise time of birth. M-65-C also has two different two-chart modules, one devoted to synastry (which looks at interaspects between charts, but without indicating orbs) and a second that combines two sets of chart data for detailed examination. Other features let you to examine the planetary data in depth; search midpoint listings for specific pairs, signs, and so on; and make harmonic analyses for one or two charts at a time. The documentation I received with M-65-C was brief but sufficient for operating the program, but it did not make obvious the full power of the program.

On the Apple II, I couldn't help noticing how slowly M-65-C operated, compared to Astro Star by AGS. Astro Star rarely makes you wait even fifteen seconds to see results, while M-65-C makes you wait at each step of the program—sometimes as much as a minute or more. Those using the soon-to-be-released IBM version of the program, however, will experience no long waiting periods. Matrix has also begun to compile Commodore versions of the program, which should speed up operation considerably, thereby making the program more interactive and enjoyable to use. The only way to speed up the Apple version so far is to get a faster processor for your computer—for example, the aforementioned SpeeDemon card from McT (at $300), which speeds up by 3.5 times all processing on Apple computers.

The version of M-65-C I examined still had quite a few bugs in it, but Matrix is continuing to revise and debug the program.

Transit Master

Matrix is developing a very powerful transit module for M-65 called Transit Master, initially for the IBM PC at $150. It will offer a large variety of static and dynamic progression and transit methods, will be compatible with the Blue Star Menu, and will read M-65 files, create output in a variety of tabulation styles and let you define entering and leaving transit (and progression) orbs.

Since Transit Master uses a disk ephemeris, which is included with the program, its accuracy is exceptional for the years 1700 to 2050 and its processing speed should be excellent. Matrix even plans to eventually include a disk-file table of planetary stations, so astrologers will finally have a program that does not ignore or miscalculate stations, but instead includes them in the printouts. No other transit-calculation program can print out transits in other than chronological order (with entering and leaving orbs for a transit many lines or pages apart), whereas Transit Master will allow you several methods of organizing and collating the transits, including printing applying, exact and separating dates on one line. The program also will be marketed in a version that prints interpretations along with the transits. Owners of M-65 for the IBM may also wish to look at the review of M-65 Horary Clock in Chapter 7.

Nova

AGS Software, $300

Principal Functions
Prints a wide variety of charts and tables, generates files for reuse

Types of Calculations

Aspects included: Major aspects plus quintile series, semisquare, sesquiquadrate, inconjunct, semisextile

Custom aspects: 20 aspects with orbs plus separate orbs for different aspecting planets and points

Number of house systems: All major systems plus Equal from any point or planet

Heliocentric charts: Yes

Methods of progression: Secondary, tertiary, minor and user-defined progressions

Methods of direction: Solar, Naibod, degree for a year, user-defined arc

Solar and lunar returns: Calculates and prints solar and lunar return charts including harmonic, kinetic, and Wynn Key Cycle returns

Timed progressed hits: Yes

Midpoint analysis: Prints midpoint structures, linear midpoint diagrams, and modular sorts for any dial

Chart comparisons: Prints interaspect table, composite and relationship charts, and tri-wheels

Harmonics: Yes

Defaults

Preset calculation defaults: TBA

Preset printout defaults: TBA

Nova (*continued*)

File Management	**Batch processing:** Limited only by size of computer's memory
	Saves files: Yes
	File access: Very good (includes file utilities)
Printouts	**Glyphs:** Yes
	Types of wheels: Closed, tri-wheels
	Quality of printouts: Very Good
Computers	**Computer required:** IBM and MS-DOS, CP/M
	Other hardware required: Two double-density drives, printer

Writing programs for small computers (e.g., Apple II or C-64) differs in two ways from writing for larger machines (e.g., IBM/MS-DOS or Macintosh). One is that the larger computers think quite a bit faster (while holding a larger chunk of the program in memory). The second is that the larger machines offer at least twice as much room on disks for program code. The storage factor is highly significant for writers of astrological programs, because they have to write programs that fit on one or two disks, otherwise the user would have to keep taking disks out and inserting others, a cumbersome process that slows down the program. They are therefore limited in what they can write for the smaller machines. Even many CP/M computers, such as Kaypro 4, which have smaller brains than the MS-DOS computers, still have twice the disk storage of the Apple and C-64. Therefore, both AGS and Matrix can offer larger and more diverse programs on CP/M and MS-DOS machines.

Early in the game, AGS recognized the significance of the disk-storage constraint and avoided writing for the Commodore line, concentrating instead on CP/M computers. Now that IBM has set a new standard of size and power in microcomputers, AGS has begun writing programs for these MSDOS machines and adapting their CP/M programs to them.

Nova is AGS's alternative to M-65 both for CP/M users, who cannot yet buy M-65, and for IBM/MS DOS users. It's even priced the same, at an introductory price of about $300. As I mentioned, AGS is only now completing its work on Nova, and I reviewed an early version of the program.

In first running the program (on an IBM computer), I was struck by how easy it was to operate. I had no documentation to start with, only the instructions to type in NOVA; yet I was able to use the entire program without trouble. For a program so powerful to be so easy to use is remarkable. A couple of modules had not yet been spliced into the main memory, so I had to call them up as separate programs, but I understand that all the modules will be accessible from the main menu in the completed version, and that even then the program will be simple to use.

Nova's entry routines are very smooth. They let you edit entries on the screen, the prompts telling you what to enter are clear, and you can to use a variety of date-entering methods. For example, you could enter June 27, 1950 or 6 27 1950 or 06.27.1950 or even 27 June 1950 and the program would process the entry correctly. And any time you enter data, the computer rewrites it in an easy-to-read form so you can verify your entry (e.g., it changes the date entry, if entered only in numbers, to June 27, 1950, and the latitude entry from, say, 40 46 or 40/46 to 40 N 46' 0").

One of Nova's nicest features is that you can automatically insert into your present entry the most recently entered data. For instance, let's say I entered my birth data and wanted next to do six relocation charts for myself. At each prompt I would simply press the correct function key, and the program would re-insert whatever I had entered last time for that item. Thus, you can zip through the whole entry routine in seconds typing in characters only where changes are necessary. In relocation, for example, you would change only the latitude and longitude.

You might also want to use this routine is in examining your chart by six different methods of progression. You could use the re-entry feature for everything except your choice of progression method. This automatic re-entry feature greatly encourages you to explore alternative methods of computation. Bravo!

Nova offers the user a large variety of house systems, including Equal Houses from any point (not just the Meridian and Ascendant, but the Sun, Vertex, Mercury, etc.). AGS plans to include *in Mundo* options—

i.e., local-space charts—in the release version, but the version I received did not yet contain them.

The first release of Nova may not have as many customizing features as M-65. It *will* allow you to set defaults, however, which is perhaps the most important type of customizing. In the default-setting process, you will be able to tell the program which house system, method of progression, zodiac, etc. you use regularly, so you won't have to make the choice each time. Also, Nova will exhibit an important advance in the area of customization—it will allow you to select different aspect orbs not only for each type of aspect, but individually for the Sun, Moon, Ascendant, Midheaven, East Point, Vertex, and Part of Fortune. For example, you can have wider orbs for the Sun and Moon than for the rest of the planets, while setting much narrower orbs for the Part of Fortune. Nova will not calculate the true node, nor will it work initially with the Uranian planets (both of which M-65 does), and neither program will do asteroids at this time. AGS is now planning to incorporate macros, a sophisticated form of program customization, into Nova. This will enable you to preselect what you want the computer to print out from entered data; e.g., a birth chart, plus progressions, plus transits, plus midpoints.

The synastry section of Nova does composite charts (with the choice of derived cusps or midpoint cusps), relationship charts (i.e., Davidson charts), and a table of interaspects and house placements (of each set of planets in the other chart's houses) that is exceptionally clear and usable (see Figure 6.13).

The progression module allows you to create secondary, tertiary, minor, and user-defined progressions with a variety of methods for progressing the angles, including Naibod in longitude or right ascension, solar arc by longitude or R.A., and a variety of Quotidian methods. Unlike M-65, Nova will allow you to progress secondary charts, e.g., solar returns, in addition to natal charts. Note that the progression module I looked at could only create progressed charts with an aspect page— that is, no progressed hits—but that AGS plans to include in Nova a dynamic progression module that will give you timed hits.

Nova can also create a remarkably large variety of return types, such as standard and harmonic solar and lunar returns, Wynn Key Cycle returns, pssrs, and a variety of kinetic returns (e.g., Quotidian) where the angles are different from standard returns. AGS is introducing so many new techniques with Nova that the documentation being prepared for the program is said to be a textbook on the new methods.

As with M-65, the version of Nova I examined required that you request a printout as well as a calculation for each job. I understand that

hank friedman
9:42: 0 AM EDT   orange n.j.
Latitude 40N46   Longitude 74W14

kathi friedman
3:45: 0 PM PST   seattle wa
Latitude 47N36   Longitude 122W20

hank friedman -- Horizontal   .   kathi friedman -- Vertical

	☉	☽	☿	♀	♂	♃	♄	♅	♆	♇	☊	As	MC	Vx	EP
☉	Tri 4 13					Con 2 06	Opp 4 35	Tri 4 20	Biq 0 58						
☽			Con 2 35				Squ 3 20		Tri 2 53	Sxt 0 54			Ssx 1 21	Qnx 1 06	Sxt 3 34
☿			Squ 2 59						Biq 0 28			Sxt 4 13			
♀			Biq 0 52	Tri 4 58								Qnx 0 24			
♂				Squ 3 03								Opp 1 31			
♃				Opp 2 52				Qnt 1 09	Biq 1 56			Squ 1 42			
♄	Tri 0 56			Sxt 2 48	Sxt 3 30	Biq 1 30			Qnt 0 22		Tri 0 14				
♅			Con 2 18		Squ 3 37				Tri 3 10	Sxt 1 11			Ssx 1 04	Qnx 1 23	Sxt 3 51
♆	Squ 4 53			Con 3 46					Con 4 22			Ssq 0 22			
♇				Qnt 0 34					Sxt 3 00	Con 4 59					Con 2 19
☊	Ssx 1 42	Opp 3 09			Tri 0 35	Squ 0 25			Ssx 1 49			Sxt 4 19			
As			Sxt 2 46						Sxt 2 42	Con 0 43	Sqq 0 26		Squ 1 32	Qnx 0 55	Con 3 23
MC	Sxt 1 13	Qnx 0 14	Ssq 0 56				Sxt 3 20		Sxt 1 06		Ssx 1 24				
Vx	Opp 2 47			Biq 1 58	Squ 1 40	Sxt 0 40			Opp 2 54						Biq 0 13
EP		Tri 4 11			Sxt 0 27	Biq 1 45	Ssq 0 34				Tri 3 01	Qnt 1 07			
⊕				Squ 4 15	Squ 2 26				Sxt 2 53	Tri 4 52					Tri 2 12

hank friedman's PF to kathi friedman's planets.   PF-PF!

	☉	☽	☿	♀	♂	♃	♄	♅	♆	♇	☊	As	MC	Vx	EP
PF				Tri 3 52	Squ 1 57	Opp 1 46	Sxt 3 54				Qnt 0 32				Sxt 0 39

hank friedman Planets	kathi fried Houses		kathi friedman Planets	hank friedman Houses
Sun	is in the Eleventh House.		Sun	is in the Seventh House.
Moon	is in the Fourth House.		Moon	is in the Tenth House.
Mercury	is in the Eleventh House.		Mercury	is in the Seventh House.
Venus	is in the Tenth House.		Venus	is in the Fifth House.
Mars	is in the Second House.		Mars	is in the Seventh House.
Jupiter	is in the Seventh House.		Jupiter	is in the Fourth House.
Saturn	is in the First House.		Saturn	is in the Twelfth House.
Uranus	is in the Eleventh House.		Uranus	is in the Tenth House.
Neptune	is in the Second House.		Neptune	is in the Second House.
Pluto	is in the Twelfth House.		Pluto	is in the Twelfth House.
Nodes	is in the Eighth House.		Nodes	is in the Tenth House.
Ascendant	is in the First House.		Ascendant	is in the Twelfth House.
Midheaven	is in the Tenth House.		Midheaven	is in the Ninth House.
Vertex	is in the Fifth House.		Vertex	is in the Fifth House.
East Point	is in the Twelfth House.		East Point	is in the Twelfth House.
P. of Fort.	is in the Tenth House.		P. of Fort.	is in the Fourth House.

Figure 6.13: Nova's interaspect table. Note how well it is designed for chart comparison.

the release version of Nova will allow you simply to enter a single command to print all the jobs just entered, which should simplify processing considerably.

The chart-wheel module, which does the printouts, creates very clear chart wheels (see Figures 6.14 and 6.15) with an optional second-page printout of dignities, elements and modalities, and an aspect table (with or without midpoints inserted). AGS still does not proportionally space planets on the wheels in its programs (Matrix has done so for years), but the printouts are still very good. My only quibble with the aspect table as it now stands is that there is no key to the abbreviations for aspect names (e.g., what is a bis?). This will not be a problem in the release version, since the latter will include an aspect-customizing routine with which you can select up to twenty aspects, complete with orbs and your choice of abbreviations.

Nova also includes a file-manager routine that transfers the jobs you've entered (which the program stores in a temporary chart file) into a permanent file, and allows you to store only certain of the files you've created, to inspect files, and to delete files.

In general, Nova's file-handling routine is a vast improvement over AGS's previous efforts, as it lets you access a file directory with a single control character (at the point in the entry routine where you need to select the file), and to select a file by number. Remarkably, Nova even allows you to list only the files containing a certain name or set of letters, instead of all the files in the directory. For example, if you named all your solar-return files "SR" followed by dates or a person's name, you could call them up by instructing the directory to list only file names with SR in. (Nova would then list all the files with SR even if SR appeared at the end or the middle of the file name instead of at the beginning. Thus, for example, SR 84 Hank, 84 SR hank, and Hanks 84 SR would all be listed). Note, however, that while M-65 labels charts for you as progressions, solar returns, and so on as they are stored, Nova requires that *you* enter all the labels yourself and keep track of the abbreviations (e.g., SR for solar returns) if you want consistent labeling, which is an unfortunate deficiency of the program.

Nova has a midpoint module that both lists and sorts midpoints for whatever dial you specify, and creates midpoint trees and linear midpoint diagrams. (See Figures 6.16, 6.17, and 6.18). There is also a tri-wheel module, like CCRS's, which prints three charts within one wheel (see Figure 6.19).

AGS is just finishing a dynamic transit module for Nova, very much like the Apple Transit Package but with the capacity to select the time zone for which the transits are calculated. The firm also plans to include

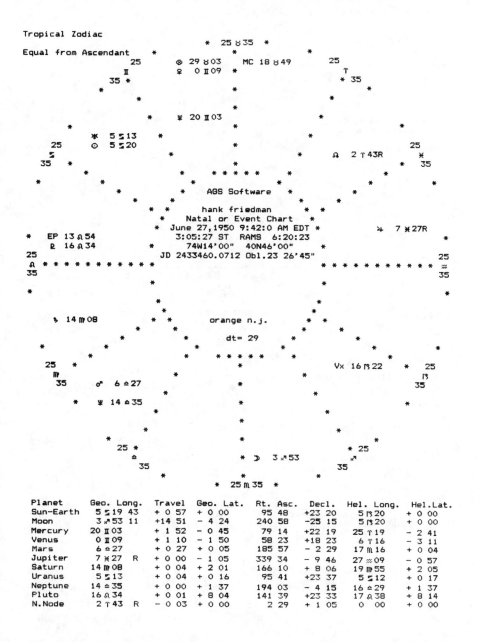

Tropical Zodiac
Equal from Ascendant

Planet table:

Planet	Geo. Long.	Travel	Geo. Lat.	Rt. Asc.	Decl.	Hel. Long.	Hel.Lat.
Sun-Earth	5 ♋ 19 43	+ 0 57	+ 0 00	95 48	+23 20	5 ♑ 20	+ 0 00
Moon	3 ♐ 53 11	+14 51	− 4 24	240 58	−25 15	5 ♑ 20	+ 0 00
Mercury	20 ♊ 03	+ 1 52	− 0 45	79 14	+22 19	25 ♈ 19	− 2 41
Venus	0 ♊ 09	+ 1 10	− 1 50	58 23	+18 23	6 ♈ 16	− 3 11
Mars	6 ♎ 27	+ 0 27	+ 0 05	185 57	− 2 29	17 ♏ 16	+ 0 04
Jupiter	7 ♓ 27 R	+ 0 00	− 1 05	339 34	− 9 46	27 ♒ 09	− 0 57
Saturn	14 ♍ 08	+ 0 04	+ 2 01	166 10	+ 8 06	19 ♍ 55	+ 2 05
Uranus	5 ♋ 13	+ 0 04	+ 0 16	95 41	+23 37	5 ♋ 12	+ 0 17
Neptune	14 ♎ 35	+ 0 00	+ 1 37	194 03	− 4 15	16 ♎ 29	+ 1 37
Pluto	16 ♌ 34	+ 0 01	+ 8 04	141 39	+23 33	17 ♌ 38	+ 8 14
N.Node	2 ♈ 43 R	− 0 03	+ 0 00	2 29	+ 1 05	0 00	+ 0 00

Figure 6.14: *A Nova chart wheel.*

hank friedman — Natal or Event Chart

Planets in Elements and Modalities

Fire	☽ ♇ ☊ As EP	Total No.= 5 Weighted Score= 7
Earth	♄ MC Vx ⊗	Total No.= 4 Weighted Score= 4
Air	☿ ♀ ♂ ♆	Total No.= 4 Weighted Score= 7
Water	☉ ♃ ♅	Total No.= 3 Weighted Score= 5
Cardinal	☉ ♂ ♅ ♆ ☊ Vx	Total No.= 6 Weighted Score= 7
Fixed	♇ As MC EP ⊗	Total No.= 5 Weighted Score= 7
Mutable	☽ ☿ ♀ ♃ ♄	Total No.= 5 Weighted Score= 9

Weights used above: ☉, ☽,AS,MC=3 ; ☿, ♀, ♂=2; ♃, ♄, ♅, ♆, ♇ =1; ☊,VX,EP, ⊗=0

Planetary Dignities

Planets in Rulerships ☿ ♃

Planets in Exaltations ♇

Planets in Detriments ♂

Planets in Fall

There are no Mutual Receptions

Geocentric Aspects and Midpoints

	☉	☽	☿	♀	♂	♃	♄	♅	♆	♇	☊	As	MC	Vx	EP
☉	----	19 ♍ 37	27 ♊ 42	17 ♊ 45	20 ♌ 54	6 ♏ 24	9 ♌ 44	5 ♋ 17	24 ♌ 58	25 ♋ 57	19 ♉ 02	0 ♌ 28	12 ♊ 05	10 ♎ 51	24 ♋ 37
☽		----	11 ♍ 58	2 ♍ 01	5 ♏ 10	20 ♑ 40	24 ♎ 01	19 ♍ 33	9 ♏ 14	10 ♎ 14	3 ♌ 18	14 ♎ 44	26 ♌ 21	25 ♐ 08	8 ♎ 54
☿			----	10 ♊ 06	13 ♌ 15	28 ♎ 45	2 ♌ 06	27 ♊ 38	17 ♌ 19	18 ♋ 19	11 ♉ 23	22 ♋ 49	4 ♊ 26	3 ♎ 13	16 ♋ 59
♀		Opp 3S44		----	3 ♌ 18	18 ♎ 48	22 ♋ 09	17 ♊ 41	7 ♌ 22	8 ♋ 22	1 ♉ 26	12 ♋ 52	24 ♉ 29	23 ♍ 16	7 ♋ 02
♂	Squ 1A07	Sxt 2A34			----	21 ♐ 57	25 ♍ 18	20 ♌ 50	10 ♎ 31	11 ♍ 31	4 ♋ 35	16 ♍ 01	27 ♋ 38	26 ♏ 25	10 ♍ 11
♃	Tri 2A07	Squ 3A34	Bis 0A15			----	10 ♐ 48	6 ♏ 20	26 ♐ 01	27 ♏ 01	20 ♍ 05	1 ♐ 31	13 ♎ 08	11 ♒ 55	25 ♏ 41
♄							----	9 ♌ 41	29 ♍ 22	0 ♍ 21	23 ♊ 26	4 ♍ 52	16 ♋ 29	15 ♏ 15	29 ♌ 01
♅	Con 0S07				Squ 1S14	Tri 2S14		----	24 ♌ 54	25 ♋ 54	18 ♉ 58	0 ♌ 24	12 ♊ 01	10 ♎ 48	24 ♋ 34
♆				Sqq 0S34		Biq 1S08	Ssx 0S27		----	15 ♍ 35	8 ♋ 39	20 ♍ 05	1 ♌ 42	0 ♐ 29	14 ♍ 15
♇			Sxt 3S29						Sxt 1S59	----	9 ♊ 39	21 ♌ 05	2 ♋ 42	1 ♏ 28	15 ♌ 14
☊	Squ 2S37	Tri 1S10		Sxt 2A34	Opp 3S44			Squ 2S30		Sqq 1S09	----	14 ♊ 09	25 ♈ 46	24 ♌ 33	8 ♊ 19
As				Squ 4A34							Biq 1A08	----	7 ♋ 12	5 ♏ 59	19 ♌ 45
MC						Qnt 0A38	Tri 4S41	Ssq 1A24	Biq 1A46	Squ 2S15	Ssq 1S06		----	17 ♍ 36	1 ♋ 22
Vx			Tris 0S36	Sqq 1S13		Sep 0S21	Tri 2S14		Squ 1S47	Qnx 0A12			Tri 2S27	----	0 ♏ 08
EP				Qnt 1S45			Ssx 0A14		Sxt 0A41	Con 2S40			Squ 4A55		----
⊗		Opp 4A50		Con 1S06					Sqq 0A32		Sxt 3A40	Squ 3S28			

Declinations not given on page 1

AS 13N00 MC 17N26 VX 22S27 EP 16N40 ⊗ 19N57

AGS Software

***Figure 6.15:** A Nova aspects page.*

Natal or Event Chart

hank friedman June 27 1950 9:42: 0 AM EDT

Midpoints (Halfsums)

						As	MC	Vx	EP	♈	
☉	5 ♋ 20					25 ♌ 35	7 ♋ 12	5 ♏ 59	19 ♌ 45	12 ♊ 48	As
☽	19 ♍ 37	3 ♐ 53					18 ♉ 49	17 ♍ 36	1 ♋ 22	24 ♈ 25	MC
☿	27 ♊ 42	11 ♍ 58	20 ♊ 03					16 ♑ 22	0 ♏ 08	23 ♌ 11	Vx
♀	17 ♊ 45	2 ♍ 01	10 ♊ 06	0 ♊ 09					13 ♌ 54	6 ♊ 57	EP
♂	20 ♌ 54	5 ♏ 10	13 ♌ 15	3 ♌ 18	6 ♎ 27					0 ♈ 00	♈
♃	6 ♏ 24	20 ♑ 40	28 ♎ 45	18 ♎ 48	21 ♐ 57	7 ♓ 27					
♄	9 ♌ 44	24 ♎ 01	2 ♌ 06	22 ♋ 09	25 ♍ 18	10 ♐ 48	14 ♍ 08				
♅	5 ♋ 17	19 ♍ 33	27 ♊ 38	17 ♊ 41	20 ♌ 50	6 ♏ 20	9 ♌ 41	5 ♋ 13			
♆	24 ♌ 58	9 ♏ 14	17 ♌ 19	7 ♌ 22	10 ♎ 31	26 ♐ 01	29 ♍ 22	24 ♌ 54	14 ♎ 35		
♇	25 ♋ 57	10 ♎ 14	18 ♋ 19	8 ♋ 22	11 ♍ 31	27 ♏ 01	0 ♍ 21	25 ♋ 54	15 ♍ 35	16 ♌ 34	
☊	19 ♉ 02	3 ♌ 18	11 ♉ 23	1 ♉ 26	4 ♋ 35	20 ♍ 05	23 ♊ 26	18 ♉ 58	8 ♋ 39	9 ♊ 39	2 ♈ 43
As	0 ♌ 28	14 ♎ 44	22 ♋ 49	12 ♋ 52	16 ♍ 01	1 ♐ 31	4 ♍ 52	0 ♌ 24	20 ♍ 05	21 ♌ 05	14 ♊ 09
MC	12 ♊ 05	26 ♌ 21	4 ♊ 26	24 ♉ 29	27 ♋ 38	13 ♎ 08	16 ♋ 29	12 ♊ 01	1 ♌ 42	2 ♋ 42	25 ♈ 46
Vx	10 ♎ 51	25 ♐ 08	3 ♎ 13	23 ♍ 16	26 ♏ 25	11 ♒ 55	15 ♏ 15	10 ♎ 48	0 ♐ 29	1 ♏ 28	24 ♌ 33
EP	24 ♋ 37	8 ♎ 54	16 ♋ 59	7 ♋ 02	10 ♍ 11	25 ♏ 41	29 ♌ 01	24 ♋ 34	14 ♍ 15	15 ♌ 14	8 ♊ 19
♈	17 ♉ 40	1 ♌ 57	10 ♉ 02	0 ♉ 05	3 ♋ 14	18 ♍ 44	22 ♊ 04	17 ♉ 37	7 ♋ 18	8 ♊ 17	1 ♈ 22
	☉	☽	☿	♀	♂	♃	♄	♅	♆	♇	☊

45 Degree Sorting of Midpoints

*Ari	0 00	♆/♈	7 18	♄/MC	16 29	♂/♇	26 31	☽/♅	34 33
♇/EP	0 14	Vx/♈	8 11	♃/As	16 31	☽/☿	26 58	☉/☽	34 37
♄/Vx	0 15	♀/♇	8 22	☿/EP	16 59	♅/MC	27 01	*Merc	35 03
☊/♈	1 22	♆/☊	8 39	☽/♀	17 01	☉/MC	27 05	♆/As	35 05
MC/EP	1 22	☽/EP	8 54	☿/♇	18 19	♂/MC	27 38	♃/☊	35 05
*Plut	1 34	♀/MC	9 29	♀/♃	18 48	As/♈	27 48	☽/♂	35 10
☿/♆	2 19	☊/Vx	9 33	*Moon	18 53	☿/♃	28 45	As/Vx	35 59
♅/♈	2 37	♅/♆	9 54	☿/MC	19 26	*Sat	29 08	♃/♅	36 20
☉/♈	2 40	☉/♆	9 58	♄/As	19 52	☊/As	29 09	☉/♃	36 24
♇/MC	2 42	☽/♇	10 14	☽/♃	20 40	♆/EP	29 15	♂/♃	36 57
*Node	2 43	♂/♆	10 31	EP/♈	21 57	♀/♈	30 05	♄/♈	37 04
☿/Vx	3 13	*Asc.	10 35	♀/♄	22 09	Vx/EP	30 08	♀/♆	37 22
♂/♈	3 14	♃/EP	10 41	*Jup	22 27	♅/As	30 24	♀/Vx	38 16
*M.C.	3 49	♅/Vx	10 48	☿/As	22 49	☉/As	30 28	♄/☊	38 26
♅/☊	3 58	☉/Vx	10 51	♇/♈	23 17	♆/♇	30 35	☽/♆	39 14
☉/☊	4 02	☽/MC	11 21	☊/EP	23 19	♂/As	31 01	♄/♅	39 41
♂/☊	4 35	♂/Vx	11 25	☽/♄	24 01	♀/☊	31 26	☉/♄	39 44
As/EP	4 45	♃/♇	12 01	MC/♈	24 25	♇/Vx	31 28	☿/♈	40 02
*Uran	5 13	♀/As	12 52	♅/EP	24 34	♆/MC	31 42	☽/Vx	40 08
☉/♅	5 17	♃/MC	13 08	☉/EP	24 37	☽/♈	31 57	♂/♄	40 18
*Sun	5 20	♄/EP	14 01	♇/☊	24 39	☿/♄	32 06	♃/♆	41 01
♂/♅	5 50	*Nept	14 35	☿/♀	25 06	MC/Vx	32 36	☿/☊	41 23
☉/♂	5 54	☽/As	14 44	♂/EP	25 11	♀/♅	32 41	♃/Vx	41 55
♇/As	6 05	*Ven	15 09	☊/MC	25 46	☉/♀	32 45	☿/♅	42 38
*Mars	6 27	♄/♇	15 21	♃/♄	25 48	♀/♂	33 18	☉/☿	42 42
♀/EP	7 02	♆/Vx	15 29	♅/♇	25 54	☽/☊	33 18	☿/♂	43 15
As/MC	7 12	*Vert	16 22	☉/♇	25 57	♃/♈	33 44	*E.P.	43 54
								♄/♆	44 22

Figure 6.16: *A Nova midpoint table with sorting.*

a harmonic package that will function like the Harmonics program for the Apple. (For a description of the transit package, see the section on the Apple Transit Package (#113) in Chapter 4. See the description of the Harmonic program following the review of Apple Star Track in Chapter 3). Neither of these modules was completed as of this writing.

AGS has announced that it will include the following features in the Nova package:

a three-thousand-year ephemeris for the outer planets;

```
                              Natal or Event Chart

hank friedman                     June 27  1950                9:42: 0 AM EDT

                       Linear Printout of Planetary Axes

                      45 Degree Pictures with 60 Minute Orb.

+--------+-------------------------------------------------------------------+
| Aries  | = ♄/♆-0 38 = ♇/EP+0 14 = ♄/Vx+0 15                                |
+--------+-------------------------------------------------------------------+
| Pluto  | = ☊/♈-0 12 = MC/EP-0 12 = ☿/♆+0 45                                |
+--------+-------------------------------------------------------------------+
| Nodes  | = ☿/♆-0 24 = ♅/♈-0 06 = ☉/♈-0 03 = ♇/MC-0 01 = ☿/Vx+0 30          |
|        | = ♂/♈+0 31                                                        |
+--------+-------------------------------------------------------------------+
|  M.C.  | = ☿/Vx-0 36 = ♂/♈-0 35 = ♅/☊+0 09 = ☉/☊+0 13 = ♂/☊+0 46           |
|        | = As/EP+0 56                                                      |
+--------+-------------------------------------------------------------------+
| Uranus | = ♂/☊-0 38 = As/EP-0 28 = ☉/♅+0 04 = *Sun +0 07 = ♂/♅+0 37        |
|        | = ☉/♂+0 41 = ♇/As+0 52                                            |
+--------+-------------------------------------------------------------------+
|  Sun   | = ♂/☊-0 45 = As/EP-0 35 = *Uran-0 07 = ☉/♅-0 03 = ♂/♅+0 30        |
|        | = ☉/♂+0 34 = ♇/As+0 45                                            |
+--------+-------------------------------------------------------------------+
|  Mars  | = ♂/♅-0 37 = ☉/♂-0 33 = ♇/As-0 22 = ♀/EP+0 35 = As/MC+0 45        |
|        | = ♆/♈+0 51                                                        |
+--------+-------------------------------------------------------------------+
|Ascend. | = ♅/♆-0 41 = ☉/♆-0 37 = ☽/♇-0 21 = ♂/♆-0 04 = ♃/EP+0 06           |
|        | = ♅/Vx+0 13 = ☉/Vx+0 16 = ☽/MC+0 46 = ♂/Vx+0 50                   |
+--------+-------------------------------------------------------------------+
|Neptune | = ♄/EP-0 34 = ☽/As+0 09 = *Ven +0 34 = ♄/♇+0 46 = ♆/Vx+0 54       |
+--------+-------------------------------------------------------------------+
| Venus  | = *Nept-0 34 = ☽/As-0 25 = ♄/♇+0 12 = ♆/Vx+0 20                   |
+--------+-------------------------------------------------------------------+
| Vertex | = ♆/Vx-0 53 = ♄/MC+0 07 = ♃/As+0 09 = ☿/EP+0 37 = ☽/♀+0 39        |
+--------+-------------------------------------------------------------------+
|  Moon  | = ☿/♇-0 34 = ♀/♃-0 05 = ☿/MC+0 33 = ♄/As+0 59                     |
+--------+-------------------------------------------------------------------+
|Jupiter | = EP/♈-0 30 = ♀/♄-0 18 = ☿/As+0 22 = ♇/♈+0 50 = ☊/EP+0 52         |
+--------+-------------------------------------------------------------------+
| Saturn | = ☿/♃-0 23 = ☊/As+0 01 = ♆/EP+0 07 = ♀/♈+0 57 = Vx/EP+1 00        |
+--------+-------------------------------------------------------------------+
|Mercury | = ☽/♅-0 30 = ☉/☽-0 26 = ♆/As+0 02 = ♃/☊+0 02 = ☽/♂+0 07          |
|        | = As/Vx+0 56                                                      |
+--------+-------------------------------------------------------------------+
|  E.P.  | = ☿/♂-0 39 = ♄/♆+0 28                                             |
+--------+-------------------------------------------------------------------+
```

Figure 6.17: *Nova's new linear planetary-axes diagram.*

the capacity to choose the symbols you want for the chart spokes (e.g., a period for spokes that are unobtrusive, or a star for more clearly defined house cusps);

a planetary-picture routine;

a screen module that will work with chart files on the screen;

hard-disk compatability;

a printer-installation routine (to customize the program for a particular printer);

extension files for each chart file (both enabling you to attach an "unlimited" number of notes to a chart file and to hand-enter additional points, such as asteroids, to a chart file;

and storage of progression ephemeride (to speed up subsequent progressions for the same person).

The last of these options might use too much disk space if you kept track of a great many people's progressions, but the error trapping in Nova seems very good, and I expect the program will indicate a full disk without crashing.

Natal or Event Chart

hank friedman June 27 1950 9:42: 0 AM EDT

Tree-Style Printout of PLanetary Axes

45 Degree Pictures with 60 Minute Orb.

Aries	Pluto	Nodes	M.C.	Uranus	Sun	Mars	Ascend.
♄-+-♆	☊-+-♈	☿-+-♆	☿-+-Vx	♂-+-☊	♂-+-☊	♂-+-♅	♅-+-♆
♇-+-EP	MC-+-EP	♅-+-♈	♂-+-♈	As-+-EP	As-+-EP	☉-+-♂	☉-+-♆
♄-+-Vx	☿-+-♆	☉-+-♈	♅-+-☊	☉-+-♅	Uranus	♇-+-As	☽-+-♇
		♇-+-MC	☉-+-☊	Sun	☉-+-♅	♀-+-EP	♂-+-♆
		☿-+-Vx	♂-+-☊	♂-+-♅	♂-+-♅	As-+-MC	♃-+-EP
		♂-+-♈	As-+-EP	☉-+-♂	☉-+-♂	♆-+-♈	♅-+-Vx
				♇-+-As	♇-+-As		☉-+-Vx
							☽-+-MC
							♂-+-Vx

Neptune	Venus	Vertex	Moon	Jupiter	Saturn	Mercury	E.P.
♄-+-EP	Neptune	♆-+-Vx	☿-+-♇	EP-+-♈	☿-+-♃	☽-+-♅	☿-+-♂
☽-+-As	☽-+-As	♄-+-MC	♀-+-♃	♀-+-♄	☊-+-As	☉-+-☽	♄-+-♆
Venus	♄-+-♇	♃-+-As	☿-+-MC	☿-+-As	♆-+-EP	♆-+-As	
♄-+-♇	♆-+-Vx	☿-+-EP	♄-+-As	♇-+-♈	♀-+-♈	♃-+-☊	
♆-+-Vx		☽-+-♀		☊-+-EP	Vx-+-EP	☽-+-♂	
						As-+-Vx	

Figure 6.18: *Nova's midpoint tree pictures.*

If indeed Nova is released with all these features, then it will be a very good buy indeed, but at least some of the modules will probably have to be upgraded after the first version is released. While Nova lacks a research module at present, AGS plans to allow you to convert chart files into files that can be read and therefore researched using commercial data base programs and will eventually release its own research and statistical packages.

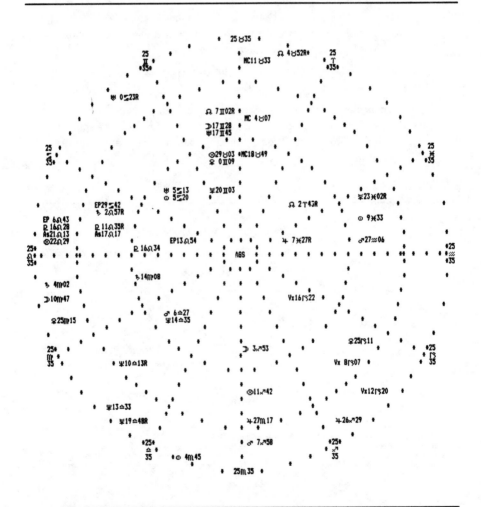

Figure 6.19: The Nova tri-wheel.

I was struck by how well the test version of Nova functioned. This prerelease version was better than many programs are when first sold. It is clear that AGS does extensive debugging before releasing its programs, and this says a lot for the organization. AGS plans to provide thorough documentation for Nova.

Only IBM/MS-DOS users have the choice between M-65 and Nova at present. If I owned an IBM/MS-DOS machine and was trying to decide between Nova and M-65, I would take note of both program's printouts and itemize the features of each that the other lacked. If I were primarily printing out a variety of astrological charts and tables and wanted a program that offered a longitude/latitude/time changes module, and that would calculate the parallax-corrected Moon position, and had an already-functioning research module, or some of Matrix's unique local space options, I would select M-65. Because Matrix has a head start on AGS with respect to programming at this level of sophistication, Matrix will probably continue for the time being to offer new modules before AGS does.

On the other hand, if I wanted to generate files that could be read by other programs (from other companies); that could do dynamic transits at no extra cost (a feature that Matrix is working on in a separate, albeit much more powerful, add-on program); that could do kinetic returns, tri-wheels, Equal Houses from many points, or new sidereal techniques—i.e., features that only Nova has—or that allowed me to save to disk only the charts I tagged instead of all the charts from each batch, I would choose Nova. Nova is easier to use than the version of M-65 I am familiar with. As I indicated, I did not even need to read any documentation to use Nova. However, I have not yet seen the new Blue Star Menu in action, and the additional modules already prepared for M-65—for example, the research module and the time changes/longitude/latitude module—offer advantages not to be overlooked. For a summary comparison of the two programs, see Table 6.1.

CP/M and IBM/MSDOS users should also look at Astro Star II (reviewed in Chapter 3), as this update to Astro Star is actually as powerful in many ways as M-65 and Nova, and is more screen-oriented for those astrologers who want an interactive program of great speed that also has powerful customizing and batch-processing features. The weaknesses of Astro Star II compared to Nova and M-65 are its lack of dynamic progressions and directions—that is, its inability to calculate timed progressed (and directed) aspect hits—and its lack of a dynamic transit module and of some options found in the other programs: the eclipse module, the variety of local space options, planetary pictures, multiple wheels, extended files, and carefully designed printouts. The

CCRS program (also reviewed in Chapter 3) is also powerful as well as inexpensive and well worth evaluating.

Eventually, when Matrix adapts M-65 for CP/M computers and AGS implements what it can of Nova for the Apple, there will be more competition and more choices for every computer astrologer. Meanwhile, both systems are excellent for the computers they run on, and they are the most powerful astrology programs ever written for microcomputers.

	M-65	*Nova*
Parallax Moon	Yes	No
Works with hard disk	No	Yes
Progress secondaries	No	Yes
Research module	Yes	No
Open wheel	Yes	No
Bi-wheel	Yes	No
Tri-wheel	No	Yes
Uranian planets	Yes (option)	No
True Node	Yes	No
Proportional spacing	Yes	No
Onscreen editing	Yes*	Yes
Kinetic returns	No	Yes
Top accuracy range	1700-2300	3000 years
Date released	1981	Late 1984
Time change atlas	Yes*	No
Orbs by planet	No	Yes
Custom aspects	15	20
Auto-label secondaries	Yes	No
Linear midpoint chart	No	Yes

*IBM version only.

Table 6.1: *M-65 compared to Nova.*

Chapter Seven

Software for Specialized Applications

Since astrology is a field with many sub-specialties, it should be no surprise that there are many programs with specialized applications. I will review three of the larger specialized programs here: M-86 Synastry Video Package, M-73 Natal & Progression Package, and Blue Star 6 Solar & Lunar Return Package, all from Matrix Software. I will also look at several special-order programs obtainable from Matrix and AGS.

M-86 Synastry Package

M-86 is a screen-oriented program ideal for the astrologer who wants to inspect relationships in depth. It is available for Commodore and Apple computers at $100. It creates no files, and cannot be customized, so you have to use its aspect set, which comprises the major aspects plus semisquare, sesquiquadrate, inconjunct, and quintile. M-86 will "dump" screen displays to a printer for those who want printouts, but it is clearly designed primarily for screen use.

At the same time, M-86 gives you a lot to work with. You can calculate two natal charts, and from those charts create two secondary progressed charts, plus a composite and a relationship chart, and a progressed relationship chart, and you can work with all of them at the same time. In other words, M-86 will store all seven in memory, for you to work with in a variety of ways.

You can choose among converse and relocated progressions, Koch and Placidus houses (although you could probably special order the program for other house systems if you wished to), and can switch to any of the seven charts created.

There are many ways to compare two charts using this Synastry Package. You can place one chart's planets in the other's houses. You can see how the planets, house cusps, and midpoints in one chart connect to the planets, house cusps, and midpoints in the other chart using whatever dial you wish, as shown in Figure 7.1. You can compare aspects between the two charts, complete with orbs as Figure 7.2 illustrates. You can even combine many charts in a single midpoint listing, if you wish.

Unfortunately, Matrix has not, to date, compiled the program and many steps take a minute or more to execute, with *no* indication that the computer is doing anything. If you purchase M-86, I suggest requesting an unprotected version and compiling it yourself. Otherwise, the waiting might take some of the fun out of using the program. The program could also flow a little more smoothly. It isn't obvious how to get midpoint listings for one or both charts, for example. Nevertheless, many astrologers would enjoy adding this program to their library, especially if it were compiled.

M-73 Progressed Hits Printing Package

This program is designed primarily to aid you in calculating progressions for several years at a time. It is available for Commodore and Apple computers at $150. M-73 can print out a series of progressions for as many years as you specify, complete with a bi-wheel chart for each year, and a table of dates when each progressed aspect enters and leaves a 1 degree orb and becomes exact (see Figure 7.3).

The bi-wheel chart places the natal chart inside the wheel and the progressed chart outside the wheel, will print glyphs with certain printers, and includes a list of the natal and progressed positions. You can have an open wheel (without house lines) or a standard wheel chart, and you can choose secondary progressions, or solar arc, Naibod arc, or degree-for-a-year directions. M-73 uses the major aspects plus semi-square, sesquiquadrate, quincunx, and quintile, and lists both mutual aspects (progressed-to-progressed) and progressed-to-natal aspects.

M-73 will also print out natal charts (in this case not a biwheel, but with the natal data repeated twice at the bottom of the chart), complete with a second page of aspects, and will batch process about ten jobs at a time. In calculating the natal aspects, all of the aspects are listed as

JU/SA B	00AR07	*UR/NO A	18TA57	48*MA/NO A	04CN35	94*PL/AS B	14LE26	134
MA/MC B	00AR36	*SU/NO A	19TA01	49*SA/NO B	05CN00	95*ME/VT B	15LE34	135
VE/NO B	01AR06	1*MA/PL B	19TA20	49*URA A	05CN12	95*JU/MC B	15LE42	135
NOD A	02AR43	2*NO/MC B	20TA34	50*SU/UR A	05CN16	95*PLU A	16LE33	136
ME/VT A	03AR12	3*SU/SA B	21TA15	51*SUN A	05CN20	95*ASC B	17LE17	137
JU/PL B	04AR26	4*MA/AS B	22TA11	52*AS/MC A	07CN12	97*ME/NE A	17LE18	137
MO/VE B	06AR18	6*NE/VT B	24TA10	54*VTX B	08CN07	98*SU/VE B	17LE22	137
MAR A	06AR27	6*VE/MC A	24TA29	54*VE/PL A	08CN21	98*MA/UR A	20LE49	140
VE/UR B	06AR28	6*SU/PL B	25TA34	55*NE/NO A	08CN39	98*SU/MA A	20LE53	140
SU/MC B	06AR50	6*MO/MC B	25TA47	55*PL/NO B	09CN18	99*PL/AS A	21LE04	141
JU/AS B	07AR17	7*UR/MC B	25TA56	55*MO/SA B	10CN12	100*ME/VE B	24LE06	144
NEP B	10AR13	10*MA/VT A	26TA24	56*SA/UR B	10CN21	100*NO/VT A	24LE32	144
MO/PL B	10AR15	10*JU/PL A	27TA00	57*NO/AS B	12CN10	102*UR/NE A	24LE53	144
MA/NE A	10AR31	10*JUP B	27TA17	57*MA/JU B	12CN11	102*SU/NE A	24LE57	144
UR/VT A	10AR47	10*ME/SA B	27TA59	57*VE/AS A	12CN52	102*ASC A	25LE35	145
SU/VT A	10AR50	10*SU/AS B	28TA25	58*MO/PL B	14CN31	104*H07 A	25LE35	145
JU/MC A	13AR08	13*VEN A	00GE09	60*UR/PL B	14CN40	104*H01 A	25LE35	145
ME/MC B	13AR34	13*NE/VT A	00GE28	60*VTX A	16CN21	106*MO/MC A	26LE23	146
NEP A	14AR35	14*JU/AS A	01GE31	61*SA/MC A	16CN29	106*MAR B	27LE05	147
MO/AS A	14AR45	14*ME/PL B	02GE18	62*VE/VT B	16CN38	106*SA/PL A	00VI21	150
MA/NO B	17AR03	17*VE/NE B	02GE42	62*MO/AS B	17CN22	107*MO/VE A	02VI02	152
VE/JU B	18AR48	18*MON B	03GE56	63*UR/AS B	17CN31	107*JU/NO B	02VI09	152
SA/VT B	20AR32	20*ME/MC B	04GE26	64*ME/PL A	18CN18	108*SU/MA B	03VI19	153
H03 A	21AR14	21*ME/AS B	05GE09	65*SU/JU A	18CN25	108*AS/AS A	04VI51	154
H09 A	21AR14	21*NOD B	07GE02	67*MO/JU A	20CN41	110*MC/VT A	06VI07	156
MO/MA B	22AR16	22*PL/NO A	09GE38	69*VE/SA A	22CN08	112*SA/NE B	06VI35	156
MA/UR B	22AR25	22*ME/VE A	10GE05	70*NE/MC B	22CN10	112*MO/JU B	07VI22	157
SU/NO B	23AR17	23*JU/SA A	10GE47	70*ME/AS B	22CN48	112*JUP B	07VI27	157
MO/SA A	24AR02	24*UR/MC A	12GE01	72*ME/JU B	25CN09	115*JU/UR B	07VI31	157
PL/VT B	24AR51	24*SU/MC A	12GE04	72*VEN B	25CN10	115*SUN A	09VI33	159
NO/MC A	25AR46	25*MO/NO B	12GE14	72*UR/PL A	25CN53	115*ME/MA B	10VI03	160
AS/VT B	27AR42	27*UR/NO B	12GE23	72*SU/PL A	25CN56	115*NE/PL B	10VI54	160
SU/MO B	28AR30	28*NO/AS A	14GE09	74*MA/MC A	27CN38	117*MA/PL A	11VI30	161
SU/UR B	28AR39	28*MON B	17GE27	77*H06 A	27CN56	117*MO/ME A	11VI59	161
ME/JU A	28AR44	28*MO/UR B	17GE36	77*H12 A	27CN56	117*NE/AS B	13VI45	163
VE/SA B	29AR04	29*VE/UR A	17GE40	77*UR/AS A	00LE23	120*SAT A	14VI08	164
ME/NO B	00TA01	30*JU/VT B	17GE42	77*SU/AS A	00LE27	120*VE/MC B	14VI39	164
VE/NO A	01TA26	31*SU/VE A	17GE44	77*NE/MC A	01LE42	121*NE/PL A	15VI34	165
PL/VT A	01TA27	31*URA A	17GE45	77*ME/SA A	02LE05	122*MA/AS A	16VI01	166
VE/PL B	03TA23	33*SA/MC B	18GE32	78*MA/VT B	02LE36	122*SU/NE B	16VI17	166
JU/NE B	03TA45	33*MA/NE B	18GE39	78*SAT B	02LE58	122*MC/VT A	17VI35	167
MC B	04TA07	34*MER A	20GE02	80*VE/MA A	03LE18	123*MO/UR A	19VI34	169
MO/MA A	05TA12	35*MA/JU A	21GE57	81*MO/NO A	03LE19	123*SU/MO A	19VI38	169
MO/ME B	05TA14	35*PL/NO B	22GE51	82*SA/PL B	07LE16	127*JU/NO A	20VI05	170
ME/UR B	05TA23	35*SA/NO A	23GE25	83*VE/NE A	07LE22	127*NE/AS A	20VI05	170
AS/VT A	05TA58	35*SU/NE B	24GE53	84*NE/NO A	08LE37	128*NO/VT B	22VI34	172
VE/AS B	06TA14	36*MO/VT A	25GE09	85*SU/VT B	08LE50	128*MER B	23VI01	173
JU/UR A	06TA19	36*AS/MC B	25GE42	85*SA/UR A	09LE40	129*VE/VT A	23VI15	173
SU/JU A	06TA23	36*JU/NE A	26GE01	86*SU/SA A	09LE44	129*H02 A	23VI20	173
MO/NE A	09TA15	39*VE/JU B	26GE14	86*AS/AS B	10LE08	130*H08 A	23VI20	173
ME/NO A	11TA22	41*ME/UR A	27GE37	87*VE/MA B	11LE08	131*MA/SA A	25VI17	175
MA/SA B	15TA01	45*SU/ME A	27GE41	87*PLU B	11LE35	131*MO/VT B	27VI47	177
SA/VT A	15TA15	45*H05 A	28GE01	88*JU/VT A	11LE54	131*UR/VT B	27VI56	177
MC A	18TA49	48*H11 A	28GE01	89*ME/MA A	13LE14	133*SA/NE A	29VI21	179
H04 A	18TA49	48*ME/NE B	01CN37	91*MO/NE B	13LE50	133*		
H10 A	18TA49	48*PL/MC A	02CN41	92*UR/NE B	13LE59	133*		

Figure 7.1: M-86 midpoint table for two natal charts, including house cusps.

```
          ASP BETWEEN A   AND B
     A \B SUN     MON     MER     VEN     MAR
     SUN 4TRI14
     MON 5SQR37                             6SQR51
     MER         2CON35  2SQR59
     VEN                         4TRI58  3SQR04
     MAR
     JUP 2CON06                  2SSQ44
     SAT 4OPP35  3SQR19
     URA 4TRI21
     NEP         2TRI52                  2SES30
     PLU         OSXT53
     NOD         2QNT44
     ASC                 2INC34  OINC24  1OPP30
     MC  2QNT44          4SXT12  6TRI21
     VTX         1INC05                  4SSQ16
     LEFT RIGHT VERT ASP SEP MDPT EXIT
```

Figure 7.2: M-86 screen dump of interaspect table.

```
#ASPECTS FOR HANK FRIEDMAN  1985 SECONDARY
+--------+--+---+--+---+-+-+-+        +--------+--+---+--+---+-+-+-+
!MM-DD-YY!PR!ASP!RD!P/R!X!E!L!        !MM-DD-YY!PR!ASP!RD!P/R!X!E!L!
+--------+--+---+--+---+-+-+-+        +--------+--+---+--+---+-+-+-+
! 1-08-85!MO!INC!NE!P>P!X! ! !        ! 5-30-85!MA!SXT!AS!P>R! !E! !
! 1-15-85!MO!OPP!SA!P>R! ! !L!        ! 6-04-85!MO!SQR!ME!P>R!X! ! !
! 1-15-85!AS!QTL!MO!P>R! ! ! !        ! 6-30-85!ME!SQR!VE!P>R! !E! !
! 1-21-85!MO!SXT!VT!P>R! !E! !        ! 6-30-85!JU!INC!MA!P>R! ! !L!
! 1-27-85!MO!INC!NE!P>R! ! !L!        ! 7-03-85!MO!SQR!ME!P>R! ! !L!
! 1-27-85!MO!INC!PL!P>R! !E! !        ! 7-09-85!MO!SQR!MC!P>P! !E! !
! 2-06-85!MO!INC!NE!P>P! ! !L!        ! 7-24-85!VE!TRI!VT!P>P!X! ! !
! 2-15-85!MO!OPP!SA!P>P! !E! !        ! 7-24-85!VT!TRI!VE!P>P!X! ! !
! 2-19-85!MO!SXT!VT!P>R!X! ! !        ! 8-09-85!MO!SQR!MC!P>P!X! ! !
! 2-22-85!ME!SSQ!NE!P>R! !E! !        ! 8-10-85!MO!OPP!AS!P>P! !E! !
! 2-23-85!SU!INC!JU!P>R! ! !L!        ! 8-25-85!MO!SES!SU!P>P! !E! !
! 2-23-85!MO!INC!PL!P>P! !E! !        ! 9-09-85!MO!SQR!MC!P>P! ! !L!
! 2-24-85!MO!INC!PL!P>R!X! ! !        ! 9-10-85!MO!OPP!AS!P>P!X! ! !
! 3-13-85!MO!QTL!VE!P>R! !E! !        ! 9-19-85!MO!INC!MA!P>P! !E! !
! 3-16-85!MO!OPP!SA!P>P!X! ! !        ! 9-25-85!MO!SES!SU!P>P!X! ! !
! 3-19-85!MO!SXT!VT!P>R! ! !L!        !10-05-85!ME!SSQ!NE!P>R!X! ! !
! 3-24-85!MO!INC!PL!P>P!X! ! !        !10-11-85!MO!OPP!AS!P>P! ! !L!
! 3-25-85!MO!INC!PL!P>R! ! !L!        !10-12-85!MO!INC!AS!P>R! !E! !
! 4-02-85!MO!SXT!MC!P>R! !E! !        !10-19-85!MO!INC!MA!P>X! ! ! !
! 4-11-85!MO!QTL!VE!P>R!X! ! !        !10-26-85!MO!SES!SU!P>P! ! !L!
! 4-14-85!MO!OPP!SA!P>P! ! !L!        !11-10-85!MO!INC!AS!P>R!X! ! !
! 4-20-85!VE!SSQ!AS!P>R! ! !L!        !11-18-85!MO!INC!MA!P>P! ! !L!
! 4-22-85!MO!INC!PL!P>P! ! !L!        !12-09-85!MO!INC!MA!P>R! ! !L!
! 4-30-85!MO!SXT!MC!P>R!X! ! !        !12-13-85!AS!SQR!MC!P>P! !E! !
! 5-06-85!MO!SQR!ME!P>R! !E! !        !12-13-85!MC!SQR!AS!P>P! !E! !
! 5-10-85!MO!QTL!VE!P>R! ! !L!        !12-24-85!ME!SSQ!NE!P>P!X! ! !
! 5-10-85!ME!SSQ!NE!P>P! !E! !        !12-31-85!MO!QTL!VT!P>R! !E! !
! 5-29-85!MO!SXT!MC!P>R! ! !L!        !12-31-85!ME!INC!NO!P>P! !E! !
! 5-30-85!MA!SXT!AS!P>R! !E! !        +--------+--+---+--+---+-+-+-+
+--------+--+---+--+---+-+-+-+        +--------+--+---+--+---+-+-+-+
X=EXACT E=ENTER ORB L=LEAVE ORB P=PROGRESSED R=RADIX T=TRANSIT
```

Figure 7.3: M-73 progressions.

exact—they are not—and there is no indication in the documentation as to the size of orb used. The aspect table for natal charts is not useless, but without orbs it is certainly not very useful.

A third function of M-73 is comparing a second date (called a *transit* by the program) with a natal chart. Unfortunately, you cannot enter longitude or latitude for the second entry, and the M.C., Ascendant, and Vertex are all listed as zero degrees Aries. As a result this function is not suitable for comparing charts. It does print a second page of aspects (both transit-to-transit and transit-to-natal). You can select whatever orb you wish for this function.

I was concerned that, unlike most Matrix programs, which are exceptionally accurate, the version of M-73 I examined incorrectly calculated my Jupiter by 3 minutes of arc, and I wonder if any other positions might be miscalculated. Clearly, for most purposes, such a small error is negligible, but I suggest you test the program for a few charts before fully trusting it.

I also was amazed at how slowly M-73 calculates progressions. It would take all day to calculate and print out 30 years of progressions— at least an hour for every twelve years of progressions, *with* a printer buffer. M-65 prints out the same type of information much more quickly. The Progressed Hits package has other drawbacks as well. It does not save files, and it doesn't even let you use the same birth data for different jobs. In other words, if you want to create a natal chart, prepare a transit, calculate a couple of years of secondary progressions, and examine a solar arc chart for the same person, you have to re-enter the person's birth data four times, (and the program must recalculate the chart each of the four times, which is time-consuming). The programmers at Matrix could easily speed up M-73 many times if they reworked it. Until they do upgrade M-73, I can't recommend the program unless you have lots of time and don't mind re-entering data frequently.

Blue Star 6

At first glance, Blue Star 6 looks like everything an astrologer interested primarily in solar and lunar returns might want. It is available for Commodore computers at $100. It can use Tropical, Sidereal, and Precessed Tropical zodiacs, and the four most popular house systems (Equal, Campanus, Placidus, and Koch) plus Aries, Solar, and user-defined (Ascendant) houses. It will calculate fractional returns (e.g. demi-returns), converse as well as direct returns, search point returns

(returns to any point), relocated returns, and successive returns (i.e. returns for several years).

The program is quite accurate. A table displayed on the screen allows you to sort the planetary positions by longitude, latitude, right ascension, and declination, and you can look at charts from any harmonic you wish. You can also customize the program to run with the house system, harmonic, and zodiac you use, and with precession, search point, and increments turned on or off (as you wish); and can select the 15 aspects (and orbs) you want the program to use.

Unfortunately, the program doesn't print full-page chart wheels, only screen dumps of the tables and forty column square wheels. As a result, you cannot print out the aspects for all of the planets in the return unless you dump 12 wheels (with aspects in a small square in the center of the square wheel) for each planet one at a time. There is no provision for aspects to the node, and most important, there is no way to compare aspects (or anything) between the return chart and the natal chart. The net effect of these deficiences is to greatly reduce the value of this program for most potential buyers.

Special-Order Programs

It would be impossible to either review or examine closely the wide range of specialized software Matrix has produced, but I will introduce some of the more important offerings. I will also review a few of AGS's additional programs.

Horary Astroclock Program

This program places on your screen a new chart for the time at your location at least twice a minute. The original version, M-009, (for the Commodore PET and C-64) did little else, but Matrix has developed a new version for the IBM PC and PC*jr* at $50 that gives beeps when planets cross the mundane angles, Ascendant and M.C., and the compass points (North, South, East, and West), so that you can keep track of what is happening when these crossings take place. The new version, called the M-65 Horary Clock, allows you to use the PC as an alarm clock, set orbs for the crossings, and choose your house system. (What better way to test the value of various types of house cusps!) At this point, the documentation needs to be rewritten, as it tells you to hit some incorrect keys, but this is an easy problem to fix, and I suspect IBM users have a real find here.

Planetary Nodes

While only a very small fraction of astrologers pay attention to the planetary nodes, Matrix has three programs for Commodore PET and C-64 that calculate them. The M-19 Interface program ($30) calculates and sorts heliocentric nodes, and creates tree diagrams. Both M-201 ($30) and M-202 ($50) accurately calculate geocentric planetary nodes plus the Sun's nodes and the geometric and apparent positions of the Sun for dates from 1600 to 2100. M-202 also allows you to store 100 client files as a part of the program and uses a harmonic graphic display (for any dial) to analyze the nodal positions.

Arabian Parts

For those who work extensively with the Arabian Parts, Matrix publishes (again only for the PET and C-64) a program, M-43 (at $50), for nine house systems that will calculate and print out a sorted list of 73 Arabian Parts complete with keywords. It has no screen display of results.

Comets

Many astrologers of old paid great attention to the comets and their orbits, and today's astrologers can use the M-47 Comet Ephemeris ($100, for the PET and C-64) to compute the position of any comet at any moment in time. The program will generate a tabulated ephemeris for the specified time span with intervals of your choice. In order to use the program, you have to enter the orbital elements for the comet under study (obtained from the *Catalog of Cometary Orbits* by Brian Marsden).

Super-Accuracy

Although most astrologers need to know where planets are only to the nearest minute of arc, M-79 ($100, for C-64 and PET) will calculate planetary positions to the nearest second of arc. It also calculates right ascension, declination, and latitude.

Cycle Graphs

John Townley has written a program that allows you to look at the long term cycles of the planets graphically, and lets you combine the cycles of two planets at a time and graph the resultant wave. This program, M-200 ($30 for Apple computers), allows you to examine a span of 70 years for the cycles under examination, and prepares high-resolution printouts.

Hindu Astrology Packages

Both AGS and Matrix publish small packages for those interested in investigating Hindu astrology. AGS's program, #131 Vimshottari Dasas (for Apple computers at $35), allows you to choose among 5 ayanamsas and lists planetary periods in chronological order. You can use the screen display with or without printout. The Matrix program, M-213 Hindu Astrology Package for the PET only ($50), offers a choice of ayanamsas, birth time or Sunrise chart, and Sayana or Nirayana systems, and in addition to listing planetary periods (Vimshottari Dasa), places planets in the appropriate lunar mansions, and does Shodsavargas and Dwadashamas.

Sunrise/Moonrise

Not only fishermen and astronomers want to know the times for Sunrise, Sunset, Moonrise, and Moonset. Matrix's M-215 calculates these times, as well as the Moon's overhead transit. It will run on the PET and C-64 ($30).

Solar Arcs

AGS publishes this small ($25) program for Apple users who wish to examine several years of solar arcs. It does not calculate planet positions and cannot use the files of other programs, but simply lists, for whatever consecutive years you ask for, the Sun's movement since birth, to the nearest minute the nearest second of arc.

This program should be used in conjunction with other programs to have full value. As you might guess, there are several more astrological software packages written for microcomputers. Many of them are no longer listed in any catalogs, and are available only for one type of computer. Matrix spent many years writing a large assortment of programs for the Commodore PET, for example, that are no longer publicly advertised in their catalogs, which perform such diverse functions as:

> rectification assist (a program that calculates a chart and then allows you to shift the Ascendant and M.C. around for different times);

> an ephemeris printing program for ancient dates (from 4713 B.C.), and more accurate geocentric and heliocentric ephemeris printing packages;

a dedicated relocation package;

astrostatistics packages (now being prepared for M-65 also, complete with tests for statistical significance and graphing);

a complete Cosmobiology system;

an astrodyne package;

a mini-graphic ephemeris program;

a harmonic analysis program (frequency distributions).

Matrix also used to program astrological software in the computer language FORTRAN, as well as for a wide variety of calculators, micro-, and mini-computers. Many of these programs may still be purchased, but some have been discontinued. If you have a specialized need (e.g., a microcomputer that will not run any of the software in this book, or an astrological application not handled by any of the programs listed here), you might call Matrix or AGS to see if they can meet your needs.

In many cases, the software no longer listed has been superseded by more powerful programs, such as M-65, which have a large variety of applications. In some cases, the software might not have functioned correctly, so be careful to test the accuracy of any software you buy.

Chapter Eight

The Future

We are at the forefront of a technological revolution whose outcome we cannot even guess. As computers become more powerful and oriented towards graphics, we will begin to see programs that will extend the range of astrology in many directions.

New Advances in Astrological Software

Both AGS and Matrix are continuing to develop programs that enable astrologers and students of astrology to use their computers even more to help them with both astrological calculations and printouts. Some of the projects in the works at this time include:

Disk ephemerides: More compact and precise tables of planetary data are being prepared by both AGS and Matrix. They allow users to employ a wider range of time periods—thousands of years—with great precision and speed. These disk tables will not only be used for natal charts, transits, and progressions, but eventually for graphic ephemerides and other graphic printouts.

Designer wheels: Matrix is completing work on a series of high-resolution chart wheels for the IBM PC. These wheels can be printed in open or closed formats, with aspect lines between planets. See Figures 8.1, 8.2, and 8.3.

Advanced predictive techniques: Astrologers can now easily study methods of progression and direction that are very difficult to compute by hand. Students of astrology will be able to test new predictive theories and techniques as they are developed, using astrological software written for that purpose.

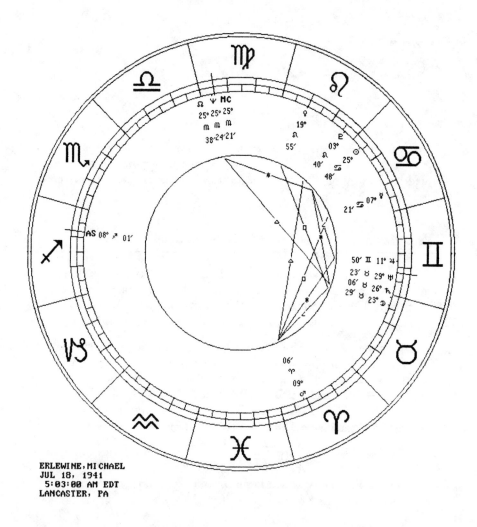

ERLEWINE, MICHAEL
JUL 18, 1941
5:03:00 AM EDT
LANCASTER, PA

Figure 8.1: Designer wheel with aspects.

Screen displays: Matrix has finally created a program (for the Commodore 64) that will display a round wheel on the screen, with planets proportionately spaced around the circle, *with* aspect lines drawn in. This advance will enable astrologers to effectively study charts and perform readings directly from the display, without first printing out hard copy.

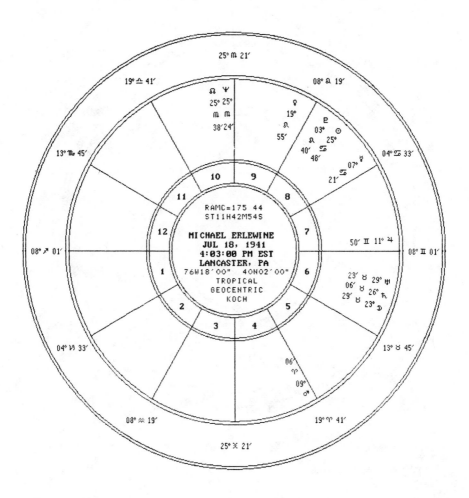

Figure 8.2: Designer wheel without aspects.

Future graphic developments: Among the projects being considered for future development are local-space maps and the implementation of Jim Lewis' Astro*Carto*Graphy maps on personal computers; star maps; transit ephemerides; chart wheels that print aspect lines in color; and graphic forms of chart comparison.

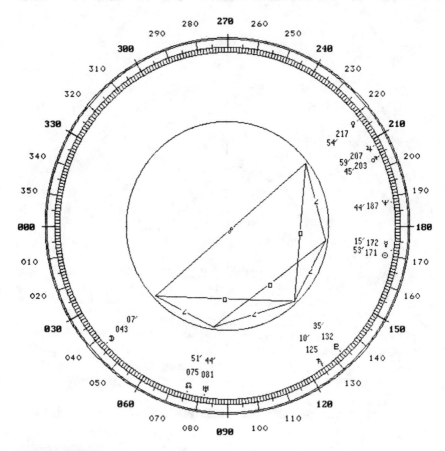

ERLEWINE, STEPHEN
SEP 15, 1946
  3:14:00 AM EDT
LANCASTER, PA

Figure 8.3: Designer wheel with 360-degree notation.

Research advances: Matrix plans to distribute file disks of famous people's birth data, and to establish an astrological network to share information, using *modems* (devices to connect computers via telephone lines). Matrix has also published a new program, called M-65 Tracker Cross-Reference System, which will enable users to keep track of a wide variety of data and retrieve it via keywords, for such purposes as correlating information, keeping a client appointment file, and sorting through the files for all references to specific astrological factors.

AGS has plans to develop a research data base for Nova, which will include the capacity to work with hard disk files, a complete statistical analysis module, and very powerful search capabilities. Nova will also include a file conversion program that will translate its files into standard files which can then be used by any commercial data base program.

M-65jr: With the help of a new compiler, Matrix has solved one of the longstanding problems of M-65 on the Commodore: slow speed of processing. The new M-65jr, at $200, has almost all of the features of M-65-A, but cannot prepare solar and lunar returns. The program allows you to process five charts at once and choose from seven house systems. Its speed of processing is many times faster on the Commodore than M-65-A.

Programming in C: Although both AGS and Matrix have worked hard to provide versions of their programs for as many computers as possible, they were often thwarted by the amount of work necessary to translate programs from one computer system to another. A new computer language, called C, enables programmers to transport software easily from one system to another. Writing programs in C will enable software publishers to create astrological programs for most computer systems.

Hardware Advances

Not only are astrological programmers moving at a rapid pace, but so are hardware manufacturers. Among the advances in the field affecting astrologers are:

Faster processors: I have just finished testing the SpeeDemon card for the Apple, and can recommend it to the computer astrologer. It not only speeds up processing three times, but it makes most screen-oriented programs much more interactive, since you don't have to wait as long for the computer to display its results. Additional speed cards are now being released for the IBM PC and compatible computers.

Color printers: We are at a turning point in printing technology, with high-speed, inexpensive color printers just being developed. Astrologers have wanted, for example, chart printouts that used color to distinguish between aspect lines, and in the near future both the printers and the necessary software will be available.

Graphics-based computers: By introducing the Macintosh, Apple Computer initiated a trend that is likely to continue: creating computers that have greater graphics capabilities and are easy to use. Astrologers can create three-dimensional chart representations, adding new perspectives to astrology.

File storage: Hard disks, bubble memory, high capacity disk drives, and laser disks are being developed to afford computer users more file storage at lower prices. These devices can be used by astrologers to store much larger multifunction programs, work with larger groups of files, and conduct more extensive research.

What's Coming

In the next few years, we will see further developments both in computer technology and in the writing of astrological programs. New companies may begin publishing software for astrology, and individuals using programs will be adding their own innovations.

Each person using astrology programs has the opportunity to change the style and quality of what we see in the future. We are limited only by our imaginations.

Appendix A

Using Computers in Astrology

The Anatomy of a Computer System

A computer system is a group of parts designed to receive information, process the information received, and then give back the results to the user. Each of these functions—*input, processing,* and *output*—is handled in different ways in different types of computer system.

Input Devices

Input—feeding information into the computer—serves two purposes. First, there must be a way of getting *programs*—sets of instructions the computer must follow—into the computer. Second, there must be a way to feed in *data*—the information you want your computer to work with. Let's consider programs first.

A few systems such as the *appliance systems* described in Appendix D have the progams stored permanently in the computer. There is no way to input additional programs into this type of systems, nor is there any need to.

Most computer systems, however, *do* need programs to tell them what to do. You can enter a program via the keyboard, of course, but in most instances that takes too much time and energy, and you would have to re-enter the program every time you wanted to use it. Therefore, as a rule, programs are *loaded* into the computer either from cassettes, by means of a tape recorder, or from *disks* (also called *floppy disks* or *diskettes*) via disk drives.

The advantage of a cassette-based system is price. Tape players and cassettes are simply cheaper. The disadvantages of this type of entry method are many: cassettes are less reliable (many systems simply cannot use cassette input for this reason), and the entry time is much longer.

Disk drives, on the other hand, are fast, very reliable for some computers (e.g. Apple, IBM), and less so for others (Commodore), can store huge amounts of information, and work with much more sophisticated software as a result. They are more expensive, and disks need to be treated with care, but the advantages clearly outweigh the disadvantages for all but the simplest systems.

Data can be entered by any of these methods. The most obvious way of entering data is typing it in from the keyboard. In choosing a computer, whether portable or desktop, pay attention to the feel of the keyboard. You should be comfortable typing on it, as you will be using it for a long time. Detachable keyboards may be particularly convenient when placed on a shelf below your computer or in your lap.

Speaking generally, both disks and cassettes can also serve as input devices for data. If your program generates *files* of information, they can be saved on disk or cassette, so that, if you want to use the same data for other purposes, you can have the computer read it back in, without entering it all over again. No astrology software, however, uses cassettes to store files, so if you want to save charts for future use, you must have a disk drive.

Output Devices

From the above, it should be clear that tape recorders and disk drives are *output devices,* as well as input devices. That is, they can receive information after the computer has processed it. But you, the user, need a method of receiving the results of the computer's processing, in a form in which you can read it. For this purpose, there are two other types of output devices; screens and printers.

Both screens and printers come in a variety of sizes. If you choose a portable system, you may be willing to work with a tiny screen and a tiny printer (or just a screen). If, on the other hand, you will be using a desktop system, you will want a bigger, clearer screen, and, if finances permit, a full size (8½ × 11) printer.

With the exception of the Macintosh screen, which is exceptionally clear, most buyers find 12" screens with non-glare finishes and green or amber displays much easier to read than black and white or smaller screens. Choosing a screen (called a *monitor* in the computer trade) is largely a matter of taste, so look carefully at a few different types, and make sure you look at an 80-column display to assess whether the resolution is sharp enough.

The price of printers has dropped sharply in the past few years, so there is no reason (other than portability) to buy a printer with smaller-than-normal-size output. There are two types of printers to choose from: *daisy-wheel* printers, and *dot-matrix* printers. (*Thermal* printers, whose printouts are unacceptably small and fade badly with time, and *ink-jet* printers, which are just being produced, also exist.)

If you choose a daisy-wheel printer, you will have the advantage of typewriter-style output. But daisy-wheel printers are slow, need servicing frequently, and cannot print any kind of graphics, such as astrological symbols.

Dot-matrix printers, on the other hand, may have slightly rougher-looking characters, but are faster, cheaper, and more reliable, and can print graphics. They are therefore better suited for astrological use.

There is one problem that many purchasers of printers, computers, and astrological software run into, however: compatibility. As the users of word-processing software know only too well, each program works only with a limited number of computer/printer combinations. Moreover, if you want to print astrological symbols, which I highly recommend, you will not only be limited to a few brands of printers (and sometimes specific models of each brand), but will also need to use a specific brand of connector (called *printer interface*) to join the computer to the printer. For instance, if you use the Matrix M-65 system on a Commodore 64 computer and want to print astrological symbols, you must use a Microworld interface and either an Epson MX-80 or Gemini 10X printer.

Too many people buy all the parts of a system (called the *hardware*) and expect the programs to work with them. It is much wiser to decide what your needs are, find the specific software that fulfills these needs, and then purchase the computer system that will work with the software.

Nonetheless, if you do not need glyphs or other graphic output, you can use almost any combination of computer and printer with at least some astrological software.

The Processor

The final part of a computer system is the processor itself. Most computers available for astrology today have an *8-bit processor*. This type of processor typically takes between 20 and 40 seconds to calculate a natal chart with good precision. In addition, some computers have processors that can perform only one function at a time (e.g., the Commodore 64) which slows down certain operations a great deal, while others can do many operations at the same time (e.g., the Apple II).

With the introduction of the IBM PC, astrologers have access to a *16-bit* computer, which runs ten times faster than the 8-bit machines, and can use even more complex software. Once the astrology programs are written for the 32-bit Macintosh, even more powerful software will become available.

A computer system, then, consists of a keyboard, processor, screen, cassette- or disk-based entry device, and (optionally) a printer.

Guidelines for Using Computers

As mentioned above, computers are not invulnerable. Taking good care of your system will ensure not only accuracy, but a long life to your system. Books such as *Don't!* by Rodnay Zaks (SYBEX, 1981) discuss computer care in depth but a brief review here won't hurt.

Caring for Your System

First, unless your computer is specifically designed to be portable or transportable, you should make a point of moving the system as little as possible. Cables and connecting wires are sensitive and should not be crimped or bent unnecessarily, and if the system has to be moved, disconnect them first and reconnect them later.

Floppy disks are very sensitive to dust, grease and magnetism, so keep them in a cool, dust-free place when you are not using them. Always keep backup copies of your programs and files, and keep telephones and other magnetic/electric equipment away from your disks.

When you use an astrological program—or any type of program—you should work from a backup copy and not the original disk sent to you. Since no astrological software is copy-protected (made difficult to copy), you can use commercially-available programs, or programs included in the astrological package, to make as many copies as you like. The reasons for working from copies are twofold: to ensure that you still have access to the program if your disk is damaged, and so that if the program can be customized, you can produce a variety of differently customized copies for different purposes. For example, I keep different versions of a printwheel routine on different copies of the main program (with backups for each): some include many minor aspects, others have different tabular output, and one version even lets me use two different file disks to calculate chart comparisons.

In addition, in order to keep track of your chart files effectively, it is good to keep printouts of the files on your disks.

To keep your disk drives functioning properly, you should clean the drive heads monthly (many stores sell head-cleaning kits) and the drive speed should be checked once a year and adjusted if necessary.

If your neighborhood is on the same line as any heavy equipment users, power surges and dips can wreak havoc with your system. Surge protectors—devices that protect your computer and printer from such extremes—can now be purchased for under $50 and are a worthwhile addition to your system.

If you have to open up your computer for any reason, first touch grounded metal (such as the power supply in the computer) before touching any of the boards or chips. This will discharge static and keep the chips safe. You should never plug the three-prong plug that grounds your computer, printer, and other equipment into an adapter or output that is not grounded.

Finally, if you are having trouble with your system, ask for help. Most dealers and computer clubs are very happy help you keep your system up and running.

Software Capacities

The programs you buy for astrological and other uses may or may not be everything you hoped for. It is wise to examine a program firsthand, either before buying or immediately upon purchase, to see if it really meets your needs. Most companies will let you return software provided you do so within a short period of time.

If you are buying more expensive software, you may be able to get upgrades for a minimal fee, or a discount on any new, advanced software that comes out. These possibilities are worth exploring before spending too much money.

It is very important—for the new user especially—to realize that new software often has "bugs" in it; and there are more bugs in the larger and more sophisticated software packages. Therefore, if your needs are simple, you may want to get something less powerful but that has been around for awhile, and is therefore debugged. Otherwise, be prepared to work around bugs for the first year of software release.

In other words, don't expect the most sophisticated software to perform like a perfect new car would. Expecting software to be perfect is like expecting a twenty-volume encyclopedia to have no errors. Nonetheless, also know that as a consumer you have a right to software that does at least most of what it is supposed to do, even with the bugs.

Most of the less expensive programs (under $60) for astrology are accurate for the twentieth century. Like walking off a cliff, going beyond the year 2000 (or before 1900) can result in highly inaccurate computations. Other programs are highly accurate from 1700 to 2300, while others can be quite precise for the inner planets (through Saturn) as far back as 4000 B.C. Be sure to check the reviews to see if the software you are considering is accurate for the dates you intend to use.

This book examines software from the two major astrological software houses, Matrix and AGS. A few other firms market astrological software, but the little I have seen has not been accurate or powerful to meet most astrologers' needs.

Be aware that speed (and to a lesser extent, precision) of calculation varies greatly, depending upon the machine and software you use. Compiled programs run faster, but are impossible to "break into," i.e., to fix if they contain errors or to modify to suit your own needs.

User friendliness refers to the ease with which a program can be understood and used, and the ease of recovering from errors. While none of the astrological software is perfect in this regard, the programs available now are much better than those on the market a few years ago.

Nevertheless, you should not depend too much upon your computer for accuracy. Just as when you drive the same route in your car many times, it is easy to become overconfident, and make mistakes in entering birth data. Therefore, you should always double-check your work.

Getting the Most from Your System

In most cases, the programs you purchase are designed to run as fast and effectively as possible. Nevertheless, as a user of astrological software, you can optimize your work in a variety of ways.

Software Enhancements

Each computer system is set up differently, and for any system there are programs whose sole purpose is to make other programs run more efficiently. One prime example is a compiler, which translates other programs into a language that runs much faster than the original language in which the program was written. Because both AGS and Matrix have spend much time and effort designing programs that process data

228 Astrology on Your Personal Computer

quickly and efficiently, many of their programs are already compiled. Therefore, you should not try to compile their programs on your own.

Since you will be making copies of your astrological programs, you can benefit by using copy programs, which are available for most computers, and will quickly and easily make error-free copies of files and whole disks. Take the time to find the best copy program for your machine. For the Apple II computers, for example, Super Disk Copy III is an excellent program. (However, since M-65 has specially packed files, you should use only the file copy program included with M-65 to copy the file disks it creates.)

Another method of improving your software is to use a faster disk operating system (DOS) than the one that comes with the computer. this is only worth doing if you want to use the larger programs, which take some time to load. For Matrix programs on the Apple, for instance, PRONTO-DOS is as good choice. Not all DOS enhancers are compatible with astrology programs, however, so you should test an enhancer on a backup copy of your program before relying on it.

Finally, if you buy a program that comes on many disks, such as M-65, you might consider preparing single-disk versions (by using a file copy program), to eliminate the need for swapping disks. For example, I prepared an M-65 disk containing the calculation modules (M000, M001, M002), the printing modules (M021, M022) and the machine codes (CODE 1, and HEX21 + HEX22); and added the file inspection/ deletion module from the Research Disk (R000) to give me a very usable file printing and inspecting disk that requires no swapping.

IBM users who have enough memory in their system, can use programs to transfer entire disks into RAM, which also makes programs run much faster. Be careful, however, to find out whether the program you want to use will work if placed in RAM before going to the trouble of buying extra memory and a transfer routine.

Hardware Enhancements

If you initially purchased a computer system with a single disk drive, the most obvious enhancement is a second disk drive. Not only does a two-drive system speed up the backup process considerably, but many of the more sophisticated astrological software packages either require two drives or work much more smoothly with a two-drive system.

RAMdisks, which store the entire contents of a disk in the computer's memory, are also available for Apples and other computers, but for most users the price is not worth the time saved.

If you expect to do a lot of printing, a *printer buffer* can save you a great deal of time. A printer buffer holds the output from the computer while the printer, which runs more slowly, catches up. Otherwise, the computer has to pause until the printer has finished printing, which slows down both the computer and the printer. Using a buffer can double the speed of output on programs with glyphs, for instance, while returning the computer to you long before the printing is completed. A printer buffer is a must if you are planning to print out interpretive reports.

I recommend a free-standing 64K printer buffer, because printer buffer cards that fit into the computer or printer are not always compatible with astrological software, and can cause overheating. In addition, such a buffer can be used with any combination of printer and computer, so you can use it even if you replace your printer or computer.

While the IBM and Macintosh computers are fast, Apple II and Commodore and CP/M users could use some extra processing speed. For example, some interpretive programs take upwards of 20 minutes to process a printout. Without a printer buffer, your computer is tied up completely for that period of time. Most batch processing also takes many minutes, so a faster processor could be a valuable commodity. For the Apple II, there are several fast processor boards. They speed up all calculations about 3½ times. The newly released SpeeDemon board from McT costs $300, and is a worthwhile investment for the busy astrologer, businessman, or other Apple II user.

Finally, a keyboard that sits on your lap may be more comfortable, and may allow you to type more quickly with less fatigue. A D-Tach kit for your Apple II enables you to remove the keyboard from the Apple II (II + or IIe) and install it in a separate unit that fits comfortably in your lap. At $89, this is definitely a worthwhile investment. You can purchase other keyboards for your Apple, but make sure that they have as good a feel as the original keyboard before buying one.

Modifying the Programs

If you already know how to program a computer in BASIC, you may want to modify the actual program code for some of the programs you buy. If you think you might, first find out if the program you have or are about to buy can be modified. With direct permission from Matrix, you can order modifiable versions, but check before purchasing. Many programs from both AGS and Matrix are sold in compiled form, or are written in machine language, neither of which can be modified from

BASIC. You may, however, be able to obtain unprotected, uncompiled versions, with direct permission from the manufacturers.

If you overcome these hurdles, you may want Matrix's *Manual of Computer Programming for Astrologers,* by Michael Erlewine, the first, only, and best manual for learning the basics of astrological programming. You may also want back issues of *Matrix* magazine, a journal for astrological programmers. It has been discontinued, but back issues are available from Matrix. They are excellent, albeit a bit technical.

Obtaining Accurate Data

When you use astrological software for generating charts, transits, and other applications, the results are only as good as the data you enter. You should therefore be very careful to verify the data at each step of the way. When you first get birth information from someone, repeat it back to them for confirmation. When you enter data into your computer, double-check the entry before or after the calculation process, and in looking up time-zone information, again recheck your work.

If your work depends so heavily on the accuracy of the birth data you use, then your reference books must be of the highest caliber. Fortunately for the astrologer, excellent references do exist. For births in the U.S., the *American Atlas,* by Neil Michelsen is the most accurate reference for longitudes, latitudes, time zones, and standard vs. daylight time corrections. For locations outside of the U.S., any of the better world atlases (e.g. Goode's) will be more accurate sources of longitude and latitude than the outdated *AFA Longitudes and Latitudes Throughout the World* by Dernay, and although Doris Chase Doane's books *Time Changes in Canada and Mexico* and *Time Changes in the World* are the best sources for time zone information outside the U.S., they contain some incorrect longitudes and latitudes, so do use world atlases instead for longitudes and latitudes.

Appendix B

Advanced Uses for Astrological Software

Even the most basic astrological calculations are simplified by computers. As a result, with a computer to do your calculations, you gain more time to think about and work with astrology. Once you begin using a computer for astrology, you open the door to many of its branches, including those that were inaccessible before. This appendix is designed to introduce you to some of the areas in astrology that computers can help you to explore.

Relocation and Astrology

When people think of moving, or traveling for business or pleasure, they often use astrology to determine the best places to go to. The methods used by astrologers in ascertaining a place's effect upon a person are varied, and I will not attempt to review them all.

Here are a few of the most common methods. You can look at the transits of the person for the dates of travel to decide both if it is a good time to travel and what moods the person is likely to experience. A strong transit in water signs might incline someone towards more natural settings and a quieter itinerary, while fire transits might encourage a more lively vacation spot, for example. Programs such as M-91 Transit Writer, M-65 Transit Master, Transit Package 113, Nova's Transit Module, and The Daily Astro-Report can help you by calculating transits.

Alternatively, you can use an Astro*Cart*ography map, which focuses on the ascending and culminating lines for each planet, and the places on Earth that they cross, to discover where a particular influence is amplified. The AstroMapping add-ons for AGS Apple Star Track and Astro Star calculate these lines.

A second method is to compare the chart of the person to the charts of the places under consideration. Books such as *Horoscopes of the U.S. States & Cities* by Dodson are of value with this approach, and many programs will let you compare two charts, including Apple Star Track, CCRS, Astro Star, Nova, M-65, Blue Star 10, and M-86.

The most commonly used method is to recalculate the birth chart for the locations being considered. This can be done with any of the programs described in Chapters 3 and 6, as well as by the smaller packages M-31, M-30, M-0, M-1, Astrotalk, and AstroScope.

In a *relocation chart,* which is a birth chart reworked for a new location, you enter all of the original birth data except the longitude and latitude of the new place. This new chart will change only the angles (the Ascendant and Midheaven) and house placements, not the planetary aspects or sign positions. In order to evaluate the relocated chart, one notes which planets have become emphasized by position, i.e., in close aspect to the Ascendant or M.C. A common failing among those evaluating relocation charts is to judge places where Jupiter or Venus is emphasized as good, and places where Neptune or Saturn are strong as bad. Much depends upon the natal aspects of the planet in question, and on what you want to accomplish by going to a new place.

Midpoints

Ever since Ebertin published *The Combination of Stellar Influences,* the astrological world's interest in midpoints has grown. The Cosmobiologists of Germany use midpoints in synastry (chart comparison), predictive work, birth chart analysis, and medical astrology, among other things, with very effective results.

You need to learn to form your own interpretations of midpoint meanings, because every astrologer interprets the meanings of each planet differently, and you can form your own synthesis based on your experience of the planetary energies.

Most of the programs discussed in this book will calculate midpoints for you, and M-30, M-64, M-65, AstroStar, Nova, CCRS, and Apple Star Track will sort midpoints and calculate midpoint dials.

Midpoint trees are the patterns drawn for occupied midpoints. M-65, Astro Star, and Nova will construct these patterns for you, to facilitate looking at the interactive effects of midpoint structures.

Those who use midpoints construct a 45-degree dial to better indicate the relationship between the conjunctions, squares, oppositions, semi-squares, and sesquiquadrates of the occupied midpoints. These aspects, which are called *eighth harmonic aspects* because they all are based on the number two (2, 4, 8), have been found to have the most predictive value and impact in Cosmobiological work. Reinhold Ebertin has written many books on the subject, including *Applied Cosmobiology.*

Astrological Prediction

Two of the most common uses of astrology are preparing for the future, and understanding the present. The areas to which astrological prediction are applied vary greatly, from telling others when to get their hair done or go to the race track, to helping people see the psychological and metaphysical significance of present events. In any case, astrologers have at their disposal a number of tools for predictive work. Some of the techniques available to the astrologer are transits, progressions, returns, directions, and eclipse cycles. I will review the techniques here.

Transits

The astrological prediction method of using transits is perhaps the most logical technique in use today. The positions of the planets at any given moment (past, present, or future) are compared with their positions at birth. Astrologers have observed that as a planet in the sky approaches an exact angle (aspect) to a planet in the natal chart, the transit's intensity increases, peaking around the time of exactness and subsiding rapidly thereafter. Most astrologers would agree that transit effects may be experienced when the transiting planet (the one in the sky) is a few degrees before exact contact, but it is most important to watch transits once they are within one degree of exact contact. Within a couple of weeks after exact transit, the effect becomes negligible. As a planet enters the degree before contact, should it happen to slow down and stand still (called a *station,* as in stationary), the effect can be very great indeed.

Because the outer planets (Pluto, Neptune, Uranus, Saturn) move so slowly, they take longer than the inner planets to approach a transit. As a result, transits by the outer planets are more potent in the events that they signal. (I do not believe that the planets cause events, but rather that they are indicators of cycles with a Greater Cause.)

Because the Earth moves much faster than the outer planets, outer planet transits will happen more than once. For example, Pluto could conjunct the Sun in a chart, then retrograde (move backward due to the Earth speeding by) and conjunct the Sun a second time, then go direct (begin to move forward again) and conjunct the Sun a third time. Since each of these transit swings might be potent for a month or two (for the period from one degree applying to exact), with breather periods in between, some cycles last for more than a year. You must not presume that each swing of a transit will be as potent as every other swing, as they will vary in both flavor and intensity.

Pay attention to overlapping transits to the same natal planet, for example Pluto square Mars during the same time period that Saturn sextiles Mars. If two or more cycles overlap to the same planet in a chart, the effect is both increased and altered by the blending energies of the transiting planets.

The majority of astrologers, and of books on transits, ignore the effect of the natal planet's sign on the expression of the transit. Although some books on transits are excellent, they all fail in cases where the planet's sign is not consistent with the presumed nature of the planet. They treat Uranus square Mercury, for example, the same regardless of the sign that Mercury is in, even though the sign it is in affects the transit more than the fact that it is Mercury being transited! If Mercury were in Gemini, curiosity, restlessness, and communication might be amplified, but if the Mercury were in Taurus instead, you could expect increased resistance to communicating, stubbornness, and perhaps financial issues. In sum, the effect would be completely different. Almost none of the transit books even mention this fact, while those that do don't indicate the effect of signs on the expression of transits.

Two of the best books on transits are *Forecasting by Astrology* by Martin Freeman, and *Planets in Transit* by Robert Hand. You might wish to begin paying attention to semisquare and sesquiquadrate transits, as they can be quite significant at times. There are a number of programs that calculate transits, including Nova, Daily Astro-Report, Transit Package 113, and M-65 Transit Master.

Progressions

In the early days of Western astrology, when Kepler would have given his eyeteeth for accurate knowledge of the planets' positions in a year's time, astrologers had to resort to means other than transits to predict the future. The mainstay of medieval predictive astrology is called *progressions,* or more specifically, *secondary progressions.* This method works on the principle that the day after birth symbolizes a year of life. In other words, the location of the planets on the second day of life would be used to determine what the second *year* of life would be like. Although empiricists might find this very speculative, secondary progressions can accurately indicate cycles and changes in the life of a person.

Early books on progressions, unfortunately, were very melodramatic, predicting gloom and doom for certain progressed aspects. Alan Leo's *The Progressed Horoscope,* for example, has a great deal of useful information, but gets much too negative at times.

In today's computer age, astrologers have considerably expanded the variety of progressions used. Besides secondary progressions, astrologers can investigate tertiary progressions (a day for a lunar month), minor progressions (a lunar month for a year), converse progressions (progressions based on days or months *before* the birth, instead of after the birth), and new methods of progression that are being invented by computer astrologers. Contemporary books of quality on progressions include *The Technique of Prediction* by R.C. Davison, *The Expanded Present* (Volume VI of Principles and Practice of Astrology) by Noel Tyl, and the sections on progressions in Stephen Arroyo's *Astrology, Karma, and Transformation* and Martin Freeman's *Forecasting by Astrology.*

When a planet changes direction by secondary progression, there are often marked changes in the person's orientation towards life. There is great value in watching the progressed Moon's movement through the natal houses, the progressed Ascendant, and the progressed aspects. As opposed to transits, where the outer planet movements are most significant, in progressions one pays attention to the inner planets, because the outer planets move so slowly that they form almost no secondary progressed aspects at all. It is customary to place much more weight on aspects between the progressed planets and the natal planets than to "mutual" aspects (the aspects in the progressed chart itself).

Apple Star Track, CCRS, and Astro Star will create progressed charts, while M-31, Nova, and M-65 will additionally list timed progressed hits. The latter two programs can calculate a very wide variety of progressions.

Returns

The use of solar and lunar returns in astrology is becoming more common. The solar return, or birthday chart, is a symbolic representation of the year ahead. It is calculated by looking at the moment the Sun returns to the exact position it occupies in the birth chart (which it does every year within 48 hours or so of your birthday). It is as if the soul reconnects to itself at that moment, and steers a course towards the coming year. Lunar returns, on the other hand, are calculated for the time when the Moon returns to its natal placement. Therefore, lunar returns are used as monthly predictors.

Tropical and sidereal astrologers disagree strongly on whether or not to adjust for the effects of precession, which changes the Earth's position relative to the constellations. Since tropicalists use the Sun's orbit rather than the constellations to determine the positions of the signs, most of them don't correct for precession. Siderealists, on the other hand, base their work on the way precession alters stellar sign positions. They therefore must—and do—correct returns for precession.

As a result of including precession correction, sidereal returns differ considerably from those done by tropical astrologers. Nowadays, many siderealists urge tropical astrologers to precess their returns even if they use a tropical zodiac. When evaluating the meaning of a solar return, you should pay attention to the focal planets, the strong (one degree or less) aspects, the rising sign of the return, and the overall patterns in the return chart.

Several of the computer programs reviewed in this book will allow you to test the relative merit of the tropical, precessed tropical, and sidereal returns yourself, including M-32, M-65, Nova, CCRS, Astro Star, and Apple Star Track. Good books on solar returns include *The Solar Return Book of Prediction* by Raymond Merriman, and (for siderealists) *Interpreting Solar Returns* by James Eshelman.

Solar Arc Directions

The technique of solar arcs involves adding to each planet the distance the Sun has moved since the birth (or event). Some astrologers add the Sun's average yearly movement (called Naibod arc) to the planets, others add one degree for each year, while true solar arc directions add the actual distance the Sun has traveled. Many astrologers have found this method of directing the planets very useful in predictive work. A common facet to focus upon in using this technique is the conjunctions between directed planets and those in the birth chart. You can use Nova, M-65, M-35, Astro Star, and CCRS to evaluate solar arcs.

Eclipses

Throughout the ages, astrologers placed much emphasis upon eclipses that conjuncted or opposed planets in a person's chart, and many astrologers have begun to focus attention upon eclipses again. Robert Jansky's *Interpreting the Eclipses* spearheaded the new interest in this field.

At present only M-65's eclipse module allows you to calculate precise eclipse timings. AGS intends to include an eclipse module in Nova, but it is not yet completed.

Testing Predictive Methods

One of the best ways to test the value of the wide variety of predictive methods in astrology is to go back to important times in your past (or the past of those you know well) and see what each method of prediction (solar arcs, returns, transits, and progressions) does or does not indicate about the time period in question. For the predictive method to be of true value to you, it must help you to recognize the purpose and value of the events, and give you assistance in dealing with present and future occurrences.

A second method of testing predictive techniques is to read the biographies of famous people whose birth data is published, and compare the events in their lives with what occurred astrologically at the time. You can find birth information for public figures in books like *The American Book of Charts* and *Profiles of Women* by Lois Rodden, *2001: The Penfield Collection* by Marc Penfield, and *The Gauquelin Book of American Charts* by Michel and Francoise Gauquelin; as well as *The Mercury Hour,* an excellent information-sharing newletter for astrologers.

Alternate Frames of Reference in Astrology

For at least 2000 years, astrologers have drawn all of their charts from the geocentric point of view. This means that charts are constructed as if the Earth were the center of the universe, with planetary positions computed from the center of the Earth in relationship to the ecliptic plane (defined by the Sun's apparent orbit around the Earth). There is nothing wrong with this method, but today's astrologers have at their disposal, via computers, a number of additional frames of reference to test and employ.

One frame of reference worth examining (since we don't live at the center of the Earth) is the *topocentric* perspective, i.e., calculating astrology charts from the surface of the Earth. (This has no relationship to the Topocentric House System, which is only a modification of the house system of Placidus.)

Only the Moon's position changes significantly when measured from the surface of the Earth instead of its center. The *parallax-corrected Moon position,* as it is called, can be up to a degree off from the geocentric Moon position. To test the validity of parallax correction, you can look at charts where the Moon changes sign. In my experience, this testing validates using the parallax correction. If you wish to examine the parallax Moon, you will have to purchase M-65, as no other programs calculate its position.

It would seem logical to use a local reference plane (such as the equator, the local horizon, or the prime vertical) as opposed to a celestial one (the ecliptic), in preparing charts for mundane astrology (including geophysical studies such as earthquake correlations) and perhaps even in relocation work. This is a fresh area for research in astrology, pioneered by Michael Erlewine of Matrix, Charles Jayne (see his *Introduction to Locality Astrology*), and others. Programs such as M-64 and Nova make these locality charts available at the push of a button.

Another perspective that is rapidly gaining popularity in astrology is *heliocentric* charting. Heliocentric astrology is based on measuring positions as they actually are, i.e., with the Sun as the center of the chart. In a heliocentric chart, the Earth's position takes on a great deal of importance, while the Moon is disregarded (since heliocentrically it is at virtually the same position as the Earth), and the signs must be reassessed as having either different meanings, no meanings, or their traditional meanings. Houses are generally not used in the heliocentric system, as there is no Ascendant nor M.C., while the aspects are given primary importance.

Many people use heliocentric charts as indicators of the soul's purpose and themes on Earth, reserving the geocentric chart for the personality's traits and lessons. The heliocentric chart thus offers a different perspective, and can shed light on individuals as well as on global events. At present, there are very few books on heliocentric astrology. Neil Michelsen has published the *American Ephemeris for the 20th Century* in a heliocentric version, and T. Patrick Davis has two books on the subject, *Revolutionizing Astrology with Heliocentric* and *Interpreting Geo-Helio Planets.* The field is ripe for both research and publication. Most of Matrix's programs include heliocentric charting, and AGS's Nova and AstroStar also include heliocentric chart work.

Even within geocentric, ecliptic-based astrology, there are many divergent methods among astrologers. A major division is the one separating tropical astrologers from sidereal astrologers. The difference between the two schools hinges on their methods of determining the signs. The tropical astrologers, including most Western astrologers, emphasize the Solar

System, particularly the Sun's orbit and the resulting seasons. They define the signs by the Sun's crossings of the equator (this defines Libra and Aries), and its solstice points (defining Cancer and Capricorn). The sidereal astrologers, on the other hand, use the fixed stars in the constellations to determine the beginning of the signs (e.g., where Aries starts). Due to precession, the two zodiacs no longer coincide, but are nearly one sign apart. Siderealists correct for precession in all of their work, and also use a number of techniques in their work not commonly used by tropical astrologers (e.g., quotidians and enneads), while tropicalists, on the other hand, pay much more attention to the signs of the zodiac. Virtually all of the astrological software in this book can work with both tropical and sidereal methods.

House Systems

A second area of divergence among astrologers is the method of house division used, if any. The several methods of house division fall into two types: those that divide time and those that divide space.

Among the time-based methods, only the Placidian System is commonly used. Although the Placidus House System is still one of the most popular systems in use today, support for it is declining while other systems are gaining adherents. It has been speculated that the method of Placidus gained such popularity because it was the only system *in print* for a long time. In the 1920's and '30's, the British Faculty of Astrological Studies conducted a study involving thousands of charts (the largest study of house systems to date) and concluded that the Equal House System was more reliable for both natal work and prediction than the Placidian System.

Among the space-based house systems, three methods are in common use: the Koch or Birthplace System, the Campanus House System, and the Equal House System. The Koch House System, although in fact a minor variation on a previous method of house division, departs from all other methods in two ways. First, it does not divide any great circles to arrive at its house cusps, and second, it fails totally above the Arctic Circle. While all house systems become useless at the Poles, none besides Koch are limited to below the Arctic Circles.

The Campanus House System is the most natural division you might think of. If you were to divide the visible sky like an orange into six equal slices (and the sky on the other side of the Earth likewise), you would have the Campanus System. For this reason, it has been popular among many noted astrologers.

The Equal House System is the only method of house division that divides the plane in which the planets orbit (the ecliptic) directly, into twelve houses starting with the Ascendant. All other space methods divide up alternate planes, such as the prime vertical in the Campanus System, and then project the house boundaries onto the ecliptic. The Equal House System is the original twelve-house system used by the ancients, and is rapidly gaining popularity among metaphysical and psychological astrologers.

It is important that new astrologers study the field of house systems for themselves, as feelings run high concerning which system is best, and every few years a new system becomes the fad. I have found the most value in the original Equal House System, and strongly disagree with those that propose abandoning houses altogether. Different house systems may well be more suitable for other purposes, such as horary and mundane astrology.

The most comprehensive treatment of this topic is *Elements of House Division* by Ralph W. Holden. Except for a few of the interpretive programs from AGS, all of the programs discussed in this book will prepare charts for any of the major house systems.

Choosing a Career

For centuries, astrology has been used to assist people in discovering their talents, their optimal work setting, and the particular type of position that would best suit their needs and temperament. In examining the natal chart for career potentials, pay attention to the whole chart and not just the work-related houses, as you bring all of yourself to the job, not just your professional self. A good introduction to the topic is *In Search of a Fulfilling Career* by Joanne Wickenburg.

Synastry: Astrology in Human Interaction

You can develop a great deal of self-awareness by looking at your own birth chart. Even more can be learned by looking at the charts of people you like, dislike, emulate, and reject. Those you like often have astrological factors that connect well to your own chart, especially to the parts of yourself you favor, while those you dislike or can't tolerate trigger parts of yourself you don't accept. Instead of using the interconnections between charts to justify yourself or blame others, you can see where you connect to another person, and gain wisdom about your own dynamics. You can examine your families' and relatives' charts and learn more about the common patterns, conflicts, and astrological heritage you share, and gain insight and become able to relate to your family with more perception.

The use of astrology in examining relationships is called *synastry*, and it has been practiced so widely, and is such a popular use of astrology, that Linda Goodman received the largest advance in publishing history for her monumental and rambling book, *Love Signs*. Among the better books in the field of synastry are *Synastry: Understanding Human Relations Through Astrology* by Ronald Davison, and *How to Handle Your Human Relations* by Lois Haines Sargent.

In exploring chart comparisons, you should use tighter orbs than when examining natal charts, and focus particularly on the one degree orb aspects. Many astrologers use a 4 degree orb (perhaps a little wider for the Sun, Ascendant, and Moon). While trines between charts indicate natural blending and support, sextiles represent bridging two elements (e.g., division of labor) and may indicate the need for more work to maintain rapport. Oppositions can be either polarizing or stabilizing depending upon how they are handled, and squares demand the most diligence in learning to relate to another whose needs and style (at the time) are quite different from your own. Conjunctions vary depending upon the planets involved, but usually represent a synchronization.

Astrologers have begun to use two other methods to look at relationships: composite charts and relationship charts. Composite charts are created from the midpoints between the two charts' planets (e.g., the midpoint between both people's Suns), while relationship charts are calculated as a birth chart for the midpoint in time and place between the two people's birth data.

Programs particularly useful for synastry work include Nova, Apple Star Track, M-65, and M-86.

Minor Aspects and Harmonics

One of the newest and most exciting fields in astrology is the area of harmonics. Thanks to the power of computers, astrologers can investigate the minor angles between the planets. For centuries, astrologers focused primarily upon the five major aspects: the conjunction, sextile, square, trine, and opposition.

Next, the semisquare, sesquiquadrate, semisextile, and quincunx (also called the inconjunct) came into use. Now astrologers are focusing upon the five series (quintile and biquintile), the sevens (septile, biseptile, etc.), the nines, and so on.

There are a number of ways of working with these new angles, but most astrologers either calculate the minor aspects directly or construct *harmonic charts*. In a harmonic chart, all of the planets in a specific aspect series become conjunct in that harmonic. For example, all the planets that are quintile or biquintile become conjunct in the fifth harmonic chart. Harmonic charts reveal more than just the minor aspects, because each harmonic chart has oppositions, squares, trines and sextiles, in addition to conjunctions. Thus, harmonic charts allow you to observe in greater depth the significance of a particular number series.

John Addey initiated much of the interest in this area with his *Harmonics in Astrology*. David Hamblin has written the excellent book *Harmonic Charts,* and Alan Epstein looks at semisextiles and quincunxes in depth in his *Psychodynamics of Inconjunctions*. The more powerful astrological programs, including Nova, AstroStar, CCRS, and M-65, permit you to add minor aspects to their aspect tables, and will construct harmonic charts.

Astrology for Divination

There is a separate branch of astrology, called *horary astrology,* which uses charts the way others use Tarot cards or the I Ching. The theory behind horary astrology is that the time a question is asked contains the answer to the question. In applying this principle to astrology, the practitioner simply casts a chart for the moment a question is asked. With a computer and almost any astrology program, nothing could be simpler.

The rules for horary are *very* different than the rules for natal astrology, and therefore you should study one of the classical texts of horary (e.g., *Horary Astrology: The Key to Scientific Prediction,* by Simmonite) or one of the more modern books in the field, such as *The Art of Horary Astrology* by Sylvia DeLong.

Choosing the Right Time

Astrologers throughout history have chosen the times for coronations, weddings, business ventures, and even occasionally births. The field of *electional astrology,* selecting the time for an event to be scheduled, has its own rules, much as horary does. Two books in the field are both called *Electional Astrology*. One is by Vivien Robson, and the other is by Christine Rechter. A good transit program, such as Transit Package 113,

M-65 Transit Master, Daily Astro-Report, or Nova is essential if you intend to get involved in this field.

Studying the World

Students of astrology who study the astrological correlates of earthquakes, politics, and other world dynamics specialize in *mundane astrology.* If you become interested in looking at world events in this way, you will find it useful to have reference books of charts of countries, such as *Contemporary World Horoscopes* volumes 1, 2, and 3, by Joseph Folino, and *Book of World Horoscopes,* by Moon Moore. There are several textbooks in the field as well, among them Sylvia DeLong's *Guideposts to Mundane Interpretation.*

Medical Astrology

Medical astrologers have been able to diagnose illnesses, prescribe successful treatments, and assist in the prevention of disease by interpreting birth charts. There are many excellent introductions into the field of medical astrology, including Robert Jansky's *Astrology, Nutrition and Health, The American Book of Nutrition & Medical Astrology* by Eileen Nauman, and a little pamphlet called *Healing Herbs of the Zodiac* by Ada Muir.

Ordering Charts by Mail

One of the easiest and least expensive ways of employing computers to do astrology for you is to farm the work out to others. In today's world, there are many mail order houses that calculate and even interpret charts via computer. These firms process large numbers of charts for astrologers. They therefore offer many types of service and usually respond promptly.

Before going into detail about the services available, let's look at the advantages and disadvantages to using a mail-order chart service. First, when a company processes thousands of charts a day (which the biggest and best services do), there will certainly be some degree of error. In contrast to using your own computer, where you can correct erroneous data immediately, discovering an error may delay you several days if you use a computer mail service.

And errors can easily go undetected. You should check not only to see whether your service used the birth data you gave them, but also whether they used the correct time zone and daylight savings corrections. One mail order house used by many of my astrological students had an error rate of about ten percent! Since the busy astrologer will all too often assume these printouts are accurate, using mail services may entail more problems than you might suspect.

A second problem with most chart services is the quality of the printout. While most people ordering charts will redraw them by hand, the printouts in many cases are barely readable and esthetically distasteful, so reworking them becomes essential.

On the positive side, charts by mail can save a great deal of time for people who don't wish to do astrological computing themselves, and the largest firms make an effort to be very accurate and reliable.

The granddaddy of all mail order chart services is Astro Computing Services (ACS), run by Neil Michelsen. His printouts lack esthetic appeal, and few astrologers would read directly from them, but the firm has an excellent reputation in the field and can be trusted. (Nevertheless, you should still double-check the data used to calculate any charts you order.)

ACS offers not only a variety of natal charts, progressed charts, returns, and relationship charts, but also midpoint work, transits, graphic ephemeride, chart transparencies and color wheel printouts. They respond quickly to an order, and I have found Neil Michelsen responsive and open in personal communication.

Many local chart services that use personal computers and astrological software are coming into existence. While these services cannot compete with ACS in their variety of output, they may be more convenient. In any case, check out a service carefully before placing too much reliance on it.

Appendix D

Astrological Appliances

Astrological appliances are computers that have built-in programs, and do nothing but perform astrological calculations. Unlike most computers, they cannot be programmed. Consequently, they can never be used for other applications, such as word processing or financial analysis. Appliances cannot store any files, so you can't enter a batch of charts to process, nor reuse a chart you had previously prepared, nor do research on a group of charts.

The best astrological appliance is the DR-70 from Digicomp. It costs as much as a complete Apple IIe system, including a printer. DR-70s are still being sold even though comparable computer systems can do much more, and can produce higher-quality printouts. The appeal of appliances rests in the fact that you get a sturdy device that looks like an adding machine that can calculate charts in seconds, and gives you many other choices as well. You don't have to deal with cables, diskettes, and peripheral equipment.

The DR-70 is portable, so you can take it wherever you like, and it doesn't intimidate many people, as do more complicated computer systems. This appliance creates dot-matrix printouts of square-wheel charts, complete with astrological symbols, and also prints tables of interaspects in comparing charts, as well as tables of progressions and transits. Its forty-column printouts are easy to read, although too rough to hand out to clients. I like its style of glyphs used for signs, planets and aspects, as well as its method of tabulating aspects and transits.

It has a clear, one-line LED display that you can use not only for entering data, but also for scanning results, e.g., looking at a person's planetary aspects or house positions. Therefore you can use the DR-70 without hooking up its printer. Moreover, its keyboard is excellent.

Digicomp did their best to design a machine that could perform a wide variety of astrological calculations, including quotidians, harmonics, returns, lunations, and composites, with a choice of eight house systems. Since new routines cannot be added, users of appliances have no way to utilize new astrological techniques as they are developed.

As you begin to employ the more powerful techniques available to you with the DR-70, you may notice that it takes longer to get a response, that entry routines become more complex, and that you must follow the instructions in the manual very carefully. For instance, the transit search routine is excellent, but to use it you have to enter over 60 items of code to specify all of your choices as to how the search should be done. Then it takes about half an hour to complete a daily scan for just a few months.

Although the brochure describes the DR-70 as having a 10,000-year ephemeris, the machine's accuracy is limited to the twentieth century for the asteroids, and a few hundred years for the outer planets.

One of the prices you pay for the convenience of an appliance system is that you cannot store files of chart data, so you must re-enter all the data you need every time you want to use it. A second weakness is that it cannot be modified or expanded. It is very hard to add any new options to the DR-70 at the factory, and impossible for the user, and so the DR-70 will not change at all in the future. You will never be able to use it to correct the Moon for parallax, perform calculations involving the Uranian planets, research a group of charts, or use any new techniques that arise in astrology.

Digicomp has also released a smaller version of the DR-70 called the Astrion, which has the same astrological functions for $1000 less. The Astrion's display is barely readable. In place of a keyboard, it has a flat, touch-sensitive mat. The built-in thermal printer must be handled gently and the feel of the machine is less solid. Nevertheless, the Astrion is becoming popular because of its lower price and better entry routine. Moreover it is modular, so you can buy an even cheaper, stripped-down version first, and upgrade later. Again, you can get much more for your money with a Commodore, Kaypro, or Apple package.

Finally, the smallest and newest astrological appliance is the Compuchart-1. This $300-some-odd machine will calculate only natal charts and aspects. It can compute only one chart at a time, so it cannot perform synastry. It cannot calculate returns, progressions, harmonics, or midpoints. Moreover, the Compuchart-1 makes numerous errors in labeling planets as retrograde when they are direct, and the planetary positions it calculates are commonly off by a few minutes (up to half a degree in some cases) for twentieth century dates. Clearly it is too inaccurate for the professional astrologer.

The aspects are calculated and displayed quickly and clearly, and it is easy to walk through all the aspects to each planet. As with all appliances, however, you cannot go beyond the limits of the machine. This one uses no house systems other than Koch or Placidus, no aspects other than the majors plus semisquares, sesquiquadrates and quintiles, and its orb settings cannot be altered. Moreover, it produces no printouts.

On the positive side, the Compuchart is fast, easy to use, and light in weight. It has decent documentation and a clear screen display. I wish the designers had created more accurate routines, given the device a less plastic-looking case, and made the price reasonable for what you get ($100?) or added more options. I cannot recommend it in its present form.

Addresses of Suppliers

Matrix Software
315 Marion Ave.
Big Rapids, MI 49307
(616) 796-2483

AGS Software
Box 28
Orleans, MA 02653
(617) 255-0510

Microcycles
1056 5th St.
P.O. Box 852
Santa Monica, CA 90406
(213) 393-8401
(Apple Star Track supplier for
    AGS)

M Systems, Inc.
P.O. Box 421
Douglaston, NY 11363
(212) 428-4880
(Manufacturers of Compuchart-1)

Digicomp Research
Terrace Hill
Ithaca, NY 14850
(607) 273-5900
(Manufacturers of DR-70 and
    Astrion)

Astro Computing Services
P.O. Box 16430
San Diego, CA 92116-9987
(619) 297-9203

Index

Copy protection, 10, 225, 229
Copying programs, 228
CP/M computers, 12, 190–191, 229

Disk drives, 12, 13, 190–191, 229
Disk ephemerides, 83, 188, 198, 215
DR-70, 248–249

Eclipses, 180, 237–238
Electional astrology, 243–244

Files
   M-65, 164–165, 228
   Nova, 194, 200
   types of, 9–10

Glyphs, 10

Harmonics, 86, 177, 186, 242–243
Heliocentric astrology, 239
Horary astrology, 243
House systems, 131, 153, 177, 240,
   241

IBM/MS-DOS computers, 13–14,
   190–191, 223, 225, 229
Interpretive software, 117–159
   large report programs,
      128–159
   limitations, 118, 158
   predictive report programs,
      141–153
   small packages, 119–128
   synastry report programs,
      153–159

Keyboard, 223, 229

Local space charts, 38, 39, 171, 239
Lunar returns. *See* Returns

Macintosh, 14, 220, 223, 225, 229
Medical astrology, 244
Midpoints, 68, 73, 175, 187,
   197–199, 233, 234

Minor aspects, 84, 242, 243
MS-DOS computers, 13, 14, 190,
   191
Mundane astrology, 244

Onscreen editing, 49, 184, 191

Parallax Moon, 180, 238–239
Predictive report programs, 141–153
Printer buffers, 128, 229
Printouts, 10, 48, 165, 170, 171, 194.
   See also individual programs
Programming manuals, 230
Progressions, 34, 179, 192, 235–236

Relationship charts, 40, 41
Relocational astrology, 232–233
Returns, 36, 37, 76, 84, 150,
   151, 171, 192, 209–210,
   236–237

Sidereal techniques, 171, 192
Software/hardware compatibility, 224
Solar arc directions, 42, 43, 237
Solar returns. *See* Returns
SpeeDemon card, 14, 187, 219–220,
   229
State-of-the-art software, 160–202
Synastry, 179, 193, 241–242
Synastry report programs, 153–159

Transit calculation programs,
   153–159
Transit report programs, 141–153,
   188
Transits, 34, 105, 144–145, 188,
   234–235
Tropical and Sidereal methods,
   239–240

Upgrades, 11, 182

Vocational astrology, 241

Program Index

Selections from The SYBEX Library

Introduction to Computers

OVERCOMING COMPUTER FEAR
by Jeff Berner
112 pp., illustr., Ref. 0-145
This easy-going introduction to computers helps you separate the facts from the myths.

PARENTS, KIDS, AND COMPUTERS
by Lynne Alper and Meg Holmberg
145 pp., illustr., Ref. 0-151
This book answers your questions about the educational possibilities of home computers.

PROTECTING YOUR COMPUTER
by Rodnay Zaks
214 pp., 100 illustr., Ref. 0-239
The correct way to handle and care for all elements of a computer system, including what to do when something doesn't work.

YOUR FIRST COMPUTER
by Rodnay Zaks
258 pp., 150 illustr., Ref. 0-142
The most popular introduction to small computers and their peripherals: what they do and how to buy one.

Computer Books for Kids

MONICA THE COMPUTER MOUSE
by Donna Bearden, illustrated by Brad W. Foster
64 pp., illustr., Hardcover, Ref. 0-214
Lavishly illustrated in color, this book tells the story of Monica the mouse, as she travels around to learn about several different kids of computers and the jobs they can do. For ages 5–8.

POWER UP! KIDS' GUIDE TO THE APPLE IIe® /IIc™
by Marty DeJonghe and Caroline Earhart
200 pp., illustr., Ref. 0-212
Colorful illustrations and a friendly robot highlight this guide to the Apple IIe/IIc for kids 8–11.

BANK STREET WRITING WITH YOUR APPLE®
by Stanley Schatt, Ph.D. and Jane Abrams Schatt, M.A.
150 pp., illustr., Ref. 0-189
These engaging exercises show children aged 10–13 how to use Bank Street Writer for fun, profit, and school work.

Humor

CONFESSIONS OF AN INFOMANIAC
by Elizabeth M. Ferrarini
215 pp., Ref. 0-186
This is one woman's tongue-in-cheek revelations of her pursuit of men, money, and machines. Learn about the many shopping services, information banks, and electronic dating bulletin boards available by computer.

Special Interest

THE COLLEGE STUDENT'S PERSONAL COMPUTER HANDBOOK
by Bryan Pfaffenberger
210 pp., illustr., Ref. 0-170
This friendly guide will aid students in selecting a computer system for college study, managing information in a college course, and writing research papers.

CELESTIAL BASIC
by Eric Burgess
300 pp., 65 illustr., Ref. 0-087
A collection of BASIC programs that rapidly complete the chores of typical astronomical computations. It's like having a planetarium in your own home! Displays apparent movement of stars, planets and meteor showers.

PERSONAL COMPUTERS AND SPECIAL NEEDS
by Frank G. Bowe
175 pp., illustr., Ref. 0-193
Learn how people are overcoming problems with hearing, vision, mobility, and learning, through the use of computer technology.

ESPIONAGE IN THE SILICON VALLEY
by John D. Halamka
200 pp., illustr., Ref. 0-225
Discover the behind-the-scenes stories of famous high-tech spy cases you've seen in the headlines.

Computer Specific

Apple II—Macintosh

THE EASY GUIDE TO YOUR APPLE II®
by Joseph Kascmer
147 pp., illustr., Ref. 0-122
A friendly introduction to the Apple II, II plus and the IIe.

APPLE II® BASIC PROGRAMS IN MINUTES
by Stanley R. Trost
150 pp., illustr., Ref. 0-121
A collection of ready-to-run programs for financial calculations, investment analysis, record keeping, and many more home and office applications. These programs can be entered on your Apple II plus or IIe in minutes!

THE APPLE® CONNECTION
by James W. Coffron
264 pp., 120 illustr., Ref. 0-085
Teaches elementary interfacing and BASIC programming of the Apple for connection to external devices and household appliances.

THE APPLE IIc™: A PRACTICAL GUIDE
by Thomas Blackadar
175 pp., illustr., Ref. 0-241
Learn all you need to know about the Apple IIc! This jargon-free companion gives you a guided tour of Apple's new machine.

THE BEST OF EDUCATIONAL SOFTWARE FOR APPLE II® COMPUTERS
by Gary G. Bitter, Ph.D. and Kay Gore
300 pp., Ref. 0-206
Here is a handy guide for parents and an invaluable reference for educators who must make decisions about software purchases.

THE COMPLETE GUIDE TO YOUR MACINTOSH™
by Joseph Caggiano and Roy Robinson
350 pp., illustr., Ref. 0-204
This is an in-depth guide to the Macintosh, ideal for the intermediate and advanced user.

MACINTOSH™ FOR COLLEGE STUDENTS
by Bryan Pfaffenberger
250 pp., illustr., Ref. 0-227
Find out how to give yourself an edge in

the race to get papers in on time and prepare for exams. This book covers everything you need to know about how to use
the Macintosh for college study.

Atari

BASIC EXERCISES FOR THE ATARI®

by J.P. Lamoitier

251 pp., illustr., Ref. 0-101
Teaches ATARI BASIC through actual
practice, using graduated exercises
drawn from everyday applications.

THE EASY GUIDE TO YOUR ATARI® 600XL/800XL

by Thomas Blackadar

175 pp., illustr., Ref. 0-125
This jargon-free companion will help you
get started on the right foot with your new
600XL or 800XL ATARI computer.

Coleco

THE EASY GUIDE TO YOUR COLECO ADAM™

by Thomas Blackadar

175 pp., illustr., Ref. 0-181
This quick reference guide shows you
how to get started on your Coleco Adam
using a minimum of technical jargon.

Commodore 64/VIC-20

THE BEST OF COMMODORE 64™ SOFTWARE

by Thomas Blackadar

150 pp., illustr., Ref. 0-194
Save yourself time and frustration with this
buyer's guide to Commodore 64 software. Find the best game, music, educa-
tion, and home management programs
on the market today.

THE COMMODORE 64™/VIC-20™ BASIC HANDBOOK

by Douglas Hergert

144 pp., illustr., Ref. 0-116
A complete listing with descriptions and
instructive examples of each of the Commodore 64 BASIC keywords and functions. A handy reference guide, organized like a dictionary.

GRAPHICS GUIDE TO THE COMMODORE 64™

by Charles Platt

261 pp., illustr., Ref. 0-138
This easy-to-understand book will appeal
to anyone who wants to master the Commodore 64's powerful graphics features.

CP/M Systems

THE CP/M® HANDBOOK

by Rodnay Zaks

320 pp., 100 illustr., Ref 0-048
An indispensable reference and guide to
CP/M—the most widely-used operating
system for small computers.

THE BEST OF CP/M® SOFTWARE

by John D. Halamka

250 pp., Ref. 0-100
This book reviews tried-and-tested, com-
mercially available software for your
CP/M system.

INSTANT CP/M:® A KEYSTROKE GUIDE

by Robert Levine

250 pp., illustr., Ref. 0-132
This novice's guide includes a complete
explanation of terms and commands,
showing how they appear on the screen
and what they do—a quick, foolproof way
to gain proficiency with CP/M.

IBM PC and Compatibles

THE ABC'S OF THE IBM® PC

by Joan Lasselle and Carol Ramsay

143 pp., illustr., Ref. 0-102
This book will take you through the first
crucial steps in learning to use the IBM PC.

DATA FILE PROGRAMMING ON YOUR IBM® PC

by Alan Simpson

219 pp., illustr., Ref. 0-146
This book provides instructions and
examples for managing data files in
BASIC. Programming design and development are extensively discussed.

SELECTING THE RIGHT WORD PROCESSING SOFTWARE FOR THE IBM® PC

TRS-80

**THE RADIO SHACK®
NOTEBOOK COMPUTER**
by Orson Kellogg
118 pp., illustr., Ref. 0-150
Whether you already have the Radio Shack Model 100 notebook computer or are interested in buying one, this book will clearly explain what it can do for you.

YOUR COLOR COMPUTER
by Doug Mosher
350 pp., illustr., Ref. 0-097
Patience and humor guide the reader through purchasing, setting up, programming, and using the Radio Shack TRS-80 Color Computer. A complete introduction.

Software Specific

Spreadsheets

VISICALC® FOR SCIENCE AND ENGINEERING
**by Stanley R. Trost and
Charles Pomernacki**
203 pp., illustr., Ref. 0-096
More than 50 programs for solving technical problems in science and engineering. Applications range from math and statistics to electrical and electronic engineering.

**MULTIPLAN™ ON THE
COMMODORE 64™**
by Richard Allen King
260 pp., illustr., Ref. 0-231
This clear, straighforward guide will give you a firm grasp on Multiplan's functions, as well as provide a collection of useful template programs.

Word Processing

**INTRODUCTION TO
WORDSTAR®**
by Arthur Naiman
202 pp., 30 illustr., Ref. 0-134
Makes it easy to learn WordStar, a powerful word processing program for personal computers.

PRACTICAL WORDSTAR® USES
by Julie Anne Arca
303 pp., illustr., Ref. 0-107
Pick your most time-consuming office tasks and this book will show you how to streamline them with WordStar.

**THE COMPLETE GUIDE TO
MULTIMATE™**
by Carol Holcomb Dreger
250 pp., illustr., Ref. 0-229
A concise introduction to the many practical applications of this powerful word processing program.

THE THINKTANK™ BOOK
by Jonathan Kamin
200 pp., illustr., Ref. 0-224
Learn how the ThinkTank program can help you organize your thoughts, plans, and activities.

Data Base Management Systems

UNDERSTANDING dBASE II™
by Alan Simpson
260 pp., illustr., Ref. 0-147
Learn programming techniques for mailing label systems, bookkeeping, and data management, as well as ways to interface dBASE II with other software systems.

Integrated Software

THE ABC'S OF 1-2-3™
by Chris Gilbert and Laurie Williams
225 pp., illustr., Ref. 0-168
For those new to the LOTUS 1-2-3 program, this book offers step-by-step

instructions in mastering its spreadsheet, data base, and graphing capabilities.

MASTERING APPLEWORKS™
by Elna Tymes
250 pp., illustr., Ref. 0-240
Here is a business-oriented introduction to AppleWorks, the new integrated software package from Apple. No experience with computers is assumed.

Languages

BASIC

YOUR FIRST BASIC PROGRAM
by Rodnay Zaks
182 pp., illustr. in color, Ref. 0-092
A "how-to-program" book for the first time computer user, aged 8 to 88.

BASIC PROGRAMS FOR SCIENTISTS AND ENGINEERS
by Alan R. Miller
318 pp., 120 illustr., Ref. 0-073
This book from the "Programs for Scientists and Engineers" series provides a library of problem-solving programs while developing the reader's proficiency in BASIC.

Pascal

INTRODUCTION TO PASCAL (Including UCSD Pascal™)
by Rodnay Zaks
420 pp., 130 illustr., Ref. 0-066
A step-by-step introduction for anyone who wants to learn the Pascal language. Describes UCSD and Standard Pascals. No technical background is assumed.

Other Languages

UNDERSTANDING C
by Bruce H. Hunter
320 pp., Ref 0-123
Explains how to program in powerful C language for a variety of applications. Some programming experience assumed.

FIFTY PASCAL PROGRAMS
by Bruce H. Hunter
338 pp., illustr., Ref. 0-110
More than just a collection of useful programs! Structured programming techniques are emphasized and concepts such as data type creation and array manipulation are clearly illustrated.

Technical

Hardware

FROM CHIPS TO SYSTEMS: AN INTRODUCTION TO MICROPROCESSORS
by Rodnay Zaks
552 pp., 400 illustr., Ref. 0-063
A simple and comprehensive introduction to microprocessors from both a hardware and software standpoint: what they are, how they operate, how to assemble them into a complete system.

THE RS-232 SOLUTION
by Joe Campbell
194 pp., illustr., Ref. 0-140
Finally, a book that will show you how to correctly interface your computer to any RS-232-C peripheral.

Operating Systems

REAL WORLD UNIX™
by John D. Halamka
209 pp., Ref. 0-093
This book is written for the beginning and intermediate UNIX user in a practical, straightforward manner, with specific instructions given for many business applications.

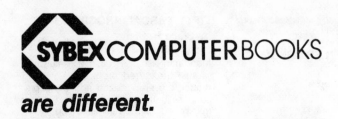

SYBEXCOMPUTERBOOKS

are different.

Here is why . . .

At SYBEX, each book is designed with you in mind. Every manuscript is carefully selected and supervised by our editors, who are themselves computer experts. We publish the best authors, whose technical expertise is matched by an ability to write clearly and to communicate effectively. Programs are thoroughly tested for accuracy by our technical staff. Our computerized production department goes to great lengths to make sure that each book is well-designed.

In the pursuit of timeliness, SYBEX has achieved many publishing firsts. SYBEX was among the first to integrate personal computers used by authors and staff into the publishing process. SYBEX was the first to publish books on the CP/M operating system, microprocessor interfacing techniques, word processing, and many more topics.

Expertise in computers and dedication to the highest quality product have made SYBEX a world leader in computer book publishing. Translated into fourteen languages, SYBEX books have helped millions of people around the world to get the most from their computers. We hope we have helped you, too.

For a complete catalog of our publications please contact:

U.S.A.	FRANCE	GERMANY	UNITED KINGDOM
SYBEX, Inc.	SYBEX	SYBEX-Verlag GmbH	SYBEX, Ltd.
2344 Sixth Street	6–8 Impasse du Curé	Vogelsanger Weg 111	Unit 4–Bourne Industrial
Berkeley,	75018 Paris	4000 Düsseldorf 30	Park
California 94710	France	West Germany	Bourne Road, Crayford
Tel: (800) 227-2346	Tel: 01/203–9595	Tel: (0211) 626441	Kent DA1 4BZ England
(415) 848-8233	Telex: 211801	Telex: 8588163	Tel: (0322) 57717
Telex: 336311			Telex: 896939